Epic and the Russian Novel

from Gogol to Pasternak

Studies in Russian and Slavic Literatures, Cultures and History
Series Editor – LAZAR FLEISHMAN (Stanford University)

ACADEMIC
STUDIES
PRESS

EPIC
and the RUSSIAN NOVEL
from GOGOL
to PASTERNAK

Frederick T. GRIFFITHS
and Stanley J. RABINOWITZ

Boston
2011

Library of Congress Cataloging-in-Publication Data

Griffiths, Frederick T.
  Epic and the Russian novel : from Gogol to Pasternak / Frederick T.
Griffiths and Stanley J. Rabinowitz.
      p. cm. — (Studies in Russian and Slavic literatures, cultures and
history)
  Includes bibliographical references and index.
  ISBN 978-1-936235-53-7 (hardback : alk. paper) 1. Russian fiction—
19th century—History and criticism. 2. Russian fiction—20th century—
History and criticism. 3. Epic literature, Russian—History and criticism.
I. Rabinowitz, Stanley J. II. Title.
  PG3098.E65G75 2011
  891.73'309—dc22
                                    2011006283

ISBN 978-1-61811-814-1

Book design by Ivan Grave

Published by Academic Studies Press in 2011
28 Montfern Avenue
Brighton, MA 02135, USA
press@academicstudiespress.com
www.academicstudiespress.com

CONTENTS

ACKNOWLEDGMENTS

We gratefully acknowledge Ian David for his unstinting efforts in preparing the manuscript in its final version.

Our deepest thanks go to Amherst College Dean of the Faculty Gregory Call for providing funds to see this project through to publication.

The following publishers have generously given permission to use extended quotations from copyrighted works:

Chichikov's Journeys: or, Home Life in Old Russia, by Nikolai Gogol, translated by Bernard Guilbert Guerney. Copyright © 1942 by The Readers Club and renewed 1965 by Random House, Inc. Reprinted by permission of Random House, Inc.

Selected Passages from Correspondence with Friends, by Nikolai Gogol, translated by Jesse Zeldin. Copyright © 1969 by Vanderbilt University Press. Reprinted by permission of the publisher.

The Iliad, by Homer, translated by Richmond Lattimore. Copyright © 1951 by the University of Chicago. Reprinted by permission of the publisher.

Remembrance of Things Past. vol. 3, *The Captive*, by Marcel Proust. translated by C. K. Scott Moncrieff and Terence Kilmartin. and by Andreas Mayor. Copyright 1981 by Random House, Inc., and Chatto & Windus. Reprinted by permission of Random House, Inc.

PREFACE

These essays address four Russian novels as they adapt a monumental tradition from outside of Russia. The readings focus not on the history of the Russian novel itself but on how these four works allusively incorporate a history of European letters so as to locate themselves within it, that is, how they trace their descent ultimately from Homer as well as from scripture. We are not concerned with the native forms of epic nor with the other writers, notably Pushkin, who framed a Russian identity within European letters, but only with what we consider the clearest cases of transforming the novel as a form by assimilating it to the epic tradition. In invoking that tradition, these novels claim position within world literature, and it is from that vantage point that we consider them: Were these writers finally within their rights in asking to be read beside Homer, Virgil, and Dante? For the burden of joining that company is not simply to be as critically esteemed as these poets or as widely read, but to continue the narrative cycle that they began.

The first chapter defines terms and explains what we take the epic tradition to be. The following chapters vary widely in format to accommodate the various novels. *Dead Souls* is considered in the context of the other works that Gogol published or burned with and after it. We include *The Brothers Karamazov* as a limiting case: Directly because Dostoevsky so notably lacks the allusive technique through which the other three invoke their predecessors, the gestures that he makes to epic conventions at the end of the novel make all the clearer indication of the pressures that he felt from that tradition. We take *War and Peace* and *Doctor Zhivago* as unities unto themselves, though unities each with a triple conclusion. A final chapter considers further permutations of the epic tradition during the Stalinist period of Russian culture in literary criticism (Bakhtin), memoir (Nadezhda Mandelstam), and narrative poetry (Anna Akhmatova).

...чаще поэты, разделенные временем
и пространством, отвечают друг другу,
как отголоски между утесами: развязка
"Илиады" хранится в "Комедии" Данте.

— В. Ф. Одоевский,
"Русские ночи" (1835)

... separated by time and space, poets quite
often answer each other like echoes among
cliffs; the denouement of the Iliad is given in
Dante's Comedy.

— V. F. Odoevsky,
Russian Nights (1835)

1. EPIC AND NOVEL

Two Romes have fallen, but a third stands
fast; a fourth there cannot be.

Rome, Byzantium, Moscow: through this prophecy the sixteenth-century monk Philotheus evades an old and still unanswered question — does Russia belong in Europe? — by proclaiming a Europe that spiritually belongs to Russia and should look to Moscow as the true and final capital of a renascent Christendom. For the Slavs to westernize has always seemed a compromise of the otherness and unworldliness that set them apart and above. By the logic of Christianity, their very innocence as outsiders can also signify spiritual election. The conversion of Christendom's northern periphery to its center and capital recalls the miracles of the rejected rock as capstone, the carpenter's son as Messiah, the meek inheriting. Something good can come from Nazareth. Indeed, it is to the Nazareths that one must look to find the future, for the old capitals, Rome as well as Jerusalem, fall prey to worldly success. Philotheus suggests how Slavophiles might welcome the prospect of leading Europe rather than joining it.

Yet danger lurks in this proud calling, for the process of redeeming publicans and sinners entails large risks of joining their number. Already by Philotheus's day the West had seen millennia of conquerors, among them the Romans themselves, battling their way to cultural enslavement. Though politically subjected, the Greeks may have prevailed culturally, as Horace already suspected: "Graecia capta ferum victorem cepit et artes / intulit agresti Latio" ("Conquered Greece conquered her fierce victor and brought the arts into rustic Latium," *Epistles* 2.1.156-57). The statuesque marble Romanness of Rome was framed by sophisticates who spoke Greek among themselves; in the best circles, Russians after 1812 both celebrated and compromised their expulsion of foreign masters by still speaking French as they pursued their own increasingly Napoleonic ambitions. The inheriting meek lose their meekness. Basic to the project of constructing the third and final Rome, in Europe but not of it, was the paradox that the wall erected against European influence would have to be built with European bricks. Perhaps the bulwark could become Russian by being grander than any wall yet built.

In the fabrication of this national identity, novelists enjoyed influence rarely seen in Western letters since antiquity, the influence of prophets. Once Napoleon was beaten, writers in Russia sought to forge an independent literature that would not only celebrate the country's new status as a world power but also allow fallen Europe to read its own destiny. For prophets, the wit or sentimentality of the novel, the bourgeois fantasy that sold books in Paris or London, was no fit medium. While the novel in its materialism and privatization portrayed the spiritual fragmentation of the West, Russian writers aimed to take the genre beyond itself by making it something greater, more public, and more primary — in a word, by making it monumental, that is, epic. It is in precisely these terms that Belinsky, the father of Russian criticism, defined the status of the novel: "The epic of our time is the novel."[1] The Homeric tradition could liberate Russian writers from the confines of the European novel by providing terms to assert the magnitude of their subject, their magnificent calling, and the finality of their inherited spiritual authority.[2] The epic, to be sure, is as European as the novel but emerged from a Europe as yet uncorrupted by the Enlightenment and by industrialization, the Europe destined to renew itself on Russian

---

[1] "Èpopeya nashego vremeni est' roman," in V. G. Belinskii, "Razdelenie poèzii na rody i vidy," *Sobranie sochinenii v trekh tomakh* (Moscow, 1948), 2:38.

[2] In a curiously Soviet interpretation of Russia's literary authority, the critic L. F. Ershov disputes all claims that modernist literature can in any way embody the epic tradition. Insisting that classical epics reconstitute the moment of unity in a nation's history such as cannot be achieved in bourgeois society, this orthodox Marxist concludes that contemporary Western literature is fundamentally incapable of producing epic novels. "However," Ershov continues, "to any unbiased observer who can recall but three literary works — "Taras Bulba", *War and Peace*, and *The Quiet Don* — it is clear that only in Russia have the lessons of universal, primarily Greek and Latin epic art been consistently and organically mastered." L. F. Ershov, "Traditsii M. Sholokhova i roman-èpopeya v slavyanskikh stranakh," *Acta Litteraria Academiae Scientiarum Hungaricae* 28, nos. 3-4 (1986): 318.

soil. The novel might become Russian by being grander than anything yet written.

The turning points in the national history — 1812 and 1917 — did in fact inspire responses that pointedly surpassed and questioned the inherited terms of the European novel by invoking the tradition of classical epic. Boris Eikhenbaum has observed that in writing *War and Peace* Tolstoy used the form of Homeric epic to escape the confines of the English family novel,[3] and we have argued elsewhere that the structure of heroism in the work owes specific and extensive debts to the *Iliad* and the *Odyssey*.[4] Pasternak's much more oblique and melancholy response to the October Revolution in *Doctor Zhivago* invokes Virgil's troubled celebration of the Roman revolution in the *Aeneid*. Pasternak in some measure defines his position (and that of his generation) in the shadow of Tolstoy by thus recalling the burdens and achievements of Virgil in the shadow of Homer. He proposes that Moscow has in fact become the Third Rome, not a final and flourishing bastion of Christian orthodoxy but the capital of a totalitarian empire. Just as Rome's empire left the city "a flea market of borrowed gods and conquered peoples," so Soviet culture may be killing Russian.[5]

Tolstoy and Pasternak were writing within an established national literature, and it is not surprising that as they looked back over the decades to turning points like 1812 and 1917 they should suggest that their works be read beside texts like the *Iliad* and the *Aeneid* that were also centrally engaged in the forming of national identities. Gogol and Dostoevsky form another strand within the great tradition of the Russian novel, one in which any trace of classicism is unexpected. Both writers address Petersburg life in their earlier short stories, and Dostoevsky's debts to Gogol on this score are well understood.[6] But as they wrote their masterpieces, *Dead Souls* and *The*

---

[3] Boris Eikhenbaum, *Tolstoi in the Sixties*, trans. Duffield White (Ann Arbor, Mich.: Ardis, 1982), 227. Originally published as *Lev Tolstoi, Kniga Vtoraya* (Leningrad, 1930).

[4] See Chapter 4 of this volume.

[5] Boris Pasternak, *Doctor Zhivago*, prose trans. Max Hayward and Manya Harari, poetic trans. Bernard Guerney (New York: Pantheon, 1958; rpt. New York: Bantam, 1985), 43. See Chapter 5 of this volume.

[6] For some stimulating thoughts on Gogol's influence particularly on Dostoevsky's early works, see Donald Fanger, *Dostoevsky and Romantic Realism* (Cambridge, Mass.;

Brothers Karamazov, they turned away from the capitals and from national watersheds, and presumably therefore from any shadows of the epic tradition.[7] Indeed, *Dead Souls* seems to deflate the high, laureate style by its mock-heroic account of unwonted excitements in the provincial village of N — , midway between somewhere and nowhere. It was in a similar turning aside from epic and playful dismissal of heroism that the novel got its start in modern literatures with Cervantes, Rabelais, Sterne, and Fielding. Yet in these other literatures epic, as inspiration or target for parody, tends to fall from sight after the first generation, while in Russia, as we have seen, it keeps coming back at the crucial points of national history. The concluding question of *Dead Souls*, "Whither Rus'?" is more serious in its implications than the preceding text has seemed to be in style, and Gogol came to see his narrative as the first canticle of a divine comedy. When Dostoevsky recalls Gogol's project, as in some measure he does in *The Brothers Karamazov*, he does so not merely to satirize but to continue it. Dostoevsky also came to view his novel as the first part of some Russian divine comedy. The question of "Whither Rus'?" rises beyond the hollow rhetoric of Dmitri's prosecutor to renew the quest for the Russian identity broadly and seriously and, as we shall argue, against the allusive background of Homer and the classical as well as the Christian origins of the European tradition. The Russian novel, unlike the European, did not invoke the epic tradition to set itself playfully apart before turning to other concerns, but rather to begin a dialogue that is most apparent in the most esteemed texts.

Before turning to Gogol and, more briefly, to Dostoevsky's reflections on the tradition that he inherited from Gogol, we shall need to consider the relationship between epics and novels and in particular the question of how novels can locate themselves within a tradition that is often argued to be antithetical to the very nature of the novel.

Harvard University Press, 1965), as well as Fanger's "Influence and Tradition in the Russian Novel," *The Russian Novel from Pushkin to Pasternak*, ed. John Garrard (New Haven and London: Yale University Press. 1983), 29-50, and in general Priscilla Meyer and Stephen Rudy, eds., Dostoevsky and Gogol (Ann Arbor, Mich.: Ardis, 1979).

[7] The most comprehensive examination of Gogol's indebtedness to the European literary tradition is Anna Yelistratova, *Nikolai Gogol and the West European Novel*, trans. Christopher English (Moscow: Raduga Publishers, 1984). She discusses no influence earlier than the "epic novel" (Cervantes, Sterne, Fielding, et al.).

The Double Plot of Epic

Epic is not only older than the novel but has a much better memory. Debts within the more idiosyncratic and mutable range of the novel conceal themselves easily, but epic has from the first been preoccupied with its own genealogy. How Aeneas will inevitably launch Rome would have intrigued the ancient reader less than whether Virgil would master or be mastered by the incomparable Homer, whom he rivaled and recreated line by line. *Hoc opus, hic labor est.* Virgil is reputed to have said that it is easier to steal the club of Hercules than to lift one line from Homer (*Vita Donati* 46). His heroic terms are apposite: Aeneas's risks rank as nothing compared to Virgil's as heir and rival to Homer. The *Aeneid* bequeathed to the West a powerful foundation myth, but one centered more on the divine Homer, "the poet," as the wellspring of literature than on pallid, pious Aeneas as the father of Rome. Aeneas does finally get free of father Anchises, but Virgil's struggle with Homer continues to the end without even a forecast of victory.

Of Dante, E.M.W. Tillyard notes that it is not the occasional Ulysses or Farinata that makes the heroic impression, "it is rather the vast exercise of will that went to the shaping of the whole poem."[8] Dante proclaims his own — Christian — victory by bringing Virgil right into the fiction with him as a guide, then leaving him behind, lamented and absorbed. The form itself becomes autobiographical in explaining the act of literary derivation that gave it birth. Speaking in the vernacular, it is Roman Virgil himself who christens Italian as a literary language. Where novels have authors, writers of epic also proclaim themselves authored by the tradition, as Dante notes when he greets his ghostly guide as "lo mio maestro e 'l mio autore." What epic uniquely can offer for glory and reproach is the ability to array All That Precedes as a foil for the current dispensation, and to do so with the particular authority of a form that was as itself in Athens, Rome, and Florence. Where the historical novel, a patently modern form, must often accept the anachronism of presenting old wine in new skins, epic offers a tradition as old as the human events described, yet one incomparably quick at recapitulating millennia of culture by the merest gesture. Devices

---

[8] E. M. W. Tillyard, *The Epic Strain in the English Novel* (London: Chatto and Windus, 1958), 16.

like rosy dawns, adjectives suspended to mock epithets ("Stately, plump..."), comparisons of a warrior to a flame or a lion, or the image of a flickering bough draw the knowledgeable reader into an underworld of fallen empires and their unfading literatures.

Fully realized, then, epic may be said to have a double plot: partly about heroes, partly about its own durability as a form. From the advent of literacy to the current day, epics, through their various levels of allusion, as well as through explicit acknowledgment (for example, Joyce's choice of title for *Ulysses*), have transmitted the fossilized strata of the epochs of literary development that led up to themselves, that is, of artists' picking up the work of other artists — a record that may contain a tale larger than a given work's announced plot. For that plot will concern at most the emergence of a single sense of nationhood or creed, another Rome, while the embedded record of literary genealogy traces the movement of culture from nation to nation, language to language, religion to religion: *Iliad* to *Odyssey* to *Aeneid* to *Divine Comedy*. This is not a list of separate items in the way that novels are discrete from one another, but the incremental record of a single pilgrimage to an eternally receding shrine: to Ithaca, to Rome, to the City of God, or to a Moscow or Dublin that is and is not all of these places.

Even in summoning the weight of antiquity, this tradition favors newcomers. As Vico formulated, after decadence comes a *ricorso*, another Homer in another heroic culture. The quest myths that underlie the tradition allow movement forward in time or space to become movement backward, so that the end becomes the beginning, the last stands first, and innocence constitutes authority. For both Aeneas and Moses, the long exodus to a promised but unseen land proves to be a racial homecoming. The newcomers to that land are its true and original lords. Christianity intensifies the paradox of the first and last, and of the child that shall lead them. The road to Gethsemane returns to and repairs the first garden, and the line of David ends where it began, now in an unfallen Adam. Similarly, Virgil could suggest Augustus not merely as the latest Roman strongman but as the renewal of his line, the new Aeneas. These myths of return have implications that make them central to their cultures. In combining the classical and Christian inheritances, the epic tradition enables a culture that perceives itself as somehow new, or that expresses itself in a yet unestablished literary language — as once Virgil's Rome, so later Dante's

Florence and Gogol's Russia — to claim spiritual authority beyond its years by involving itself in the very origins of this migrating, self-regenerative culture that always flowers best on its latest frontier.

Starting late and in the east, the Russian renaissance followed the Roman pattern not less but more directly than had the former provinces of the Western empire. Just as the *Odyssey* translation of Livius Andronicus inaugurated Latin as a literary language, so an early reviewer, N. Polevoi, proclaimed Gnedich's *Iliad* (1801-29) to be "a treasurehouse of language… [that] exposes the richness, power, and resources of our own language."[9] We shall shortly encounter Gogol's comparable claims for Zhukovsky's *Odyssey*. Accommodating their resistant language to the Greek hexameter signified literary legitimacy for the Russians no less than for the Romans. For most of its history, the Roman West had known Greek, that both of Homer and of the New Testament, only as filtered through Latin. The Cyrillic alphabet puts the Russians in a different and closer tradition. Of the literary inheritance, a grammarian of the sixteenth or seventeenth century remarked that "Greek and Slavonic letters are like a lamb with its mother (for the Slavonic have proceeded from the Greek) — both of them resemble and harmonize with each other."[10] Lomonosov, for Pushkin the "Peter the Great of Russian literature," was typically heir to that tradition. Educated in the Slavonic-Greek-Latin Academy in Moscow, he translated parts of Homer (as well as of Virgil and Ovid), proclaiming that "I consider the best of all poets to be Homer."[11] As Philotheus's progression — Rome, Byzantium, Moscow — indicates, literature, the empire, and the Church all passed through a formative interlude in Italy, but the Byzantine-Muscovite axis had its own unmediated proximity to Athens, as to Jerusalem. Following in Vico's footsteps, German Romanticism and the scholarship that followed on Wood and Wolf located a bardic and folkloric Homer before and outside

---

[9] Quoted in Viktor Afanasev, ed., *N. Gnedich, Stikhotvoreniya i poèmy* (Moscow, 1984), 7.

[10] Manuscript 423, Sankt-Peterburgskaya Dukhovnaya Akademiya, an untitled grammatical thesis published in M. N. Smenkovskii, *Brat'ia Likhudy* (St. Petersbrug, 1899), ix; the translation is that of Richard Burgi, *A History of the Russian Hexameter* (Hamden, Conn.: The Shoe String Press, 1954), 11.

[11] Quoted in A. N. Egunov, "Lomonosov — perevodchik Gomera," in *Literaturnoe tvorchestvo M. V. Lomonosova* (Moscow–Leningrad, 1962), 215.

of the European tradition, so that Tolstoy in "What Is Art?" could place Homer next to the Bible as the last "good, supreme art" still accessible to the masses.[12] There are independent strands of epic inheritance from Homer to the Byzantine "Epic Cycle of Digenis Akritas" and from there into the Kievan period of Russian literature (through old-Russian translations).

To give themselves a language and a literature, the Russians did have to free themselves from the dead weight of Byzantine as well as of French influence. As in the West, it was the classical grandparent that was called in to counteract the medieval parent. Homer worship was a sustained fashion in the nineteenth century. Not only did Tolstoy place Homer next to the Bible, but the youthful Dostoevsky likened him to Christ,[13] just as Gogol had marked the serious turn in his career by revising "Taras Bulba" to be more Homeric than Homer[14] and in his final published letters treated the *Odyssey* almost like holy writ in explaining the bases for patriarchal society.

Sunt lacrimae rerum: epic's excellent, if self-involved, memory also punctures the youthful dreams of national uniqueness and unending mission. A third Rome implies a fourth. In fact, it was the now much replaced Rome herself that invented the migrating capital as a propagandistic device through her claim to be the new Troy. Memory is not a natural ally of chauvinism. In succeeding as the Homer of Rome. Virgil also incited generations of pretenders to become the Virgil of Florence, or Protestant England, or Portugal, or Russia; there will be others. By a final irony, it was in some measure the enduring vigor of Virgil's influence that inspired the Romantics to redirect their emulation to Homer. Epic's second plot, its embedded genealogy, brings arguments more powerful than any creed or nationalism or individual career that it briefly serves. The official pieties

[12] Leo Tolstoy, *"What Is Art?"* and *"Essays on Art,"* trans. Aylmer Maude (London: Oxford University Press, 1929),178. See, in general, Chauncey E. Finch, "Tolstoy as a Student of the Classics," *Classical Journal* 47 (1952): 205-10. The comparison of Homer to the Old Testament and to Christ was a commonplace already in the eighteenth century; see Kirsti Simonsuuri, *Homer's Original Genius: Eighteenth-century Notions of the Early Greek Epic (1688-1798)* (Cambridge: Cambridge University Press, 1979), 145-52.

[13] Fyodor Dostoevsky, letter to M. M. Dostoevsky, January 1, 1840, in F. M. Dostoevskii, *Polnoe sobranie sochinenii v 30 tomakh*, vol. 28, pt. 1 (Leningrad: Nauka, 1985), 69.

[14] Carl Proffer, *The Simile and Gogol's* Dead Souls (The Hague: Mouton, 1967), 166-82.

about grand results rest uneasily on the tradition's accumulating and ineradicable documentation of fallen empires and vain human wishes. In conjuring up dead glories, the latter-day bard may even find that they are not quite dead enough. No later capital outshines fallen Troy.

In the central tradition that stretches from Homer to Milton, as to Tolstoy, Joyce, and doubtless beyond, it is less literary similarity that links the texts than their memories of one another in a transmission that has moved from song to written poetry to prose and sometimes back again and that, on the crucial topic of heroic engagement, oscillates unendingly between solemnity and mockery. "Memory," noted Walter Benjamin fifty years ago, "is the epic faculty par excellence,"[15] alone responsible for producing the transmission through successive generations. To compare epic and novel is not necessarily to differentiate literary kinds but to contrast the novel as a category (unbounded and indeterminate as it may be) with a tradition, the epic, that can easily flow into and out of this corpus as it has others. We might more accurately speak of epic as a cycle than as a genre, that is, as texts associated less by likeness than by a continuing thread of narrative and allusive gestures (for instance, Dante's Virgil-guide, Milton's proemia) that announce each new text as the final chapter of what precedes. There are, to be sure, continuing characteristics: a strong protagonist, breadth of canvas, some sort of divine apparatus.[16] As has been repeatedly proven, these characteristics are notoriously poor predictors of where the cycle will next turn. Crafty Odysseus is profoundly not where the *Iliad* was heading, and, detached from the inevitability of hindsight, Aeneas and Dante-pilgrim mark similarly odd jumps. The legions of poets who have rewritten the Aeneid are mostly forgotten; it was much more likely the subversive Ovid's parody of the epic project in fifteen metamorphic books of universal history that enabled Dante and Milton to reconstitute the Virgilian voice. Goethe's abandoned *Achilleid* captures less of Homer

---

[15] Walter Benjamin, "The Storyteller," in *Illuminations*. ed. Hannah Arendt, trans. Harry Zohn (New York: Schocken Books. 1969), 97.

[16] Serviceable surveys of these characteristics can still be found in Cecil M. Bowra, *From Virgil to Milton* (London: Macmillan and Co., 1945), 1-32; E.M.W. Tillyard, *The English Epic and Its Background* (New York: Oxford University Press, 1954), 4-13; Thomas M. Greene, *The Descent from Heaven* (New Haven and London: Yale University Press, 1963), 8-25; and Daniel Madelénat, *L'Epopée* (Paris: Presses universitaires de France, 1986), 17-78.

than does *Hermann and Dorothea*. Though the tradition advances by such dodges and displacements, in each new chapter the structure of allusion leaves no doubt about where it has been.

The bid for inclusion within this cycle involves claims to literary legitimacy and cultural centrality of most interest to literatures on the periphery. After an initial dialogue with heroic literature (Cervantes, Rabelais, Fielding, Sterne), the European novel ceased to be preoccupied with this inheritance, so that the double plot mostly drops out of sight. Within the English novel, Tillyard's "epic strain," Leavis's "great tradition," and Kermode's notion of "the classic" trace other forms of magnitude and ambition.[17] Manzoni's treatise on the historical novel charts how in Italy the cumulative weight of the tradition from Virgil to Tasso became too much to bear; after Tasso, "the public wanted to call the writing of such poems to a halt."[18] Yet again it is on the frontier, in colonial literatures, that the cycle reemerges. Diagnosing the death of epic in Europe, Hegel in his *Aesthetics* declared that the aspiring writer of epic "will be necessarily restricted to the portrayal of the victory of some future and intensely vital rationality of the American nation over the prison-house of the spirit which for ever pursues its monotonous task of self-adjustment and particularization."[19] Other cases in the West parallel the Russian claim to some such election. Attempting the great Irish novel in the conquerors' language, Joyce called in the epic grandparent, Homer, to cut the Englishmen's tradition down to scale, as did Melville in *Moby Dick*, his "prose Epic on whaling,"[20] a work emphatically other than the bourgeois English novel. As telling in its failed ambitions is Joel Barlow's *Columbiad* (1807), which deployed Homer, Virgil, and Noah Webster's simplified American spellings to break the ties with England.

---

[17] E. M. W. Tillyard, *Epic Strain*; F. R. Leavis, *The Great Tradition: George Eliot, Henry James, Joseph Conrad* (London: Chatto and Windus, 1950); Frank Kermode, *The Classic: Literary Images of Permanence and Change* (New York: Viking, 1975).

[18] Alessandro Manzoni, *On the Historical Novel*, trans. Sandra Bermann (Lincoln and London: University of Nebraska Press, 1984), 103. Originally published as *Del romanzo storico* (Milan, 1845).

[19] G. W. F. Hegel, *The Philosophy of Fine Art*, trans. F. P. B. Osmaston (London: G. Bell and Sons, 1920), 4:133.

[20] William A. Butler, in an unsigned review in the Washington, D.C., *National Intelligencer*, December 16, 1851, excerpted in *Melville: The Critical Heritage*, ed. Watson G. Branch (London and Boston: Routledge and Kegan Paul, 1974), 283.

The "heroic age" itself thrives best at the borders, as we see in the tendency of the last two centuries to transfer the term *epic* to oral traditions. For a period the invented bard Ossian stood as Homer's truest successor. Even in evolved literatures, bards do well to claim barbarian blood: to Irish eyes, the Celtic inheritance puts Dublin closer to Ithaca than is London and empowers Yeats to dream of Byzantium. As doomed companion, Queequeg makes a better descendent of Patroclus than could anyone who had heard of Patroclus, and it was the still unmastered wildness of Americans themselves that enabled Melville to construct the Iliadic tale of wrath, Ahab's as once Achilles', in conjunction with the biblical quest of Leviathan, now become a white whale. In its origins and evolution, the word *epic* has far more to do with the questions of formation of tradition that we are raising than with matters of form or style. For the Greeks, *epos* was an utterance — a word, a speech, a poem. In reference to verse it designated the vast body of poems in dactylic hexameter, not just the *Iliad* and *Odyssey* but other heroic poems in long and short forms, as well as hymns, some comic verse (the *Margites*), and didactic poems (Hesiod).[21] It is prestige that attaches epos more specifically to Homer, since for the Greeks Homer was simply "the poet," as Shakespeare is to us "the bard."

The use of *epic* for the center and pinnacle is more basic than whatever texts are promoted to that position at one time or another. The term is closer in use to *classic*, a perspective or sense of literary topography describing a corpus with a center, than it is to *lyric* or *drama* as they refer to original modes of performance, or even to the radically indeterminate category of the novel, a countering perspective where, though various centers and priorities can be argued (classics, a "great tradition"), the term is applied with no sense of such election and is constantly being redefined by what is produced. Unlike other things that might be called genres (or forms, kinds, species, modes), epic tends to be self-limiting — that is, restricted to its successes. The also-rans may still receive the term from their editors but do not come to mind when the "epic tradition" is being discussed. In naming an "American epic," most respondents would find prose (*Moby Dick*) less of a disqualification than failure (*The Columbiad*).[22]

---

[21] See, in general, Severin Koster, *Antike Epostheorien*, Palingenesia, vol. 5 (Wiesbaden: Franz Steiner Verlag, 1970).

[22] That the epic may be written in prose as well as verse is an article of faith already

The other identifying characteristic of epic is that it is long dead, indeed recurrently dead. In our era it is the novel that has killed it, just as in earlier times it was done in by philosophy (so declared Plato, extruding Homer from the Republic), by tragedy (in Aristotle's diagnosis in the *Poetics*), by confessional literature (so Augustine, turning from Dido in his *Confessions*), and then by romance (for example, Ariosto — but perhaps this was the same death that epic had died with Apollonius Rhodius almost two millennia before[23] or in the somewhat later Greek romances). Even in ages when it is not being written or perhaps read with much enthusiasm, epic maintains its preeminence as the victim of choice for the currently dominant literary form. As we shall soon discuss, it is as the victim of the novel that Lukács and Bakhtin present the epic to us. Bakhtin further argues that the novel is literature's ultimate because ultimately indeterminate form, that is, the infinitely flexible genre that precludes the emergence of any new genres.

Before turning to these theorists we might note the signs that epic may survive this latest death better than the novel will outlast its permanent victory.[24] Long before Eisenstein used Milton's War in Heaven as the shooting script for the battle on the ice in *Alexander Nevsky* (1938),[25] film had singled out epic as its predecessor and esteemed victim much more than it had the novel, though in practice it is the act of novel-reading that film-going replaces. For all the novels that are turned into screenplays, "epic" has currency as a mode of cinema in a way that "novelistic" does not.

The various cinematic applications of "epic" provide a telling reflection of the complexity of its literary uses. "Screen epic" is a thriving branch of popular culture that has inherited certain stereotypical qualities of literary

for Cervantes's Canon of Toledo in *Don Quixote*, pt. 1, chap. 47.

[23] See Charles Rowan Beye, *Epic and Romance in the Argonautica of Apollonius*, Literary Structures (Carbondale and Edwardsville: University of Southern Illinois Press, 1982).

[24] On the current possibilities for epic, including film, see "Forms of Modern Epic" in Paul Merchant, *The Epic*, The Critical Idiom, vol. 17 (London: Methuen and Company, 1971; rpt. 1979), 71-94, an engaging brief introduction to the whole epic tradition.

[25] On *Paradise Lost* as a textbook for montage and audiovisual relationships, see Sergei M. Eisenstein, *The Film Sense*, trans. and ed. Jay Leyda (New York: Harcourt, Brace and Company, 1942), 58- 62.

epic: scale, celebration of nationhood (*Birth of a Nation*, *Napoleon*) or creed (*Ben-Hur*, *The Ten Commandments*), and evocation of a past so closed and distant that its iconography translates easily into the future of science fiction (*Star Wars*).[26] At its best, especially in the tradition that stretches from Griffith to Kurosawa, this archaizing form maintains its currency remarkably well, especially in comparison to the rapid obsolescence of much literary experiment (the theater of the absurd, the *nouveau roman*).

Working from Brecht's concept of "epic theater," film theory uses the word quite differently to describe a self-conscious cinema unconstrained by those unities of time, place, and action that Aristotelians stipulated for tragedy. Inspired especially by screen clowns like Charlie Chaplin and Buster Keaton, Brecht saw the externality of film, its capacity for discontinuity, plotlessness, and stylization of gesture as a tool against the bourgeois mentality of the novel.[27] The audiences "alienated" and provoked to ideological reflection by such films, most notably those of Godard, are taken to be at a polar remove from the escapists lulled by the "screen epics." Whereas those costume dramas aspire without embarrassment to the prestige of monumental art, this other and didactic mode of "epic" cinema can instead provide a critique of tradition itself, as in the famous case of Godard's *Le Mépris* (1963), a film about a filming of the *Odyssey* by a Brecht-quoting director, "Fritz Lang" (played by Fritz Lang), bullied by a crass, capitalist American producer (Jack Palance).[28] In his allegory of the "shipwreck of modernity," as Godard called it, "the eye of the camera watching these characters in search of Homer replaces that of the gods watching over Ulysses and his companions."[29]

---

[26] A comprehensive survey of the American and European historical dramas in this category can be found in Derek Elley, *The Epic Film: Myth and History* (London: Routledge and Kegan Paul, 1984).

[27] See especially the excerpts from "Der Dreigroschenprozess," sections III (1) and (6) translated in Bertolt Brecht, *Brecht on Theater: The Development of an Aesthetic*, trans. John Willet (London and New York: Harcourt, Brace and World, 1964; rpt. 1984), 47-51.

[28] See the Analysis of Robert Stam, *Reflexivity in Film and Literature from Don Quixote to Jean-Luc Godard*. Studies in Cinema, vol. 31 (Ann Arbor, Mich.: UMI Research Press, 1985), 21-22.

[29] Jean-Luc Godard, *Godard on Godard*, trans. Tom Milne, ed. Jean Narboni and Tom Milne (New York and London: Viking, 1972; rpt., New York: Da Capo Press, 1986), 201. Originally published as *Jean-Luc Godard par Jean-Luc Godard* (Paris: B. Belfond, 1968).

These are but straws in the wind, though sufficient to warrant caution in diagnosing the death of cultural forms. Epic is still alive enough as a generative principle to be called in by Brecht as an antidote (and successor) to capitalist art forms and to inspire Godard's apotheosis of the camera. Differently understood, it also lives on in the popular imagination to organize production and consumption of a certain kind of commercial film spectacle. Those disparate applications of the term reflect the dialectic of the epic tradition as it has always advanced both by the big canvasses (whether of popular or high art) and by the critiques and dismantlings of them (in other words, as much by mock-epic as by achieved national epics).[30] The development of the cinema has replicated the age-old literary quandary about whether "epic" denotes the largest sweep of action and of meaning — the aspiration to totality — or the most retentive mode of artistic self-consciousness. The evolution of serious film has not been toward the anarchic and ahistorical proliferation once expected but toward the assertion of archetypes, the codification of allusion, the induction of its makers into a guild of *auteurs* celebrating their forebears. Once the streets of Los Angeles or São Paulo or Melbourne can be shot and edited as a recapitulation of the Berlin of the thirties, the Rome of the fifties, or the utopian Los Angeles of the studios, cinema acquires its own double plot: the quick, capacious memory, the latent internationalism that we have associated with epic. A rhetoric of jump cuts, voice-overs, and tracking shots serves this end neither better nor worse than do similes and epithets. Celluloid classicism works increasingly from a pantheon of Eisenstein. Griffith, Lang, Hitchcock. Godard, Truffaut. Yet, as in the literary tradition, such reflexivity does not necessarily disrupt emotional engagement and the suspension of disbelief, but in providing imaginative distance and protective irony can allow heroic fantasies new scope.

Having survived the advent of writing and then of printing, epic as a process of tradition forming and cultural centering is more resilient than

---

[30] To trace but one recent swing from dismantling to synthesis (and Left to Right), the antinarrative techniques of the French New Wave proved useful in the revival of the American film industry after 1967. The most extravagant and profitable "screen epics" in film history (for example, the *Star Wars* and *Indiana Jones* trilogies) employ overt allusiveness, stylization of gesture, and cartoonlike externality that (pace Brecht and Godard) facilitate escapism. On the first decade of this development, see Robert Ray, *A Certain Tendency of the Hollywood Cinema*, 1930-1980 (Princeton, N.J.: Princeton University Press, 1985), 272ff.

purely written forms like the novel or short story, though it must survive each transition by a kind of "grandfather clause," a bemused toleration of it as a living anachronism. Current prospects suggest that it is much more likely the novel itself will end in the graveyard of epic's other destroyers than that epic will forego the millennial parasitism whereby it thrives through the nostalgia and condescension of its various replacements until they are themselves replaced. Yet when literary theorists call epic dead, they do so at the invitation of its practitioners, who know how to exploit this nostalgia. For two and a half millennia, epic has been a song sung at its own funeral, always deepening its poignancy with the promise that any revival of it is the last, the very last, that we are to hear. The epic cycle is a book composed entirely of final chapters.

The Death of Epic

Too big to be overlooked and firmly planted at the cultural center, epics thus elude literary historians by presenting their credentials so duplicitously. From epoch to epoch the form comes unexpectedly alive only to find another consummation and die yet another final death. As such, the epic is a convenient starting point for teleological theorists, from Aristotle to Bakhtin, who need something big, simple, and defunct as a basis of comparison.[31] It is instructive to review the fate of Aristotle's dictum that tragedy had absorbed and superseded epic, for within a century after he wrote this, tragedy was reabsorbed into the main epic tradition: Medea moved from Euripides' stage to the hexameters of Apollonius Rhodius's *Argonautica* and then, after being dramatized in the interval by Ennius, lived on in Virgil's Dido. Epic would die another death, this time for doctrinal reasons, when that erstwhile intemperate admirer of Dido, Augustine of Hippo, turned from Virgil and the pagans to scripture and the new form of the confession. Yet the full literary realization of such autobiography, Dante's *Divine Comedy*, would bring Virgil and epic back from the grave. To be sure, Dante, like Augustine, was still marching past the tribe of Dido, now led by Francesca da Rimini, but Virgil the seducer

---

[31] On Aristotle's use of Homer in the *Poetics*, see, in particular, Stephen Halliwell, *Aristotle's Poetics* (Chapel Hill: University of North Carolina Press, 1986), 253-66.

(for Augustine) had become Virgil the guide, who could be left behind atop Mount Purgatory, not because his form was moribund, but because it was now securely reborn and redeemed.

This second death proved to be only the start of Virgil's modern *Nachleben*, for he was destined to be conjured time and again by allusion so that he might confess his obsolescence and once more bequeath his authority. As was noted above, such ghosts favor the frontiers and, within such emergent cultures, outcasts. In their various forms of exile and disenfranchisement, Dante, Milton, Joyce, and Pasternak all provide terms to understand what will be our central case, Gogol's removal to Rome. To this may be added a salient American example, where, as with Gogol, sexual identity plays a central role. To establish Nebraska as a literary landscape within the European canon, Willa Cather in *My Antonia* has the classicist Gaston Cleric and his pupil, Jim Burden, self-consciously reenact the Virgil-Dante relationship even as they read Virgil's *Georgics*, which introduced the Italian landscape into the same tradition. In *The Professor's House*, Tom Outland, like Burden an orphan, reads the *Aeneid* amid the ruins of Blue Mesa (a version of Mesa Verde) and imagines before him the very towers of Troy.[32] It is outsiders — Dante in his terrifying valley, Milton in his dark study, Outland on his lonely bluff, and Cather as heir to a European and male guild — who are most apt to see ghosts, as we shall find with Gogol and his dead souls.

For writers continuing the cycle, the "death of epic" is a topos.[33] When Virgil said early in his career that he would sing no "kings and battles," he may have meant it (*Eclogue* 6.3-5), since Homeric epic was for his generation unattainable and perhaps undesired. Whatever pressures of political circumstance (Augustus) and ambition intervened, he did go on to write other things, so that his statement now stands in his oeuvre as a prelude to epic. The epic pilgrimage to which Virgil was giving permanent

[32] See, in general, Paul A. Olson, "The Epic and Great Plains Literature: Rølvaag, Cather, and Neihardt," *Prairie Schooner* 55 (1981): 263-85. The scene may also recall Goethe's reading the Odyssey and discovering the *Urmensch* in Sicily.

[33] One of the earliest traces of this device is found in Thucydides. "We shall need no Homer to sing our praises," proclaims Pericles to the Athenians in his funeral oration (2.51), testifying both to the doomed self-assurance of imperial Athens and, at another level, to Thucydides' own claims as the writer of another great book about another great war (a greater war, he argues, than the Trojan).

definition thus starts with refusal, then surmounts it. Within the same tradition Dante-pilgrim similarly declines the invitation to join *la bella scuola* of Homer, Horace, Ovid, and Lucan. They stand with dignity as a closed chapter that we might call "the death of epic." Dante could join them only by foregoing the voyage to Beatrice. Yet he can arrive at Beatrice only with the help of refugees from that *scuola*, Virgil and Statius, who equally suggest the chapter as not closed or closable. A heresy larger than joining the pagan bards on their own terms would be to conclude that their art, or any art, is not capable of transfiguration.

The nearly obligatory *ecphrases* that descend from Achilles' shield in *Iliad* 18 provide a demonstration of how the cycle fails of closure. Entering Carthage in *Aeneid* 1, Aeneas sees on the temple of Juno reliefs of the Trojan War and, observing the sufferings of himself and his people thus memorialized by Dido, is heartened and seduced. Like the Sirens' song, this account of "kings and battles" can lure the unguarded audience to oblivion. By staying with Dido and marrying that glorious past, Aeneas, like Dante with the bards of *Inferno* 4, would go no farther. Yet those very bas-reliefs, Virgil's symbol of a defunct and entrapping art, are the literary stuff out of which Dante crafts the redemptive cycle divinely carved on the first ledge of the mountain (Mary, David, and Trajan in *Purgatorio*). The very rocks have risen. Epic is dead, long live epic.

On the death of literary forms, Alastair Fowler proposes the following rule of thumb: "Pronounce a genre dead if works related to it directly are no longer widely read, so that its forms have become unintelligible without scholarly effort."[34] On this score, Homeric epic remains more alive for the modern reader than many of its successors, like the Greek romances or Menippean satire. Unlike the novel, the epic lives not just because it is written and bought but also because it is taught and incorporated into central belief systems. The contrast of epic and novel misleads because only a three-way comparison — novel, epic, and scripture — begins to lead to clarity. To note that the novel comes from the Christian era as the epic does from the pagan nearly reverses their actual literary life in the nineteenth century. For the novel, especially in Russian eyes, was a secular and Western form, while the epic, even Homer and Virgil by posthumous conversion,

---

[34] Alastair Fowler, "The Life and Death of Literary Forms," in *New Directions in Literary History*, ed. Ralph Cohen (Baltimore: The Johns Hopkins University Press, 1974), 87.

had a status in Christian letters and ecclesiastical education older than Russia itself.[35] The prospect that the epic might be a dead tradition might have been less worrisome than the fact that the novel, for all its current aesthetic possibilities, had been spiritually stillborn. The sense of historical time moving to apocalypse, a place where the European novel could never go, was not outmoded for Gogol, nor is it, for that matter, for Solzhenitsyn. For such pilgrims, the novel is only a way station. To call a novel *The First Circle* suggests that a form beyond the novel impends.

Since the novel is the later and currently generative form, some theorists, like Lukács[36] and Bakhtin[37] have sought to define it by emphasizing its amorphousness, vitality, and open-endedness in contradistinction to the closed chapter that epic supposedly represents. Both assume that once material has flowed down to the novel and to the swamps of post-Enlightenment consciousness from the Pierian spring of epic, it never flows back uphill. Both theorists take epic (almost exclusively Homer) and novel as epitomes of their respective ages.[38] What sets the forms and ages apart is the onset of indeterminacy in spiritual as in political life, in literary form as in language. For Lukács the characteristic of the epic age, and above

[35] The *Nachleben* of Homer and Virgil can be traced throughout the Renaissance by reading their respective entries in the indices to Ernst Robert Curtius, *European Literature and the Latin Middle Ages*, trans. Willard R. Trask, Bollingen Series 36 (Princeton, N.J.: Princeton University Press, 1953), and R. R. Bolgar, *The Classical Heritage and Its Beneficiaries* (Cambridge: Cambridge University Press, 1954). On Virgil, see Domenico Comparetti, *Vergil in the Middle Ages*, trans. E. F. M. Benecke (London and New York, 1895). Simonsuuri summarizes Homer's role in the earlier conturies (*Homer's Original Genius*, 3-16) before his survey of the eighteenth century.

[36] Georg Lukács, *The Theory of the Novel*, trans. Anna Bostock (Cambridge, Mass.: MIT Press, 1971). Originally published as *Die Theorie des Romans* (Berlin: P. Cassirer, 1920). A helpful introduction to these theories is provided by Michel Aucouturier, "The Theory of the Novel in Russia in the 1930s: Lukács and Bakhtin," in *The Russian Novel from Pushkin to Pasternak*, ed. John Garrard (New Haven and London: Yale University Press, 1983), 227-40.

[37] Mikhail M. Bakhtin, "Epic and Novel" and "From the Prehistory of Novelistic Discourse," in his *The Dialogic Imagination*, ed. Michael Holquist, trans. Caryl Emerson and Michael Holquist (Austin: University of Texas Press, 1981), 3-83.

[38] As a spokesman for his age, Homer is in considerable decline among classicists. Archeologists no longer feel compelled to heed him at all. Already twenty-five years ago Emily Vermeule, in introducing her important *Greece in the Bronze Age* (Chicago and London: The University of Chicago Press, 1964), wrote, "Homer has been rejected as evidence, with a pang" (p. x).

all Homer, is "the adequacy of the deeds to the soul's inner demand for greatness, for unfolding, for wholeness.... Being and destiny, adventure and accomplishment, life and essence are then identical concepts."[39] Yet the stable, fulfilling age thus described is not a heroic age so much as a patriarchal and hierarchical one, whereas the *Iliad* at least is more insistently antiauthoritarian. Lukács's description fits the well-meaning Hector far more than it does Achilles. Consider the arc of Achilles' journey to "fulfillment": his murderous wrath against Agamemnon is turned against the whole Achaean army, which is saved only when he finally turns it against Hector and himself. What modern readers tend to find compelling in the conclusion is the remarkable scene where Achilles and Priam, momentarily but with profound understanding, step outside destinies that they both regret. Lukács's hazy ideal scarcely surprises, of course, since it was only under some such protective mist that pagan epic could be allowed to enter Christian classrooms.

In fact, the heroes of classical epic, though not necessarily the secondary characters, tend to embody just those characteristics that both theorists see as setting the novel apart from the epic. The "spiritual homelessness," the ruptured linkage of code to feeling that Lukács sees as the death knell of the heroic age is in fact what sets Achilles apart from his peers,[40] as it does Aeneas and Dante-pilgrim from theirs. Indeed, such spiritual crises may have been the integrating theme that allowed shorter lays to be organized into the larger structures of Homeric epic. The *Iliad* strings together various duels and days of glory (for Diomedes, Agamemnon, Hector, Patroclus) that enact heroic values straightforwardly enough and would seem to represent the earlier tradition. Yet the larger tale in which these elements are embedded, the wrath and revenge of Achilles, pivots on questioning, rejecting, and in some measure finally ignoring the very code that he supremely embodies.[41] It is the critique of war that enables the poem to become the great tale of war.

[39] Lukács, *Theory of the Novel*, 30.

[40] How much alienation we may see in Achilles and how much we should suspect modern biases in doing so remains the slipperiest of Homeric questions. For the state of the controversy, see James M. Redfield, *Nature and Culture in the* Iliad: *The Tragedy of Hector* (Chicago and London: The University of Chicago Press, 1975), 3-29.

[41] This position is argued concisely by Adam Parry, "The Language of Achilles,"

Similarly, the new scale allows the traditional trickster of folklore not just to overcome witches and ogres along the way, as Odysseus does Circe and the Cyclops, but to rejoin a whole family turned deceivers (Penelope and Telemachus), so that the intricate process of recognizing one another goes beyond the magic tokens and dropped masks of trickster tales to become a complex analysis of epistemology of memory and desire. Odysseus, famous now and battered, finds himself in competition with the image of the beloved king and father who had left home twenty years before. The requisite happy ending, stable and complete, of an "epic age" is attained in Ithaca only when the notion of happiness itself has been permanently destabilized by the new subjectivities discovered in memory, dreams, and deceit in a text that is itself a self-conscious response to the *Iliad*.[42] In Homer, the glorious past does, as Lukács observes, maintain its absolute superiority over the present; but it is a glory that instructively dismantles, discredits, and analyzes itself. If the "epic age" is prephilosophical and unreflective, the great epics are its most philosophical and least characteristic part.

Lukács justly observes that between antiquity and the modern era (as epitomized by the epic and the novel) stands a vast increase in literary attention to alienation and spiritual homelessness. He describes thereby one of the attractions of the epic tradition for novelists who want to overcome the indeterminacy of the novel, the anomie of their age, or their own marginality or that of their culture. Epic does — if only in the retrospect that makes it seem fixed, confident, and official — promise focus and structure. Yet when these great works are executed, tendencies emerge for the wrong hero to carry the tale, for the oldest and doctrinally least acceptable stratum of material to seem the freshest and most appealing, often the pagan rather than the Christian. This most traditional of forms may celebrate some new

Transactions and Proceedings of the American Philological Association 87 (1956): 1-7, reprinted in *The Language and Background of Homer: Some Recent Studies and Controversies*, ed. Geoffrey S. Kirk (Cambridge: Heffer; New York: Barnes and Noble, 1964), 48-54, and in Homer, ed. Harold Bloom, Modern Critical Views (New York: Chelsea House Publishers, 1986), 109-13. For a wider development of this approach, see Cedric H. Whitman, *Homer and the Homeric Tradition* (Cambridge, Mass.: Harvard University Press, 1958). See, most recently, Stephen A. Nimis, *Narrative Semiotics in the Epic Tradition: The Simile* (Bloomington and Indianapolis: Indiana University Press, 1987), 63-73.

[42] For the fullest and most recent interpretation of that literary relationship, see Pietro Pucci, *Odysseus Polutropos: Intertextual Readings in the* Odyssey *and the* Iliad (Ithaca and London: Cornell University Press., 1987).

dispensation in its overt plot but make quite a different argument in the internationalism and ungovernable self-regeneration of the allusive style, that second plot of epic which does not respect shifts of doctrine or politics or fashion. It was Dante's intention to move his readers beyond his lively, pagan Inferno, as it was Milton's to get them past the antique heroics of Satan. Not all readers stay the course.

In this early work on epic and novel, Lukács is following in the tradition of Goethe, Schiller, and most immediately Hegel by romanticizing Homer's era and reasserting the ancient habit of leading universal history from some golden age. Lukács harbors hopes of revolutionary change in bourgeois culture that will restore such an epoch, and the epic that expresses it. Though such nostalgia has more sources than can here be disentangled, it is clear that for the theorist this lost paradise provides a manageable basis of comparison for the complexities to follow. Moreover, even Romantics and socialists could not quickly cut lose from pagan literature's long cohabitation with scripture and its notion of innocent and fallen ages. Thanks to the curriculum, epic is wedded to the youth of the reader as to the youth of the race, a process that Joyce depicts in Stephen Dedalus's classroom in the second chapter of *Ulysses*. Lukács was not yet thirty years old when he wrote his celebration of Homer. As Macaulay in 1825 observed of the names in Milton's catalogues:

> Like the dwelling-place of our infancy revisited in manhood, like the song of our country heard in a strange land, they produce upon us an effect wholly independent of their intrinsic value. One transports us back to a remote period of history. Another places us among the novel scenes and manners of a distant region. A third evokes all the dear classical recollections of childhood, the schoolroom, the dog-eared Virgil, the holiday, and the prize.[43]

These habits affect writers of epics and the audiences for which they see themselves as writing, even as they affect theorists. Even if there had been no "epic age," the assumption that there was one shapes the tradition and glamorizes epic ambitions, as they mix cultural imperialism and a quest for lost innocence.

---

[43] Thomas Babington Macaulay, *Critical and Historical Essays Contributed to the Edinburgh Review* (London: Longmans, Green, and Company, 1909), 1:13, quoted by Donal M. Foerster in *The Fortunes of Epic Poetry: A Study in English and American Criticism 1750-1950* (Washington. D.C.: Catholic University Press, 1962), 149.

Perfidious and uncontrollable as it may prove to those who try to master it, epic has a tendency to become fixed and monolithic when viewed over the shoulder. Its definitive heroes are volatile, treacherous, or neurotic (Achilies, Odysseus, Aeneas); from afar, they are often mistaken for patriarchs, much as Apollo and Dionysus snatched from context have been made to serve iconographically for Christ. Inscribed in the canon, translated, and taught in school, its great successes seem sedate.

Indeed, they do lose something in the original: certainty. The "realms of gold" that Keats found in Chapman's Homer may have seemed a splendid monstrosity to a Greek audience used to short heroic lays. As Kirk observes of the monumental poem, "by the normal canons of heroic song this kind of poem is an aberration."[44] Some singer, either heroically ambitious or assisted by the new technology of writing, was stringing together a week's entertainment from Trojan tales, borrowings from other cycles, catalogues, riotous *Götterkomödie*, self-parody (Thersites, Nestor), *ecphrasis*, and a hero, given to tantrums and existential speculation, who actually fights for only four books out of twenty-four. Legions of textual surgeons have not belabored the "Homeric question" for two centuries to cure an excess of uniformity. Virgil wrote by the thousands a neoteric verse form developed to be read by the dozens and, through this massive miniature, refracted his encomium of Rome into myriad congruent and dissonant voices, not so much sung as quoted, overheard, dreamt, meant, and not meant. Beneath the stately and unified diction are a welter of generic influences: Homeric, Alexandrian, and Roman epos; Greek and Roman tragedy and lyric; oratory and decrees. Dante mixed satire, pagan heroics, scripture, lyric, Ovidian metamorphoses, and homilies as he circumnavigated the cosmos in the vernacular and wrote universal history as autobiography. Had they not come to define the tradition, these experiments might rank as travesties.

Polyphony and Pentecost

Mikhail Bakhtin centers his analysis not on genres but on the opposed generative principles of all literature, the "epic" and the "novelistic." The now

---

[44] Geoffrey S. Kirk, *The Songs of Homer* (Cambridge: Cambridge University Press, 1962), 280. See, in general, 271-300.

defunct "epic" derives from a monoglot culture (Bakhtin cites only Homeric Greece) that can express its central values in a "high and straightforward word without the interplay of voices, ironies, and languages of the "novelistic" as it emerges from periods of linguistic mixture and confrontation. The "novelistic" consolidates itself in the orientalizing ("Hellenistic") mode of Greek culture (after Alexander, third century B.C.E. onward) and in bilingual Rome, then reasserts itself strongly in the linguistic struggle that brought the vernaculars out of Latin in the Renaissance. Interestingly, the polyphonic forms that Bakhtin sees as the telos of literary development are those satiric, personalistic, many-voiced texts that Gogol a century before had described, in his survey of poetry from Lomonosov to Pushkin and Zhukovsky, as being distinctively Russian. The penultimate chapter of his final work, *Selected Passages from Correspondence with Friends*, entitled "On the Essence of Russian Poetry and on Its Originality," locates quintessential Russianness in polyglossia, the power of language as it is only now being discovered by the Russians themselves:

> After all, our extraordinary language is itself a secret. In it are all the tones and all the shades, all the transitional sounds from the solidest to the tenderest and softest; it is unlimited and can, living like life, at every moment be constantly enriched, drawing, on the one hand, from the sublime words of the biblical language of the Church, and, on the other, choosing to select accurate terms from the innumerable dialects scattered through our provinces, thus having the possibility in one and the same speech of ascending to heights inaccessible to any other language and of being lowered to a level of simplicity appreciatively felt by the dullest of men....[45]

Gogol's history organizes itself around an absence: Russian literature does not have at its center a work to pull the pieces together. "It [poetry] has accumulated only in one pile innumerable little hints of our diverse qualities; it has brought together in one depository various unconnected sides of our many-sided nature" (p.243). The problem for the Russians strikingly parallels the bilingualism that Bakhtin finds generative for the Romans, the incorporation of a more evolved literary language (French,

---

[45] Nikolai V. Gogol, *Selected Passages from Correspondence with Friends*, trans. Jesse Zeldin (Nashville. Tenn.: Vanderbilt University Press, 1969), 248. When necessary, we have altered Zeldin's translation to provide more accuracy.

like Greek) that forces the new literature to proceed with particularly acute self-consciousness — to speak, as it were, always in the mode of quotation.

Gogol is a particularly interesting source because he initiates an epic project that is inimical to Bakhtin's values. His attempt to move the novel toward being authoritative, culturally central, and nationalistic, as in some measure Gogol does, is to Bakhtin a betrayal of what is lively, subversive, and anti-authoritarian in the "novelistic." Bakhtin considers *War and Peace* monophonic and claims that Gogol "lost Russia" in trying to work the "novelistic" beginning of *Dead Souls* toward some kind of monumentality.

"Epic" as defined by Bakhtin may prove to be a phenomenon of reception more than a generative principle. As Morson has shown, as a narrative *War and Peace* responds fruitfully to Bakhtin's theory.[46] Yet the book has another life, for when it is taught in translation with classroom materials that gloss over its pointed anomalies, this once aberrant and provocative unmaking of the novel stands as an unproblematic and definitive "classic." The now canonical epics themselves came from the very moments of linguistic "interanimation" that Bakhtin emphasizes. Greek lurks behind the Latin of Virgil and Ovid, as does Latin behind Milton's English and Dante's Italian. When Gogol himself, in his retreat to Rome to write the great Russian novel, used Italian to liberate Russian from French, his gesture seemed as much a part of the Virgilian-Dantesque tradition as of "novelistic" tendency. All such works are received as monophonic and authoritarian once they have been flattened by translation, removed from the controversies of their time, and imposed on the young. Even Bakhtin's beloved Rabelais and Dostoevsky experience that dull fate when they become required reading as classics — that is, in Bakhtin's terms, as "epics."

Bakhtin's field theory of literary production so powerfully discredits the pieties and simplifications of literary historians, those purveyors of category and period, that it thwarts even his own attempt to locate "epic" and "novelistic" as historical principles. He skirts the historical paradox of how "novelistic" are the processes by which the cultural center gets constituted in the first place. To take a turning point that is paradoxical in all such histories, his Socrates midwifes "dialogism" as Plato's does philosophy. Yet

---

[46] Gary Saul Morson, *Hidden in Plain View: Narrative and Creative Potentials in War and Peace* (Stanford, Calif.: Stanford University Press, 1987).

a contradiction lurks between these claims: Plato's dialogues may be the prototype of "novelistic" style, as well as of free inquiry, but they scarcely serve the spirit of carnival. To be sure, Kristeva sees Bakhtin's analysis as a corrective to Nietzsche's attack on Socrates as a destroyer of some such tendency (that is, the Dionysian as it anticipates Bakhtin's "carnivalesque").[47] Yet, in the larger historical perspective, Nietzsche's critique retains its power. The primordial spirit of Dionysus (or of carnival) has no enemies more potent than the Academy, the transcendencies of Platonism, and, ultimately, Christian theology.

We are left with an ineradicable paradox: the basic pattern of Bakhtin's larger history is contained and reversed already in the distance traversed between Socrates in the marketplace, affirming nothing but the value of questioning, and Plato, who passed down his esoteric doctrines, the absolutes of Platonism, behind the walls of the Academy. A public gadfly inspired the foundation of the Ivory Tower; free inquiry hardened into a party line; the "popular" prose form of the dialogue supported intellectual, political, and, eventually, theological elitism. In a word, the polyphonic gave birth to the monophonic. Part of the codification that simultaneously killed and immortalized Socrates' liberating assault on received wisdom and social convention was Plato's "novelistic" gift (and he has few rivals in prose) of capturing on paper the polyphony of Socrates as he is reported in action.

Bakhtin observes, "Neither an epic nor a tragic hero could ever step out in his own character during a pause in the plot or during an intermission: he has no face for it, no gesture, no language."[48] In contrast, Socrates presides over a world that has no conventional plot, only intermissions. Here the great players in history, like the *Symposium*'s drunken Alcibiades before the Sicilian expedition, come stumbling in with their masks a-kilter, and the gap between self and society becomes the beginning of wisdom. Yet in making Socrates' life the new plot, the only true plot, Plato created a world incomparably more seamless and uniform, more ranked, centered, and organized than Homer's. Achilles only *exemplified* the old heroism (and that but fitfully); Socrates was coextensive with the new, the flesh

---

[47] Julia Kristeva, *Sēmeiōtikē: recherches pour une sémanalyse*, Collection "Tel Quel" (Paris: Editions du Seuil, 1969), 163.

[48] Bakhtin, "Epic and Novel," 36.

made spirit. Plato's playful, richly voiced prose promoted the very cultural monolith that the "novelistic" dismantles.

Bakhtin's stylistic analyses of seriocomic forms in antiquity remain unsurpassed, but ideologically he nods, and recent scholarship leaves little to support the history that he implies. Popular laughter, daily life, and the open-ended present come into literature with Aristophanes' comedies, as they do in Plato's dialogues, and Aristophanes leaves no doubts: Socrates is no friend of the *dēmos*. The comedian does not restrict his characters or his audience to an elite, but Old Comedy is something of a literary dead end. As in the Platonic dialogues, popular laughter is destined to be memorialized mostly in libraries. Another of Bakhtin's central examples, Petronius also promotes popular forms into artistic prose but, as a courtier of Nero, is presumably not expressing the *Volksgeist* in any simple way. Scholarship since Bakhtin has undermined the impression that the descent of literature into the streets and into the open-ended present might reflect movements of authorship or readership. Apart from the mostly lost farces, the emergent popular forms that Bakhtin favors tend to be regarded now as "probably written as lighter reading for the intelligentsia," as Bowie observes of Lucan and the Greek novelists.[49] It was the earlier forms like Homeric epic and Attic tragedy, which Bakhtin sees as stifling the popular imagination, that in fact entertained and unified the whole society.

As other cornerstones of Europe as the Culture of the Book, Homer and the Bible are equally involved in the paradoxes of the oral passing into the written, in this case the process of folklore becoming textually fixed and scriptural.[50] Much of Bakhtin's project can be seen as tracing the recovery

---

[49] E. L. Bowie, "The Greek Novel," in *The Cambridge History of Classical Literature*, vol. 1, Greek Literature, ed. P. E. Easterling and B. M. W. Knox (Cambridge: Cambridge University Press, 1985; rpt. 1987), 688.

[50] Bakhtin discusses the influence of the Bible, but not its creation (see "From the History of Novelistic Discourse," 69-71). Writing before this essay was published, Erich Auerbach, in *Mimesis*, contrasted the externality of Homeric characterization with a more mixed and inward-looking style first exemplified in Genesis. Auerbach's characterization of Homeric style has largely been dismissed by classicists; see, for example, Jasper Griffin, *Homer on Life and Death* (Oxford: Clarendon Press, 1980; rpt., 1983), 50-80 (earlier critiques cited, p. 70, n. 37). On Bakhtin and Auerbach, see Tzvetan Todorov, *Mikhail Bakhtin: The Dialogical Principle*, trans. Wlad Godzich, Theory and History of Literature, vol. 13 (Minneapolis: University of Minnesota Press, 1980), 89-90. Originally published as *Mikhaïl Bakhtine: le principe dialogique* (Paris: Editions du Seuil, 1981).

in prose of the "voice" lost as oral forms reduced themselves to the silent page. Just as between Socratic play and Platonic doctrine, we are forced to make other distinctions: between epic as sung and created and Bakhtin's "epic" as received; between the Bible as created and scripture as imposed. Both the Homeric epics and the Hebrew Bible are aggregates of radically heterogeneous material that does not become less complex by being compiled. Even in the *Iliad* philologists have come to appreciate a quality of multivoicedness in the tension of speeches and narrative.[51]

Palestine and the Greek coast of Asia, Homer's Ionia, are Bakhtin's linguistic crossroads par excellence.[52] It seems misleading to treat either aggregate, Bible or Homer, as the dead cultural center and the outgrowth of some organized political intention when the "national" identities being asserted are more caused than celebrated by the texts themselves. In antiquity, both Greece (never a nation) and Israel have a firmer identity in these texts than they did on the map. The texts' affirmation of hierarchy often involves irony: what are we to make of the king or patriarch as trickster (Odysseus, Jacob)? The cultural reach and narrative power that render this writ holy are oral, folkloric, quintessentially polyphonic. For Bible, as for epic, the lack of "interiority" is not a safe assumption.[53] It is the processes of reception — the reduction of performances to inviolable texts, of a lively industry to a few official survivors, and of a colorful *Kunstsprache*

[51] Even three decades ago Hermann Fränkel, a scholar of Auerbach's generation and similarly a proponent of *Geistesgeschichte*, could describe what in Bakhtin's terms seems to be a dialogical quality in Homer: "The restraint which the epic poet imposes upon himself is set aside in the numerous speeches which he weaves into his work. Only so long as the singer is reporting events does he remain a mere shadow, discreet and neutral... In general the speeches are freer and richer; their style and their mode and course of thought are more modern than is narrative. In the speeches we find quite often ideas, reflections, relationships, in contradiction to those upon which the narrative and action rest. It is as if forces held in check had here broken out with elemental strength." *Early Greek Poetry and Philosophy*, trans. Moses Hadas and James Willis (New York and London: Harcourt Brace Jovanovich, 1975), 39-40. Originally published as *Dichtung und Philosophie des frühen Griechentums* (Munich: C. H. Beck'sche Verlagsbuchhandlung, 1962).

[52] That it was the very marginality of Ionia which enabled the Homeric definition of "Greekness" is a traditional speculation elegantly formulated by E. M. W. Tillyard, *English Epic*, 36-39.

[53] Along with Auerbach, see, for example, the readings of Robert Alter, *The Art of Biblical Narrative* (New York: Basic Books, 1981).

to flat, pious translationese — that create the impression of simplicity.[54] The monophony of "epic" may result more from our tone-deafness than from the processes that create the aggregations which then become the anchors of society.

Problematic as is Bakhtin's category of "epic" in historical terms, it does describe a phenomenon central to the traditions we are tracing. For the poets themselves exploit the "epic" sense of authority and centrality by parading their own grand inheritance and celebrating the canon they wish to join. Yet in the very act of pretending that their inheritance is grand and fixed, they distort it freely, as they must, and render the canon malleable. As was discussed above, the statuesque assemblage of Virgil, Homer, Horace, Ovid, and Lucan in *Inferno* 4 gives only a first and dangerous illusion of the canon, for Virgil's mobility and the encounter with the converted Statius will redeem the very concept of canon from its secular and ancient terms. Harold Bloom finds a similar freedom in Milton's adaptation of epic *ecphrasis*. Whereas Homer and Virgil miniaturized the world on their heroes' shields, Milton presents Satan's shield as a microcosm of his own literary antecedents, optically distorted (complete with Galileo's glass) to fill his own needs: "Milton does what Bacon hoped to do; Milton and Galileo become ancients, and Homer, Virgil, Ovid, Dante, Tasso, Spencer become belated moderns."[55] At key moments in the epic pilgrimage, the tradition itself steps forward to guide the seeker. Yet the tradition thus embodied may represent a reconceiving of history more radical than Bakhtin's. In the

[54] On the nature of the performances that lie behind the Homeric texts, see Eric A. Havelock, *Preface to Plato* (Cambridge, Mass.: Harvard University Press, and Oxford: Basil Blackwell, 1963; rpt., New York: Bantam, 1982), 145-64; Joseph Russo and Bennett Simon, "Homeric Psychology and the Oral Epic Tradition," *Journal of the History of Ideas* 29 (1968): 485-98; and Bennett Simon, Mind and Madness in *Ancient Greece: The Classical Roots of Modern Psychology* (Ithaca and London: Cornell University Press, 1978), 78-88.

[55] Harold Bloom, *A Map of Misreading* (New York: Oxford University Press, 1975), 138. Milton's inversion of time may derive from the scene in the *Aeneid* (8.626-728) where the baffled Aeneas looks on a divine shield summarizing the history of a Rome that has not yet been founded. Leo Bersani, "Against *Ulysses*," *Raritan* 8, no. 2 (Fall 1988): 21, observes a similar absorption and reconstitution of canon in *Ulysses*: "The Joycean intertext rescues Western literature from the deconstructive effects of the intertext itself. The parodistic replays of Homer, Shakespeare, and Flaubert — not to speak of all the authors "quoted" in "Oxen of the Sun" — are neither subversive of nor indifferent to the fact of cultural inheritance; rather, Joyce relocates the items of that inheritance with *Ulysses* as both their center and belated origin."

name of theory he may present an improbably one-dimensional Homer, but consider what Dante does to Virgil out of love: Virgilio speaks Italian, after all, and recants part of the Latin verse of Roman Virgil (*Inferno* 20). He turns out not only to have inspired Statius but to have converted him to Christianity.[56] The cultural center that epics celebrate keeps shifting, as does the frontier from which they address that center.

If we separate epics as they came to be written from the concept of monophonic "epic," which we are arguing to be largely a result of reception, we find that Bakhtin's use of counter-genre proves useful for describing the dialectic by which the tradition advances. He notes that epics generate parodies and reactions to themselves that then belong to another and "novelistic" form. Our view is that these shorter forms — mock-heroic, pastoral, and didactic poetry — regularly become reabsorbed into the larger syntheses that we are calling epic, which grow all the more "novelistic" thereby. The *Iliad* and *Odyssey* incorporate and derive from shorter forms at various levels of seriousness (for example, the *Odyssey*'s Demodocus sings a ribald tale of Aphrodite and Ares at 8.265-366). And archaic epos presents a range of didactic verse (Hesiod), as well as the *Homeric Hymns*' mixture of humor, etiology, and piety. Between Homer and Virgil lie the countermonumental short, variegated forms of the Alexandrians (Theocritus, Callimachus, Apollonius Rhodius) that are reabsorbed into the larger forms of Virgil and Ovid. Between Virgil and Dante one of the major links is the counter-epic of the insouciant Ovid.[57] Within this familiar cycle of serious monuments and the reactions thereto, even the most unlikely swings are now well studied, for instance, that between Ovid and the unsmiling Milton.[58] That successful epics temporarily exhaust the form was a commonplace assumption already in antiquity, and how a great cultural synthesis like the *Aeneid* should leave Ovid to look elsewhere as he

[56] On Dante's restaging of the tradition, see the section "Epic Resolution" in Teodolinda Barolini, *Dante's Poets: Textuality and Truth in the Comedy* (Princeton, N.J.: Princeton University Press, 1984), 188-296.

[57] On Ovid and epic, see Brooks Otis, *Ovid as an Epic Poet* (Cambridge: Cambridge University Press, 1966; 2nd ed., 1970) and Robert Coleman's review, "Ovid and the Anti-Epic," *Classical Review* n.s. 17 (1967): 46-51.

[58] See Louis L. Martz, *Poet of Exile: A Study of Milton's Poetry* (New Haven and London: Yale University Press, 1980), and Richard J. DuRocher, *Milton and Ovid* (Ithaca and London: Cornell University Press, 1985), who usefully survey work on countergenre.

constructed his fifteen books of universal history in ironic and metamorphic terms needs no further explanation.

These ironic forms are not just a medium for epic concerns to reformulate themselves between monumental syntheses — the valleys between the peaks, as it were — but are often the mode in which an opening can be made by epics or by novels in the epic tradition. Though mock heroic was the path taken by Sterne and Fielding to work forward from epic poetry to the novel, Joyce was scarcely the first to demonstrate that the same path also leads backward; we shall be arguing that case for Gogol.[59] The larger epic journey, as mapped by Dante and then Milton, begins infernally: with descent, mockery, and derision — that is, with the central mock-heroic operations of seeing the great ones of this world frozen, shrunk, and humiliated. Even the *Iliad* begins, not with battle, but with heroes throwing tantrums. Heroism manifests itself faster and more interestingly by its deformations than by its triumphs, which, narratively, must always be rare and climactic. Indeed, it has never been supposedly useful, dignified triumph that fixes the paramount heroes in the mind but, rather, peculiar scenes like Achilles' mutilation of Hector's corpse, Odysseus' being beaten as a beggar, Heracles' killing of his wife and sons. The normative hero being normatively heroic can radiate glory from a temple frieze or metope but plays no more than a supporting role in epic (see Homer's Diomedes, Ajax, Patroclus, Sarpedon): there is just no story in it. The heroism that is the simple, static, ancient thing from which literary theory traces all the interesting variations and debunkings turns out to be more like the severe and focused idealism of classical sculpture, which Hegel and Nietzsche found a more manageable inspiration than the disruptive heroes of Greek poetry. In epic, a heroic figure can include all manner of contradictions — indeed must include them — as long as they are explosive contradictions. It is scarcely out of the question for Gogol in *Dead Souls* to start with infernal descent and conceive that it might be leading somewhere higher.

The serious shorter forms also figure in the epic tradition, indeed shape the canonical epic career as, following Virgil's pattern, it progressed from

---

[59] For an astute appreciation of the interplay of the high and low mimetic modes in heroic literature, see George deForest Lord, *Heroic Mockery: Variations on Epic Themes from Homer to Joyce* (Newark, Del.: University of Delaware Press, 1977).

pastorals (the *stylus humilis*) to georgics (the *stylus mediocris*) and finally
to the *Aeneid* (the *stylus gravis*) — a course followed in various ways by
Dante, Ariosto, Milton, and Pope. We noted above that epic, though by
appearance the most encompassing and self-sufficient of forms, is uniquely
dependent on the texts that precede it — that is, can speak only as the end
and consummation of some much longer discourse over the centuries.
A second paradox now emerges about epic as a uniquely contingent form:
apart from the *Iliad*, epics have credibility only as they come at the end
of certain kinds of careers. Even the *Odyssey* was explained by Pseudo-
Longinus as the product of Homer's old age. In prose, apprenticeships that
advance from short to long, *humilis* to *gravis*, are regular: from short story
to novel in Tolstoy's case and from Joyce's *Dubliners* to *A Portrait of the Artist*
to *Ulysses*. We shall argue much the same for the progression from Gogol's
short stories to "Taras Bulba" to *Dead Souls*. The larger form can be seen to
incorporate and comment on the shorter forms.[60] With autobiographical or
semiautobiographical narratives, the career then becomes the pilgrimage
(Dante's *Comedy*). Far from becoming juvenilia, these shorter early texts
have continuing use in any oeuvre because they explain things about
the culminating masterpiece — the *Aeneid* or *Paradise Lost* — that the
text cannot explain about itself. For these minor forms, like the pastoral
and the georgic, do not so much memorialize some closed heroic age as
mediate between past and present, the grand and the everyday, the heroic
and the political. Hence it is that readers can find the "true" Virgil in the
less encumbered voice of the *Georgics* or the *Eclogues*, and more Milton in
"Lycidas" than in *Paradise Lost*. The great epics thus do not speak to their
age in isolation but in fact rely on these "satellite" forms as a kind of buffer,
a mode of translating heroic values to ordinary use in ways that go beyond
what the epics themselves can provide. Gogol's placement of "Taras Bulba"
within the *Mirgorod* cycle will provide a concrete example of this need to
cushion and insulate the boldest heroic statements.

---

[60] Ralph Cohen argues that the basis of genres in the eighteenth century was
a hierarchy in which the lower forms tended to inclusion in the higher (for example,
epigram into satire, sonnet into drama). As the highest form, epic was the most inclusive.
See "On the Interrelations of Eighteenth-Century Literary Forms," in *New Approaches
to Eighteenth-Century Literature*, ed. Phillip Harth (New York and London: Columbia
University Press, 1974), 33-78.

As with the created memory of "heroic ages," the simplicities imposed on epics — noble to Lukács, dull to Bakhtin — are themselves an important element in the tradition, for they suggest the field of reader expectations in which writers of epic operate or which they share. Bakhtin's brief analysis of *Dead Souls* reflects precisely the misapprehensions of epic that may have led Gogol himself astray: "The form of his epic Gogol modeled on the *Divine Comedy*; it was in this form that he imagined the greatness of his work lay. But what in fact emerged was Menippean satire. Once having entered the zone of familiar contact he was unable to leave it, and he was unable to transfer into this sphere distanced and positive images" ("Epic and Novel," p. 28). Bakhtin sees in Menippean satire, mixing as it does prose and poetry, high style and low subjects, an ancient precursor of the novel, a form that stands in familiar, disrespectful proximity to its subjects. What he excludes is that "the zone of familiar contact," the satirist's underworld, could be the traditional starting place of cosmic journeys. Yet may it not be the attempt to leave this fallen world that distinguishes the bard from the satirist, regardless of whether or not that attempt is successful? Dante's escape is acknowledged; Milton's remains controversial (did Satan win?); Gogol burned his sequel and turned to epistles. Bakhtin continues: "Gogol could not manage the move from Hell to Purgatory and then to Paradise with the same people and in the same work; no continuous transition was possible" (p. 28). Yet what Bakhtin expects of Purgatory, as of the whole epic landscape, is the stuff not of epic but of scripture (and of theology more than of scripture). His confusion is interesting, for it may replicate the literalism that left Gogol himself forever waiting at the gate: "It [the epic world of the absolute past] is given solely as tradition, sacred and sacrosanct, evaluated in the same way by all and demanding a pious attitude toward itself" (p. 16). But, of course, Dante's mundanely angelic Purgatory proves accessible precisely because it is such an ambiguous realm, so complexly human. It is not the world of the absolute past or the coming eternity, but proceeds, as do we, under the cycles of the sun. There is no angel at the gate, but Roman Cato; pagan history, myths, and art are not left behind but continue on, tellingly juxtaposed with biblical. Pagan Virgil is finally abandoned, but not before Roman Statius has joined up. The transitional nature of this realm is emphasized stylistically by the degree to which the style is scriptural and non-scriptural, or rather half-scriptural and entirely epic. To the large degree that Purgatory is the invention of Dante's own imagination rather than of Christian theology, it bears its own self-qualifications as metaphor and is not "given solely as tradition." Indeed, the farther Dante gets from Hell, the less tradition he has to go on. Purgatory is a poetic realm characterized by all the complicated give-and-take with contemporary reality — of spirit into flesh — that Bakhtin excludes for the epic and that Gogol himself may never have grasped as appropriate for the redemptive mode of his *commedia*. Hardest of all to portray is a second birth that is a rebirth into flesh, a promotion to humility: "Gogol lost Russia, that is, he lost his blueprint for perceiving and representing her; he got muddled somewhere between memory and familiar contact — to put it bluntly, he could not find the proper focus on his binoculars" (p. 281). To be sure, there is a muddle between the grubby particulars of Gogol's provincial N — and the vast shadow cast by a once and future Rus', but can we be sure that it is not a designed muddle? — that the blurring shift of focus, the near suddenly seen from afar, is not one of the characteristic effects of epic?

In *Selected Passages* Gogol, like Bakhtin, is a theorist trying to explain why the narrative of *Dead Souls* stalled after the first installment. As noted above, his history of Russian poetry centers on a notion of heteroglossia very like Bakhtin's, and equally teleological. The penultimate chapter of *Selected Passages*, on the originality of Russian verse, is Gogol's literary posing of the question Whither Rus'? Yet Gogol reverses Bakhtin's direction almost exactly. The lack of a monumental center is not a liberation but a captivity. Having surrendered to the French language and European writers, the Russians do not yet know their own language. It remains hidden, fractured, unresolved:

> Our poets have perceived that the time has not yet come to paint us as a whole and brag about us, that we must still be organized, become ourselves and make ourselves Russians. Our nature is still too soft, still too unprepared to take the form fitting to it; we have still not had time to take in the total of that multitude of elements of all kinds and all origins brought into our land from every place, an incoherent concurrence of alien forces within us, an unwise result of a concatenation commanded by God. (*Selected Passages*, p. 243)

The inchoate diffuseness of Russian culture is a form of Babel, and Gogol moves to the final chapter, "Easter Sunday," with a vision of the descent of the Holy Spirit that recalls the reversing of Babel at Pentecost:

This [true Russian] speech will pass into every soul, it will not fall on sterile soil. Our poetry will be imbued with an angelic passion and, having struck every string there is in the Russian, it will move the most hardened soul with a holiness with which no power and no instrument in man can contend: it will evoke our Russia for us — our Russian Russia. (p. 248)

Gogol's vision is radically centripetal. It looks, like Pentecost, to the rescinding of difference, to unification. Here we see clearly the Gogol who had left himself no human language with which to work. He was possessed of a theory whose absolute terms prevented him from speaking at the cultural center — that is, from giving Russia the monument she wanted — by the assumption that such a center must be unitary, fixed, not just stable but eternal, not entirely of this earth. His radical insistence on throwing off foreign masters leaves him with no access to the international tradition that established Greek epic at the Virgilian center of Roman letters, pagan Virgil as Dante's guide to the Christian afterlife, and Catholic, Italian Dante himself as guide to Chichikov's pilgrimage through the dead as it gave birth to the Russian novel.

Temporal Closure

If the epic tradition cannot be firmly fixed within an "epic age," it may still confine itself to describing some such thing. The handling of time has been invoked since Goethe[61] to differentiate epic from other forms — tragedy for Goethe, the novel for Bakhtin.[62] Epic is said to assume a fully distanced, completed, irrefutably glorious age that is "vollkommen vergangen," an

---

[61] In Goethe's 1797 essay (published in 1827 and cosigned by Schiller) "Über epische und dramatische Dichtung," in *Goethes Werke*, ed. Erich Trunz, Hamburger Ausgabe in 14 Bänden, vol. 12 (12th ed., 1981), 249-51.

[62] Goethe locates the distinction in the different modes of performing, not writing, epic and tragedy, that is, between the rhapsode's impersonal narration of past events and the mime's reenactment. Later work on oral poetry has largely discredited this distinction (see above, nn. 50 and 54). More than half of both the *Iliad* and the *Odyssey* consists of highly performable speeches.

In his critique of Bakhtin's failure ever to define or limit the category of "novel," Todorov (*Mikhail Bakhtin*, 89-90) discusses this transformation of Goethe's antithesis and notes that Plato would class both epic and novel as *diēgēsis*, as Bakhtin himself tends to do in his later writings.

"absolute past." The values of this age are fixed and normative and are not subject to reinterpretation by the anonymous bards who celebrate them. There are, indeed, ancient epics (the *Iliad*) and modern imitations (Gogol's "Taras Bulba") that maintain this distance; but apart from Homer they are rare even in antiquity. The interweaving of the ages of Aeneas and Augustus in the *Aeneid* typifies the etiological mode of epos that may have been dominant even before the *Iliad*.[63] As on other counts, then, the simplicities of the "epic" pole may be delusory.

The forms that replace the epic — tragedy, the novel, and arguably film — deal with the indeterminacy of the present, the "vollkommen gegenwärtig," and the ineluctable subjectivity of perceiving that present as well as of generating values for an everyday world that has not, as in epic, been fossilized into *gloire*. In Bakhtin's formulation, the open-endedness of the novel as a form responds to the open-endedness of history as we experience it. Now, the drift from the one mode to the other does encapsulate much of literary history in the period when the novel has been attaining predominance. Modern literature manifestly concerns itself with contemporary and ordinary things, "low" subjects, to a degree that ancient did not. Yet within both the epic tradition and the novelistic mode we find works that mix these two temporal perspectives and distinguish themselves in important ways along this same axis. Therein lies much of how the *Odyssey* as a sequel sets itself apart from the *Iliad*, for it shifts the focus from battle to marriage and housekeeping, slaves and peasants, the foolishness of taking risks and the glories of one's own backyard. To be sure, the events recounted officially belong to an age as distant and closed as that of the *Iliad*, yet nothing delineates Ithaca as lost or unattainable in quite the way that Troy is. Conversely, some historical novels, like those of Sir Walter Scott, present a kind of temporal closure, an "absolute past," in contrast to the contemporaneity and subjectivity of *Ulysses*, where the pervasive evocation of Homer serves not to distance and separate past and present but to entangle them in poignant confusion. Certain subjects too lowly for the bourgeois sensibilities of the novel can be accommodated precisely to the extent that the novelist aspires to the "high" form of the epic, with its greater interest in myth and fantasy. For it is as part of an

---

[63] This possibility has been explored most fully by Gregory Nagy, *The Best of the Achaeans* (Baltimore and London: The Johns Hopkins University Press, 1979; rpt., 1981).

enchanted landscape, an escape from urban, middle-class conventionality, that Tolstoy's wise peasants, Platon (Plato) Karataev in *War and Peace* and Platon Fokanich in *Anna Karenina*, emerge to prophesy and redeem, as descendents commonly of Christ as shepherd and the wise Odyssean herdsman, Eumaeus.

In their fullest forms, epics and novels combine both senses of time, and it may not be the proportions that qualify any given work as epic or novelistic, but rather the direction charted between past and present. That is, it is not the lack of connection with the current time that characterizes the epic so much as the appropriation of contemporary realities to create an importance like that of the past, a raid conducted on the present by a grander past. Writers may permit themselves surprising turns on this issue or, to use Bakhtin's image, refocus their binoculars. Dante's first audience might well have been surprised to find something as immemorial as Hades filled with Florentines whom they may have known personally. His larger intention was not to bring great traditional ideas like Heaven and Hell down to the level of daily reality but, on the contrary, ultimately to claim that near and credible reality for the larger eschatological perspective. We must be alert to the possibility that Gogol did not just betray epic in order to look satirically at contemporary Russia but ended up by claiming the satirized countryside for the eternal notion of Rus'.

In respect to the sense of time, one can find this doubleness in all epics after Homer as a result of the double plot discussed above. Even when the action transpires in some decisively closed age, the allusiveness of the language, the degree to which it renews rather than remembers what has been said before (or rather how it has been said), contradicts the whole notion of closure. Writing as he does, Virgil is a more material reincarnation of Homer than Augustus is of Aeneas, for words can be preserved and reused in a way that power cannot. In all Christian epic, even when the argument declares pagan antiquity to be a closed chapter, that past culture lives on as a generative principle in the style. The notion of the Epic Muse baffles the modern imagination in instructive ways. Does she symbolize the weighty authority of received tradition, the certification of accurate memory, or, on the contrary, some liberating access of inspiration? Does she serve *ars* or *ingenium*? Are her gifts agelessly fresh or long fossilized? Faced with these contradictions the epic poet addresses the fixity of the past in a constantly transmuting poetic medium that itself eludes fixity and even (in the Grecizing Latin of Roman epic, the Latinate Italian of Dante, and un-Englished English of Milton) the separate identity of particular languages. Though the novel may be the fruit of a polyglot era, as Bakhtin observes, it can and usually does speak in a single language in a way that fully realized epic cannot. Quite unlike its plot *in illo tempore* (when such it is), the language of epic is all history and no past — or rather, a past not remembered but spoken. As is the nature of prose, the language of the novel ages far more quickly and conspicuously than the atemporal artificialities of epic discourse. In incorporating epic tones, obsolete as the theorist may find them, the novel does not become instantly antiquated in its discourse so much as it strives to agelessness and insulation from its own passing moment. In other words, anachronism may be an active defense against obsolescence.

Novels, like all modern literature, explore subjectivity more intensively than does ancient poetry. Yet one cannot therefore claim that the movement toward subjectivity is necessarily a movement away from epic, for in the Christian system the mind as a place unto itself becomes the true and only site of heroic endeavor, and therefore a fit ground for epic struggles. Confessional literature, starting with Augustine, provides one of the purest embodiments of novelistic tendency. Dante turned it into epic; and no one will claim that he is deficiently confessional or, in Christian terms, deficiently heroic. To deal with this problem, Lukács sees Dante as moving backward and forward simultaneously, for in him "principles of structuration which tend toward the novel are re-transformed back into the epic."[64] As noted above, epic may identify itself in contradistinction to the novel not by the proportions of its temporal and evaluative perspectives, but by the movement among them; not, that is, the net amounts of "high" and "low," "far" and "near," "then" and "now," but by a final redemptive drift (even if it seems only a blurring of focus) that snatches up humbler things to serve higher perspectives, even if those higher views are just questions and muddled hopes.

---

[64] Lukács, *Theory of the Novel*, 82. John Freccero uses Lukács's observations as the basis for a reading of *Inferno* 26. See "Dante's Ulysses: From Epic to Novel," in *Concepts of the Hero in the Middle Ages and the Renaissance*, ed. Norman T Burns and Christopher J. Reagan (Albany: SUNY Press, 1975) 101–19; reprinted in John Freccero, *Dante: The Poetics of Conversion*, ed. and intro. Rachel Jacoff (Cambridge, Mass.: Harvard University Press. 1986), 136-51.

In adopting this perspective, we shall perhaps be less baffled that the most monumental of novelistic traditions — and by including works like *War and Peace*, *The Brothers Karamazov*, *The Quiet Don*, and *The First Circle* we can reasonably call it the most epic — should take its beginning from Chichikov's visit to a village of living dead and immense pygmies. For, as we have noted, it is not unprecedented in the epic tradition, or at least around it, for smaller to give birth to larger and mockery to spawn high seriousness, that is, for heterogeneous and "low" materials to coalesce into a larger hope. As we shall see, in some ways this is the argument of *Dead Souls* itself. In presenting epic more as cycle than as genre, as a mode of other genres rather than a form unto itself, we propose a new meaning to the familiar designation of an "epic tradition" in the Russian novel. For it is not just scale and calling that define the category but the quality of memory that attaches the novels to the prophets of other nations — Homer, Virgil, Dante — and novelist to novelist, as in Dostoevsky's implicit sense that he is not just replicating or rivaling Gogol's vision but materially continuing his project, as we shall see. This is a quality of memory potent enough to transform the view even of proximate, ignoble reality.

As we noted at the outset, using the great bards entails some hidden costs. Once one has invoked Greeks, Romans, and Florentines to drive French books from Russian soil, one may find oneself still culturally enslaved to equally foreign and merely older masters. They may allow the writer to speak for the very origins of civilization, now pristinely recreating themselves on Russian soil, and may validate his prophetic tone. Yet such necromancy is easier to start than to stop, and what may be reexperienced are not just the primal virtues and vigors of Western culture but its first schisms — schisms that call into question the very act of making fictions and other false idols. The conqueror of Parnassus may regret that it was not Zion. Beyond the bards one finds the prophets; behind epic, scripture; behind heroes, patriarchs. The antique perspectives that adroitly celebrate Russian spirituality in contrast to European materialism also evoke the secular, pagan origins of epic. Though more uncontaminated than the current moment, antiquity itself proves to have its better and worse parts.

The journey beyond novelistic fiction may then continue on beyond any fiction whatsoever, as we see in the careers of Tolstoy and Solzhenitsyn in the wake of Gogol, to whom we now turn. Viewed over the shoulder, epic becomes scripture, and this, with surprising frequency, turns out to be what the epic novelists of Russia finally decide that they want to write or to have written. Yet the force and richness of the tradition is also such that the same men as theorists, Russians, or Christians may discuss epic as one thing but write it as quite another, aspire to it as monolith but execute it, necessarily, as mosaic.

2. GOGOL IN ROME

> *Of Russia I can write only in Rome,*
> *only there it stands before me in all its*
> *immensity.*
>
> — N. V. Gogol to P. A. Pletnev,
> March 17, 1842

In July of 1836, amid the stormy reception of *The Inspector General*, Gogol set off on his first trip to Rome, where he was to spend the better part of the next six years and reach the pinnacle of his career.[1] In time he called the city his spiritual home and Italian his second language. Rome proved to be the site of his greatest productivity, which climaxed in 1842 with the publication of the first part of *Dead Souls*, the premiere of *Marriage*, and a new edition of the Collected Works incorporating "The Overcoat," as well as extensive revisions of "Taras Bulba" and "The Portrait." For a writer finishing a magnum opus intended to put Russia on the literary map (as *Dead Souls* did), Rome was an obvious choice. Winckelmann and Goethe had established an Italian pilgrimage as de rigueur for Romantics.[2] For Russians, the city of Augustus and Saint Peter had long symbolized the national sense both of exclusion and of election — the heart of a Europe toward which they felt both peripheral and, in the vision of Moscow as the third Rome, proprietary. What more appropriate site than the Eternal City for inscribing Russia's great book?[3] Both writer and book (on which he had been working for two years) were to be reborn in this city that, along

---

[1] The fullest account of Gogol's sojourn is Sigrid Richter's Hamburg University dissertation, "Rom und Gogol': Gogol's Romerlebnis und sein Fragment 'Rim'" (1964).

[2] See Eliza Marian Butler, *The Tyranny of Greece over Germany*, (Cambridge: Cambridge University Press, 1935; rpt., Boston: Beacon Press, 1958).

[3] For some interesting thoughts on this subject, as well as on Gogol's narrative art in general, see Hugh McLean, "Gogol and the Whirling Telescope," in *Russia: Essays in History and Literature*, ed. G. Lyman and M. Legters (Leiden: Brill, 1972), 79-99.

with the entire country, Gogol anthropomorphized in one of his letters as "a beloved one" and "a beautiful woman." In the same letter he wrote: "[Italy] is mine. No one in the world can take her away from me. I was born here. Russia, Petersburg… were but a dream. I have reawakened and am again in my homeland."[4] Like the real inspector general, who arrives only when the false one has come and gone, the resurrected author and his great salvational novel were to appear directly after the nightmare of Russia had terminated in the spiritually renewing setting of Rome.

Gogol himself compared living in Rome to reading an epic and savored the palimpsestic quality of the city:[5] "One half of it gives off the aroma of the life of paganism, the other half the age of Christianity, and both are the two greatest ideas in the world."[6] His close companion P. V. Annenkov tells us that "he was rereading his favorite passages from Dante, Gnedich's *Iliad*, and Pushkin's poetry"[7] — that is, the wellsprings of monumental literature, respectively, for Christendom, for Europe, and for Russia. In "The Portrait," the Russian monk-painter, whose noble example haunts and finally destroys the corrupt society portraitist Chertkov, made this double pilgrimage to Italy (while Chertkov indulges himself in Petersburg) and to the classics (while Chertkov can affirm only the modern, and finally himself):

> He [the ideal painter] ended up taking for his teacher only the divine Raphael, like a great poet who, after reading many works of every kind,

---

[4] N. V. Gogol, *Sobranie sochinenii v semi tomakh* (Moscow, 1966-67), 7:177.

[5] N. V. Gogol, *Polnoe sobranie sochinenii* (Moscow, 1937-52), 11:115. For a brief survey of his classical background, see Chauncey E. Finch, "Classical Influence on N. V. Gogol," *Classical Journal* 48 (1953): 291-96.

[6] Quoted by V. V. Gippius in *Gogol*, ed. and trans. Robert A. Maguire (Ann Arbor, Mich.: Ardis, 1981), 97.

[7] P. V. Annenkov, "N. V. Gogol' v Rime letom 1841 goda," in *Gogol' v vospominaniyakh sovremennikov*, ed. S. Mashinskii (Moscow, 1952), 273. On June 3, 1837, Gogol wrote to his friend N. Y. Prokopovich about the Italian sounds of Tasso and Dante (*Polnoe sobranie sochinenii*, 11:102). On August 10, 1839, he wrote to S. P. Shevyrev to thank and heartily praise him for his translation of Dante (ibid., 11:247). It is unknown precisely when Gogol first read Dante, but the noted scholar F. C. Driessen finds a parallel between Inferno 32 and 33 and Gogol's early story "A Terrible Vengeance" (1831). See Driessen, *Gogol as Short Story Writer* (The Hague: Mouton. 1965), 109. By March 15, 1839, he had sufficient Italian to write a long letter to M. P. Balabina. For a compilation of all attributed evidence of Gogol's responses to Dante, see A. A. Asoyan, "Zametki o dantovskikh motivakh u Belinskogo i Gogolya," in *Dantovskie Chteniya* 1985 (Moscow: Nauka, 1985), 104-19.

full of many wonderful and sublime passages, leaves Homer's *Iliad* on his table as his constant book of reference, having discovered that it contains everything one can wish, and that there is nothing in the whole world that cannot be found in it expressed to perfection. And so he had gained from the study of his great master's works a sublime conception of creative art, an intense beauty of thought, and the superb loveliness of a divinely inspired brush.[8]

The classic masters, like the Holy City, bear witness to the divine even beyond what they as pagans or humanists might have quite realized. The happy coexistence of Christianity and paganism in Rome symbolized for Gogol the compatibility, perhaps the identity, of the classic with the holy.

The result of Gogol's Roman pilgrimage, the first part of *Dead Souls*, did succeed in launching a monumental tradition in Russian prose, as even the French acknowledged, starting with the Vicomte E.-M. de Vogüé.[9] *Dead Souls*, however, may be the most problematic text in monumental literature, Russian or other.[10] Labeling itself a "poèma" (monumental narrative) it proceeds to be anything but that, until it ends by prophesying national destiny as if it had been an epic all along. Mangled traces of Homer, Virgil, Ovid, and Dante are recoverable from the text and sometimes flaunted by it, but the reader seeking a national bard senses from the outset that he is being led on a wild-goose chase. But then, how is Gogol, of all writers, to affect the massive, dusty solemnities on which such national monuments repose? His contradictoriness does not stop here, for even while finishing *Dead Souls* he played the bard quite differently in other texts: the revision of the 1835 "Taras Bulba" and the preliminary sketches for a novel, *Annunziata*, published as "A Fragment" in 1841 and later called "Rome." These two texts,

---

[8] N. V. Gogol, *"The Overcoat" and Other Tales of Good and Evil*, trans. David Magarshack (New York: W. W. Norton and Company, 1965), 130.

[9] E. M. de Vogüé, *The Russian Novel* (London: Chapman and Hall, 1913), see esp. 129 and 141. Originally published as *Le Roman russe* (Paris, 1880).

[10] Gogol himself eschewed uncomplicated typologies and revealed his bewilderment over distinguishing what, precisely, he was creating, when he insisted that "the thing over which I am sitting and working [*Dead Souls*]… is not like a tale or a novel" (*Polnoe sobranie sochinenii*, 11:7). Using similar language, Tolstoy also expressed bewilderment over trying to classify *War and Peace* when he claimed that "this work of mine is not a tale… it cannot be called a novel." (Leo Tolstoy, "Draft for an Introduction," in *War and Peace*, trans. George Gibian [New York: W. W. Norton and Company, 1966], 1363).

along with *Dead Souls*, show his first direct address to national destiny and the individual's role in it. All three devolve to a narrative dead end that a moment of ecstatic vision then proclaims to be a beginning. In each case that vision looks out over an expansive landscape inscribed with Destiny; in each case the narrator sees more than his fleeing, dying, or swooning hero. Prophecy thrice gets born from the collapse of plot, and a heroic narrator springs full-blown from the head of a depleted protagonist. It is this heroic narrator, a prophet beyond fiction, who, failing to sustain the sequel of *Dead Souls*, resorts to the oracular hysteria of *Selected Passages from Correspondence with Friends* (1847).

What Part One of *Dead Souls*, the 1842 "Taras Bulba," and "Rome" commonly reveal, then, is Gogol at the end of his own fictive capacities even as he is giving the Russian novel its monumental beginning. His career, like *Dead Souls*, sets the pattern for what is to come, for the epic mode of the Russian novel regularly exacts some such price from its masters. Pursued with utmost seriousness, the form leads beyond storytelling to preaching, as with Tolstoy and Solzhenitsyn, or at the least to prophetic vision (Dostoevsky and Pasternak).

"Taras Bulba" and "Rome" interest us here chiefly as they demonstrate Gogol's ambivalences in writing *Dead Souls*, for things dizzyingly mixed in the novel sort themselves out in these two texts, the buoys, as it were, between which Gogol tacks his course in *Dead Souls*. Both "Taras Bulba" and "Rome" derive from the epic tradition, but from opposite parts of it: the one from the epic as a close approach to folk poetry; the other, from the Dantesque elaboration of the form as the ultimate expression of self-consciousness. "Taras Bulba" revives heroic literature in its most severe form — out-Homers Homer — and insists on both historical and narrative closure. The dying Cossack ends an era along with the tale. By contrast, as veiled spiritual autobiography "Rome" continues the tradition of Christian monumental literature established by Saint Augustine and brought to its culmination by Dante, a tradition that pointedly erodes such boundaries by revivifying the past so that it may draw the present backward and upward to itself. The fragment's gestures toward plot get lost in the ecstasy of perceiving: the prince's life matters only as it informs his perceptions, while the Roman past remains immanent in what is seen. The "then" constantly shapes and is shaped by the beholding eye in an inchoate narrative that evolves from romance to bildungsroman to painterly meditation. As we shall see, the structural peculiarity of *Dead Souls* partly explains itself in the shift from one narrative mode to the other — that is, from saga to confession — as closure opens out to immanence and the protagonist gives way to the narrator. Gogol's satire of provincial life by the end turns in on itself to become increasingly an account of consciousness. Though Chichikov is known to us through much of the text only as others perceive him, by the end his consciousness (or something like it) emerges to direct the action and, it almost seems, to tell the tale; he comes very close to becoming the narrator. What starts out as tourism, a veristic account of the provincial countryside, by the end penetrates the national ethos and brings us finally to the central question of national destiny. What sends the troika racing forward at the end is the force of spiritual implosion, as the powerful negativities of the Russian identity finally assert and define themselves.

"Taras Bulba"

Responding to the calls of monumentality and nationality, Gogol, in his 1842 version of "Taras Bulba," lengthened the 1835 tale by a third and supplemented his earlier Ukrainian chauvinism by celebrating the Russian struggle against the barbaric, Europeanizing, and Roman Catholic Poles. He added thirteen Homeric similes and let the dying hero proclaim the Russian destiny.[11] Along with similes, catalogues, epic scene types (warrior assemblies, the view from the wall), and surgically precise gore, Gogol imported the Homeric vision of *kleos*, the warrior immortality that exists only in the lays of bards — here bandura players. The singer's duty is to celebrate and immortalize as simply as the Cossack's is to fight; both groups must commonly denounce and oppose the demonic forces (Poles, Jews, women) in this black-and-white universe. Though the narrative voice does periodically explain the "then" in terms of the "now," until the very end it calls no attention to its own values or perceptions and affects a bardic anonymity that allows the tale to roll relentlessly onward unencumbered by psychology, by irony, or even by any attempt to recommend the Cossacks' brutality to the readers' sympathy. Just as the iron-willed Cossacks live and

---

[11] On these similes and other Homeric devices in "Taras Bulba" see Carl Proffer, *The Simile and Gogol's Dead Souls* (The Hague: Mouton, 1967), 166-82.

die in a world of fixed values, so the narrative harbors no question about the use or value of memory.

Yet it is the Homer of bored schoolboys, father of clichés, who limps across these pages, as if Gogol were imitating his own demonic painter, Chertkov, who immortalizes his tasteless clients as Psyche, Mars, or Aphrodite. Cossacks dressed up in epithets are supposed to become statuesque and classical. The added similes of "Taras Bulba" distinguish themselves within the epic tradition only by their utter predictability, one thing that better bards and worse have managed to avoid. In the *Iliad*, of course, the vehicle often has a life of its own and goes off from the tenor in intriguing ways that lighten the mounting carnage and freshen a familiar tale. The Virgilian simile, though not digressive, does, by multiple and exact parallels, compel a sorting out of the correspondences, some of them subversive of the text's larger pieties, while the wondrous puzzles of Dante's comparisons squarely disconcert the single-minded reader.[12] The similes of "Taras Bulba," however, serve only to aggrandize the unremarkable into the obvious:

> he quietly planned to rouse them all suddenly with a great Cossack cry to chase even better cheer than ever back into their hearts — something of which only the broad, mighty Slavonic soul is capable, a soul that is to others what the sea is to shallow rivers. If the tempest blows, it howls and thunders and surges and throws up colossal waves such as powerless streams can never raise; but when it is calm, it is clearer than any river and spreads its glassy surface to the horizon, soothing the eyes that gaze upon it. (p.316)[13]

This analogy simply amplifies, concretizes, and implies as natural some threadbare chauvinism. Without individuating detail (what river? what sea? whose eyes?) the image elicits no precise and pleasurable visualization. It does not jog the mind but lulls it. Yet a look at Gogol's earlier and quirkily brilliant remakings of Homeric similes suggests how well he could rival the vigor and raw unpredictability of epic comparisons when he was not,

---

[12] The ramifying complexity of this tradition is traced from Homer to Milton by Stephen A. Nimis, *Narrative Semiotics in the Epic Tradition: The Simile* (Bloomington and Indianapolis: Indiana University Press, 1987).

[13] Translations of "Taras Bulba," "A Terrible Vengeance," and "Viy" are by Christopher English and appear in *Nikolai Gogol: A Selection* (Moscow: Progress Publishers, 1981).

as in "Taras Bulba," attempting a textbook imitation of them. Compare this simile from "A Terrible Vengeance":

> then the Dnieper is terrible to behold! Its surging waves roar as they pound against the hills, then retreat glistening and sighing, and weep and lament in the distance. Thus does the old Cossack mother weep and wail as she bids farewell to her soldier son. Full of high spirits he spurs on his sable steed, rakishly leaning to one side and wearing his cap dashingly aslant; she runs after him, sobbing, holding him by the stirrup, catching the bridle, and wrings her hands as she sheds torrents of bitter tears. (p. 193)

Since Homer's Hecuba and Hector, mothers weeping over departing sons have been inevitable fixtures of epic, and Gogol was to write that cliché into the plot of "Taras Bulba." This river simile, however, turns convention upside down. Where classical similes typically figure human reactions in terms of nature (for example, eyes like blazing fire), Gogol reverses the process by comparing the river to human behavior, indeed, a highly particular example thereof. The pathetic fallacy thus acquires, as it rarely does, dramatic specificity. As often in Homer, the parallels remain problematical: "A Terrible Vengeance" in fact has no Cossack mother dispatching her son. The simile adds to the perplexing nexus of family relationships in the tale and, in further personifying the Dnieper, elaborates the projection into that river of human personality, demonic will, or perhaps both. The Dnieper in this story is only the most complex working out of a motif developed throughout *Evenings on a Farm near Dikanka*, the river as a mirror concealing the inner, hidden, perhaps satanic realities of the soul, the very symbol of the unseen. But when the Dniester provides the culminating image of the 1842 "Taras Bulba," Gogol excludes everything below that glassy surface and makes the river a monolithic symbol of Russian character:

> The Dniester is a fair-sized river, with many inlets, rushy patches, sandbanks and deep pools; its mirroring surface shines and echoes the call of the swans, the proud golden-eye duck glides across it, and a host of snipes, red-cropped ruffs and all kinds of other birds hide in its reeds and on its banks. The Cossacks sailed swiftly in the narrow boats, plying the oars together, steering clear of the sandbanks, startling the birds, and speaking of their ataman. (p. 353)

The familiar pun on Gogol's own name in "golden-eye duck"[14] invites many interpretations, but one of the most attractive, given the obviousness and simplicity of the heroic scene, is to see the author himself for once simply gliding over the glassy surface of things (though, as we shall see, this self-consciousness itself does ruffle the surface). In the technique, then, as in the substance of "Taras Bulba," Gogol has for once resisted his penchant for stepping through the looking glass and, taking epic directness as an excuse for viewing the world as pure surface, has subjugated Cossacks, similes, and his own persona to the overriding imperatives of Russia and Orthodoxy.

Epic thus distilled ceases to be epic, and in both versions "Taras Bulba" conspicuously lacks the ability to stand on its own.[15] Epic, for all of the gods and national destinies that it has served, may be the least monolithic of forms. Its great scope can accommodate something like a fair fight among the various principles at play, as no text demonstrates better than *Dead Souls* itself. The *Iliad*, amid all its glory-mongering, also and oppositely denounces war as has never been done since; Homer blames no one for being Trojan, and his cruel, randomizing Olympians unwittingly shepherd all afflicted mortals toward a common sympathy. Unlike tragedy, for example, it creates space within a single text for the Achilles that kills Hector and the Achilles that welcomes Priam. Virgil's Rome comes triumphantly to birth amid a primeval landscape that might have thrived better without her, and in the invasion of Italy, as at Homer's Troy, we can feel on both sides of the battle. Milton, as Blake speculated, may have been of the Devil's party without knowing it. And though Dante distilled the essence of Christendom, he did so as an exile, and at moments as a heretic.

Whatever epic affirms, then, it affirms only on balance and with gallant regard for the losing side. "Taras Bulba," admitting no ambiguities, deflates such nobility by mean-spirited abuse of the enemy. The seduction of the

---

[14] The passage in question reads in Russian: "Nemalaya reka Dnestr, i mnogo na nei zavod'ev, rechnykh gustykh kamnei, otmelei i glubokodonnykh mest; blestit rechnoe zerkalo, oglashennoe zvonkim yachan'em lebedei, i gordyi *gogol'* bystro nesetsya po nem…" (our italics).

[15] That Gogol himself found the work flawed is seen in his confession to Zhukovsky that "all of the shortcomings that 'Taras Bulba' and 'Old World Landowners' abound in were totally unnoticeable to everyone except you, me, and Pushkin." N. V. Gogol, letter to V. A. Zhukovsky, April 6, 1837, in *Polnoe sobranie sochinenii*, 11:98.

younger son by a Polish beauty and his betrayal of his father constitute a tragic plot only in the most superficial sense. The inner conflicts of the participants, even those of Taras in executing his son, scarcely figure. That the younger and more aesthetic of the sons should be the weak link in the chain seems entirely inevitable and devoid of irony. In denying any currents under the mirrored surface, Gogol excludes both tragedy and the latent restorative powers of comedy. The primitivism of "Taras Bulba" seeks to revive the folklore prior to either mode. Yet the strong, simple, manly truths here uttered sound more like those of boys deploying tin soldiers about a cardboard field.

Already the 1835 story, however, is a simple text in a complex position. "Taras Bulba" stands as the second tale in the *Mirgorod* cycle, four contrasted views of the Russian past that variously explore what we may call the satellite forms of epic. These forms include the pastoral, the georgic, and the mock epic, all of which treat the heroic world, but without the closure toward which epic finally tends; that is, they constantly mediate between the "then" and the "now," the large and small, the heroic and the everyday, by locating themselves in some fantastic middle distance.

Poggioli has discussed the first story in the cycle, "Old World Landowners," as a pastoral, or rather as a deformation of pastoral.[16] The narrator's most extensive philosophical intrusion into the text, before the black cat somehow dooms Pulkheria, seems programmatic both for the tale and the cycle:

> Some conqueror rallies all his country's forces, wages war for several years, his generals cover themselves with glory, and it all ends with the acquisition of a patch of land on which there is barely room to plant potatoes; while sometimes two sausage-makers have a fight over some trifle and in the end their quarrel spreads over cities, big and small villages and finally, the whole kingdom.[17]

Remembering this digression, the reader will at the very least see the heroic simplifications of "Taras Bulba" in more complex terms. This observation, which of course will find a large working out in the historical

---

[16] Renato Poggioli, "Gogol's 'Old-Fashioned Landowners': An Inverted Eclogue," *Indiana Slavic Studies* 3 (1963) 54-72.

[17] "Old World Landowners," in Nikolai V. Gogol, *Mirgorod*, trans. David Magarshack (New York: Noonday, 1962), 18.

philosophy of *War and Peace*, descends from Virgil's scheme for the *Eclogues*, "to compare large things with small" (1.23), by way of the mock-heroic assumption that proportions in the world are hopelessly confused. It does much to explain Gogol's puzzling comparison of Afanasii and Pulkheria, human vegetables, to the rustic nobility of Ovid's Philemon and Baucis.[18] The point is that in this topsy-turvy world, the large has been trivialized — man becomes merely a mouth — and the trivial, the mere act of eating, takes on the appearance of a consuming, world-controlling passion. The traditional catalogue of heroes has become a monumental menu, as in *Dead Souls* it will become a listing of the contents of Chichikov's trunk. This passage captures the once and future Gogol in a moment of transition. The fatal cat typifies the peripeties of his earlier short stories, where the demonic suddenly irrupts into a world of dull routine, a plot that Gogol is abandoning. The orderly epic universe toward which he now moves suffers disruption only from the tamperings of Olympians of the invisible hand of national destiny. Invoking the strong sense of scale and proportion of that epic view, Gogol here manages to see the sinister cat as a form of mock-heroic overthrow. As we shall see, the resulting tone, at once demonic and deflating, in fact will play a large role in *Dead Souls*.

Later, in *Mirgorod*, the agon of the two Ivans, faded epigones of Cossackdom, similarly epitomizes triviality, a mock-heroic battle of legal memos. Here the dominant concerns of "Taras Bulba" — militarism, comradeship, orthodoxy — show up as sordid miniatures,[19] yet in a way that somehow generates a genuine sense of tragedy at the end. Similarly, "Viy" begins with an overtly mock-heroic battle of the various orders (that is, classes) of seminarians with their pompous titles: "Then Philosophy would go to war, with their long black moustaches, and last of all Theology, in their baggy trousers and with their beefy necks" (p. 356). In calling his protagonist, Khoma Brut, "the philosopher," the narrator provides the seminarian with a comically oversized title that nonetheless

---

[18] The addition of gluttony to Ovid's charming tale about the old couple (Met. 8.618-724) might well have been inspired by the following tale of Erysichthon (8.738-876), whose impiety was punished by a voraciousness climaxing in autocannibalism.

[19] Further illumination of this point can be found in Richard Peace, *The Enigma of Gogol* (Cambridge: Cambridge University Press, 1981), 87.

deepens the allegory of a tale seriously involved with the nature of evil. Like the pastoral pleasance and the mock-heroic barnyard, Gogol's Ukraine exists in the middle distance, described to an urbane audience by a self-conscious narrator yet overshadowed in the background by an earlier and lost heroic age, Cossackdom. Virgil's poetic herdsmen similarly find themselves somewhere between Troy and Augustan Rome, Achilles and the divine Caesar. Both the lost heroic grandeur and the author's urbanity are necessary for providing scale to the descriptions.

"Taras Bulba," then, provides the cycle with the heroic standard against which the forces of burgeoning decline can be judged in the other tales. By holding simplistically to the most conventional sense of heroic grandeur, the tale provides a foil for the tricks of proportion in the other tales. Similarly, Virgil set off his bucolics by including toward the middle of the collection the "Messianic" Fourth Eclogue, a fully prophetic and patriotic piece against which the much more ambiguous surrounding pieces can be judged. In much the same way, the great epics after Homer regularly include condensed reminders of traditional militarism to provide scale for their real subject, some new and more complex form of heroism. In making this comparison, flashing armor becomes a shorthand for a simpler past. Apollonius gives his Argonauts a battle or two at the start of their voyage as a foil for his innovative depiction of the warfare of love between Jason and Medea. Virgil includes some bloodthirsty Greeks (Pyrrhus, Diomedes) to clarify what is noble and onerous in the new Trojan-Roman heroism. The firebrand Ulysses in *Inferno* 26 sets off the vast wickedness of Satan, and Milton's War in Heaven prepares us for the subtler battle waged in Eden. Although Dante's Ulysses and Milton's Satan capture and hold some readers' imaginations, these epics mean to keep us marching past the old glories to a more complex set of values. Collections like the *Eclogues* and *Mirgorod*, with the contrastings of old and new, high and low, present similar dangers to the reader who stops short or excerpts. It is no fairer to judge Virgil's radically ambivalent view of Augustus's Rome and of heroic literature from his Fourth Eclogue than it is to judge Gogol's view of Russia from "Taras Bulba," though audiences have misread and cherished both pieces in isolation from the surrounding cycles.

Mirgorod as a cycle suggests that already in 1835 Gogol was aware that the deformations of the heroic (sentimentally as something like the pastoral, comically as mock-heroic), for which he had particular talent, were hindered by the lack of an evolved heroic tradition in Russia. There being no other monument for him to chip away at, he provided one himself. If readers otherwise lack an Achilles in Russian garb, let them read "Taras Bulba." Is it surprising, then, that in 1842 *Dead Souls*, as a yet larger assault on the heroic vanities of the culture, should be in need of a yet bigger foil and therefore confront a potentially hostile audience in tandem with an even more monumental and strident "Taras Bulba"? If readers do not know what the crazy, proliferating Homeric similes of *Dead Souls* are parodying, let them look at the thirteen new ones in "Taras Bulba." Gogol's heroic text thereby makes possible the ironies of *Dead Souls* by supplying the normative tradition from which it can then proceed to make the most inventive deviations.

Gogol may also have aimed to mollify as well as educate the Russian audience by this text. Proffer has recently argued that "Taras Bulba," along with other 1842 works, "Departure from the Theater" and the revision of "The Portrait," serves to protect the author from the doubts about his patriotism and artistic seriousness that he knew *Dead Souls* would inevitably provoke.[20] These works allow him a measure of patriotic and artistic self-certification to bolster the apologia offered by the authorial voice in the final chapters of *Dead Souls*.[21] In these shorter works of 1842, especially in "The Portrait," he articulates a redemptive vision where the artist, through self-purification and denial, enables himself to turn even the meanest subject matter to pedagogical purpose. As we mentioned at the start, the artist-monk who retreats to Italy to perfect his own art in contrast to the hapless Chertkov provides a particularly flattering image of Gogol's own Roman pilgrimage.

If "Taras Bulba" is a gesture to the national audience, it is a guilty gesture, and one whose exaggerations of epic technique establish how unnatural they were to the author. It could well be that, in order to get from the

---

[20] Proffer, *The Simile*, 183-200.

[21] Gogol admitted to the "safe" nationalist politics of "Taras Bulba" when he asked Zhukovsky: "Find the occasion and the means somehow to show the Czar my tales 'Old World Landowners' and 'Taras Bulba.' These are the two fortunate pieces that have totally satisfied all tastes and all temperaments" (*Polnoe sobranie sochinenii*, 11:337).

phantasmagoria of the short stories with their exquisite normlessness to the orderly or at least potentially organizable cosmos of monumental literature, Gogol might for once have designed a universe where norms prevailed to the exclusion of personality. Even this saga does not end without puncturing those orderly surfaces, however. The golden-eye duck on the glassy surface of the final river is, after all, the author's pun on himself, a signature on the canvas such as bards are strictly not allowed. That Taras himself dies a good deal more complexly than he has lived compromises the tale's strong principles of closure. For his final concussion not only induces second sight, but a notion of Russia and nationhood glimpsed centuries too early.

In any case, true epic heroes are not prophets, even at the stake; that role properly falls to Teiresias and Merlin, along with various ghosts and angels. Heroes regularly grasp only with difficulty the history that they are shaping. The meaning that Gogol imposes here compensates for the plot's failure to show Taras's own action as leading to his demise and thereby to reveal his greatness as it self-destructs. It is no tragic decision that fells him, but age, obsolescence, the movement of history, a lost pipe. That he should fall victim to the standard decaying universe of heroic poetry makes it all the more anachronistic for him to foresee progress, unification, and autonomy. It is not the Poles who do him in, but a narrator who has run out of episodes and wants to derive more meaning from this tale than it has quite supplied.

"Rome"

On first view, "Rome" seems as private and self-indulgent as "Taras Bulba" is stiffly official. Where "Taras Bulba" presents a view of an absolute past that is fixed, complete, and not subject to reinterpretation or diminution of its spiritual authority, "Rome" views the past as entirely immanent in the present moment and contingent on the receptivity of the observer. In short, Gogol's fragment offers a near literary antithesis to the flatness, stolid heroism, and historical closure of "Taras Bulba." Gogol claimed that it appeared in 1841, largely against his wishes, in payment of a debt, though its inclusion in the 1842 Collected Works suggests less abashment about its publication.

Gogol's descriptions of Rome closely parallel the letters he wrote home, as Richter has established,[22] and show the author shunning his monumental vocation for more private and aesthetic fantasies. He transparently veils his spiritual tourism with the fiction of a Roman prince, educated abroad, who returns to see his city through fresh and historically informed eyes. For Baroti, who has studied Dantesque motifs in Gogol's tale, the prince's four-year stay in Paris and his subsequent disillusionment can be compared to the misguided Dante's state of confusion and loss of moral foundation at the beginning of the *Inferno*.[23] Not surprisingly, then, a Beatrice-figure, Annunziata from Albano,[24] waits offstage to consummate his spectatorship; but the narrative leaves off as the nobleman prepares his approach to her. An actual encounter with this madonna would obviously unsettle the fantasy of a life purged of other annoyances (authority figures, money problems, friends, and artistic talent) and compromise the protagonist's rapturous passivity. It would scarcely do for the redeemer in the piece to intrude more than does the tyrannical father, who dispatches his timorous son to Paris at the moment when he would have wished to go and then obligingly dies to bring him back when the city's Parisian excitements prove hollow. As nowhere else in Gogol's fiction, Russia does not figure in this tale, nor do the burdens of prophecy. The Eternal City has seen too many laureates to need more at this point; it welcomes artists, but observers will do. Gogol's Rome, then, is a literary world on holiday from the issues that otherwise vex him. The faint gestures to plot give way to his most extensive portrayal of a single (and positive!) character's psychology, even though the nobleman's inner world involves little beyond connoisseurship. Whereas the heroic world is all mythos, an unstoppable chain of events, "Rome" restricts itself to the novelistic world of observation and self-creation. The episodes of this fragment hang together no more tightly — and perhaps less interestingly — than do the short story collections, but their unification

[22] Richter. "Rom und Gogol': Gogol's Romerlebnis und sein Fragment 'Rim,'" 126-44.

[23] T. Baroti, "Traditsiya Dante i povest' Gogolya 'Rim,'" *Studia Slavica Hungarica* 29 (1983): 171-83.

[24] Annunziata appears first on a wagon in Carnival, as Beatrice does in the Procession of the Host (Purg. 30). So it will be later with the redemptive Ulinka, in *Dead Souls*, Part Two.

around a single personality in a biography-cum-monologue makes a bridge to the continuities of *Dead Souls*.

As the text nowhere admits, however, it is a Russian tourist who is writing, and one intent on taking this utopia home with him.[25] Just as the titillations of Paris opened the prince's eyes to the timeless values of his own city, though now a backwater, so Gogol, anticipating his own homecoming, presents Rome as spiritual preparation, a prototype for the Third Rome.[26] Moscow and Rome are both excluded from the faddish and atheistic Europeanness of which Paris is capital, since the pope has shielded his city from the Enlightenment, which Russia also missed. Emperors and popes have come and gone, but the *popolo romano* endures as a counterpart to Russian collectivism. The vitality and essential orderliness of the state derive from the Romans' creative and stable anarchy, a political form whose essential formlessness precludes the kind of revolution *à la française* that the Russians had reason to fear. Having not only seen but caused so much of European history, the Romans now find themselves beyond the inflammatory issues that ignite wars elsewhere. The rich, jumbled accumulation of pagan and Christian monuments resists sorting out; by analogy, the doctrinal differences of Catholicism and Orthodoxy also lose their urgency, even as Gogol's letters in this period reveal a flirtation with the Roman church quite opposite to the orthodoxy of "Taras Bulba."[27] His prince perceives secular France as the antithesis of his homeland, as did Slavophiles. In this godless, materialistic age, provincialism becomes a sign of spiritual election. By the pastoral logic that links the center and

---

[25] In one of the most informative analyses of "Rome," Louis Pedrotti writes, "Although Gogol later asserted that the views of his anonymous prince should not be confused with his own, there is little doubt that there are strong autobiographical elements in the story." For further treatment of this issue, and many others, see Louis Pedrotti, "The Architecture of Love in Gogol's *Rome*," *California Slavic Studies* 6 (1971): 17-27.

[26] Dania Borghese, *Gogol a Roma* (Florence: Sansoni, n.d.), 57, argues that Gogol converted the Italian baroque style into Russian: "Questo linguaggio è un vero prodigio di stile barocco italiano interpretato in lingua russa." Does this style not constitute a surface reflection of the larger ambition of transferring Rome's spiritual authority to its final home, Russia?

[27] See Richter, "Rom und Gogol'," 24-37. For an enlightening discussion of Gogol's attraction to Rome and Catholicism, see Victor Erlich, *Gogol* (New Haven and London: Yale University Press, 1969), esp. 158-65.

the margins and puts kings in particular sympathy with shepherds and fishermen, the Roman sense of being so central to history as to be beyond it recalls the Russian sense of being outside it. The king is not a citizen, and Rome is no more part of Europe than Russia is. Rather, Rome and Moscow stand as the once and future capitals of a Christendom that lies beyond that secularized Europe. Their strength commonly lies in the people, in the earth, in the respect for tradition, in latent vigors apparent only to the prophetic artist.

"Rome" merges two views of history that figure in *Dead Souls*. The first is history as comedy, a natural outgrowth of the collectivist perspective. The comic sense of the Ukrainian short stories had found little that was redemptive in the steady decline they chart. But in Rome, the decline and fall of everything in sight reassures and inspires the observer, leading, as it does, to a superior grade of ruins. No building is complete until the perfecting hand of nature has covered it with moss. The lime burners have turned boring imperial symmetries into invitingly broken facades. Where a romantic might give way to tragic thoughts on loss and the vanity of human wishes, Gogol sees ruin as the ideal human setting and the ultimate symbol of human community. For the principle of decline (which spares the self-regenerating *popolo*) functions like a millennial humorist, bringing the great ages down to the level of the current inhabitants. The age-old dialectic of natural force and human artifice resolves itself as moss and erosion mute the hard edges of human designs.

What it all adds up to is an Eden after, not before, history, and a better paradise for lacking the fatal choices of the first garden. The collapsed facades and slow-grinding mills of history have united appearance and substance, punctured the vanities of power, but proved the durability of the race. The realities lurking in the inner, terrifying under-river world of Gogol's Ukrainian landscapes have now emerged into the bright light of day; the demons glimpsed there must now learn to take their place among the legions of other gods, spirits, ghosts, and saints who claim space in the city. The aesthetics of rot perfected in the Ukrainian stories now become a principle of historical continuity, and the faded Cossacks of those tales find much more positive counterparts in the Roman streets. The factotum Peppe, for instance, is the degeneration of so many different possibilities from the republican, imperial, Christian, and medieval periods that the issue can scarcely be raised. He is simply a Roman, a type that has been declining for so long and with so little apparent impairment that the whole notion of decadence is called into question. Decline itself, that is, may be in the eye of the beholder. The effect reverses that of mock heroic, for the present is not a betrayal and cheapening of lost glory but a rich outgrowth of it.

By the logic of that perception, all historiography aspires to autobiography, the second and more influential view of history in the tale. On such a note the fragment ends with Gogol's prince (or is it the narrator? the two have now merged) swept away by a prospect of the city: "Lord, what a vision! Seized by it, the Prince forgot himself and the beauty of Annunziata, the secret destiny of his people, and everything else which existed on earth."[28] What can finally terminate this series of descriptions is the paradisiacal self-actualization of the observer in the completed ecstasy of observing. The nobleman has felt vague stirrings about the Beatrice figure, as well as about his responsibility to the destiny of his people, but these tangible externals would only impede the convergence of observer and observed here achieved. Annunziata, did she but know it, has served her function as spiritual guide by leading to something beyond herself. History has figured in the narrative only as handmaiden to the self-perfecting eye, a means of feeling the Roman landscapes more perfectly. The city becomes utopian as the young man learns to perceive it as such, and its triumphs and defeats become real to him as they inform the disposition of marble and moss. Indeed, his intuitions about its lurking powers of renascence may only express his own gestating powers of perception. What ends the narrative, as in "Taras Bulba" and *Dead Souls*, is an observing consciousness that has perfected its passivity into an omnipotent will to perceive, leading to the capacity to confer absolute value on what it perceives. The final accommodation of history, even the endless eventfulness of the Eternal City, to individual responsibility is in the shattering of boundaries, a mystical absorption of the observer into the observed that issues in prophecy. There is no absolute "then," only a constantly unfolding present.

With all of the open-endedness of a journal, "Rome" eludes closure as deftly as "Taras Bulba" imposes it. The several narrative false starts, however, lead to the visionary conclusion far more efficiently than "Taras Bulba" and

---

[28] Gogol, *Sobranie sochinenii v semi tomakh* (Moscow, 1966-67), 3:247. The translation is our own.

Dead Souls do to theirs. The visionary voice that intrudes to end and valorize the other two narratives here has held center stage from the first. Whereas Chichikov and his narrator, like Bulba and the bard, end up awkwardly yoked together, here the protagonist and the narrator have merged. Writer and audience did stand apart from the prince as he succumbed to Parisian sham, but the overwhelming spectacle of Rome reduces the several perspectives to only one. That single view is at once the solipsism of the travel diary and, thanks largely to Dante, the capping epiphany of Christian epic. Gogol's fictionalization of himself as the Roman prince, by virtue of its various denials — not a Russian, not an artist, not crazy, not sexually peculiar, not finally either rich or needy, not even named — presents an inchoate Everyman that temporarily invites the rest of humanity into the author's fantasies. Thereby Gogol may almost inadvertently lapse into his monumental vocation in the very process of momentarily escaping it; for, in making the private world of fantasy coextensive with the cosmos of national destiny, "Rome" sets the pattern for *Dead Souls*. At the midpoint of this world the Roman prince exemplifies, in briefer and more autobiographical terms, the kind of featureless catalyst, at once dreaming and dreamt, that at base Chichikov is.

Between them, "Taras Bulba" and "Rome" suggest the two paths that Gogol, as he was writing the first part of *Dead Souls*, saw opening to him as he approached Parnassus. Both works acknowledge, as did his Roman pilgrimage, the necessity of responding to the very heart of the European tradition — Homeric epic and the Eternal City, respectively. Both presume that human experience can be organized in terms of the identity of a people — not the family or village nor Christendom or mankind, but Rome and Russia. Both acknowledge that preceding heroic ages prepare and define national identities, though the historical record is as much an open book in "Rome" as it is closed and immutable in "Taras Bulba." Both works presume a radical simplification of the writer's subject matter and of his social role.

In "Taras Bulba" the needs of history authorize the writer to see only the broad outlines, the magnificent surfaces of things. To the audience he sings as faceless bard in the tradition of Russian saga; they, in turn, can be expected to honor and enjoy the tale and, through it, their own Russianness. "Rome" turns just as steeply to solipsism, as if intended for no audience other than the author. Exactly unlike "Taras Bulba," "Rome" presents history as such infinite and still-evolving complication that one can only relax and enjoy the constantly mutating sense of pattern, a response as purely aesthetic as that of "Taras Bulba" is fundamentally political. Much of the riddle of *Dead Souls*, Part One, explains itself in the movement from the one world to the other, that is, from the fixed values and materialism of "Taras Bulba" (seen now with the humorous distancing found in the surrounding tales of *Mirgorod*) to the transformative vision of "Rome," from a world of inevitable decline to the gestation of a new, spiritually potent nationhood. Though the reference points for this axial shift, Homer and Dante, blur and confuse each other in *Dead Souls*, "Rome" and the revised "Taras Bulba" demonstrate Gogol's ability to confront each squarely and separately.

Dead Souls, Part One

"Taras Bulba" and "Rome" share another characteristic that sets them apart from Gogol's other early work, their comparative lack of irony. They lack it for opposite reasons but to much the same effect: the observer is too far from the Cossacks and, finally, too identified with the Roman prince to allow Gogol's usual irony to distance and dismiss the subject matter even while making it too sticky to put down. In these two cases the narrator does not conspiratorially take the audience aside with him to laugh and fear together. The customary dissonances and contradictions of Gogol's perspective — his unnerving feel for grotesqueries in which the audience, like the author, must see both absurdity and themselves — are flattened by the statuesque objectivity of the Cossack saga, then evaporate into the solipsism and self-creating subjectivity of "Rome." That is, anyone who is not a Cossack or an expatriate Russian writer will not feel the familiar seduction and betrayal of Gogolian irony, that process of being drawn into the fiction but also set grandly above it and then left wondering who was the real target.

Both tales suspend Gogol's usual ambivalence: "Taras Bulba," through total submission to patriotism and inherited form; "Rome," by casting off Russian subjects and responsibilities. Both of these texts proclaim visions that they cannot begin to explain, for as essentially static narrative forms they will not bear further extension. What makes the Cossacks staunch is their resistance to change, their superhuman voracity for risk and repetition.

If the pieties of "Taras Bulba" were taken further, the whole structure would risk seeming a joke. Similarly, beyond the achieved stasis of the observer observed in the act of observing, "Rome" could not proceed further with any claims to having a plot; the narrative has imploded.

What "Taras Bulba" and "Rome" indelibly illustrate is that Gogol, raising his sights to larger topics — from the village to the nation and to Christendom — had a sure feel for the limits of the available forms. Leaving the inward, autobiographical pressures of "Rome" to seek their natural if quick conclusion, he did not attempt to string out enough narrative to sustain the planned *Annunziata*. He revised "Taras Bulba" to be more intensely and identifiably Homeric but did not inflate it into a full-scale epic. In leaving these simpler visions as fragments, Gogol implicitly acknowledged that neither the Homeric nor the Dantesque poles of epic writing could sustain his ambitions. The way toward his chef d'oeuvre had to lie through some mixture of modes, somewhere in the more complicated middle ground of his usual evasive perspectives, but now applied more extensively and on a larger theme. Conflated, these two monumental modes create, explosively, the irony that each of them lacks in its polarized form. The tone that emerges from the first part of *Dead Souls* is neither the aestheticism of "Rome" nor the dispassionate historicizing of "Taras Bulba" but a perspective that transforms itself through repeated escapes from the reader. In that unfolding game, played with shifting rules, the narrator creates himself as bard, and the eluded audience becomes constituted as Russia, the very thing for which they are imputed to be searching. The final joke on them, as typically in Christian literature when it is ironic, is to deflate their obtuseness in awaiting some target other than themselves, in dumbly expecting to be merely the spectators of this satire rather than its true objects. As noted above, the irony of Gogol's early stories had the tendency to turn on the reader even as *The Inspector General* turns on its audience — that is, to include a mirror in the rogues' gallery so that the reader suddenly glimpses himself in bad company. *Dead Souls* returns to that technique, but now with higher stakes.

From the looming "Poèma" of the title page to the concluding hymn to Rus', the narrating voice of *Dead Souls* recurrently invites the audience to attend to his tale as the "epic" that it seems so obviously not to be. A text scuttering insignificantly through the immense shadow of epic verse automatically qualifies as mock-heroic. The author and his audience, who must know what a "real" epic is and what "real" heroism is, are at first united in looking down on this spectacle from an Olympian height.

This mode of irony in the first chapters of *Dead Souls* is well understood, but before analyzing it further we should anticipate the fact that the book shifts midway to a perspective no less ironic but entirely different. All readers note that after chapter 6 the static catalogue of rogues encountered in the first half, all frozen into their various trivial depravities, awaken and unite to pursue Chichikov or, more importantly, to fantasize about him. Finally, even the bard himself, so aloof in the opening chapters, seems to be having Chichikov's nervous breakdown for him. The unleashing of vast spiritual energy does not figure importantly in classical epic or mockery thereof, but it is the very essence of the ironic counterplot to pagan heroism that is articulated in the Gospels, most clearly in the Fourth. The meek do not inherit the earth without the surprising reversals, the recourse to a higher and less literal perspective, characteristic of ironic plots. Yet now the vantage point is not just the Olympus of sophisticated writer and sophisticated reader looking downward together. In the articulation of Christian heroism, as in mock heroic, the great of this world are not what they seem. However, what exposes and deflates them is no longer just the condescension of author and audience to the subject matter as the *miles gloriosus* trips over his sword or warrior valor adjourns to barnyard or nursery. Rather, proportion derives from the descent into the work of the Creator himself, self-conscious and disguised.

This contrast can be grasped most easily by taking a step back from mock heroic to the *Odyssey* as the masterwork of narrative irony in Greek and comparing it to the Gospels. In both, the true king restores his kingdom by traveling first among beggars and peasants. He is heroized by abuse and veils his messages for those who have ears to hear them, so that, as in any ironic vision, literalists cannot be saved. Penelope's suitors, like the scribes and the Pharisees, doom themselves by taking things at face value and failing to note that their underlings — beggars, youths, slaves, and women — may be more powerful than themselves. In the Gospels, however, the leap of faith, guile, or irony that it takes to get beyond literalism is needed not just to win the Kingdom but (probably) to experience it, for it may well be not an earthly kingdom at all. The *Odyssey*'s restored Ithaca will be as concrete and as free of disguise as it was in the good old days. Though hopes varied, the New Jerusalem boded well to be something quite different from the

Old. Therein the Christian and classical ironists part company. Both climax their stories in a moment of revelation and revolution — apocalypse and *anagnōrisis*, respectively — but Christian writers work away from locating the new dispensation in the ordinary reality from which the tale took its beginning. The distance from the Gospels is yet greater in the case of mock-heroic irony, which works at the expense of the protagonist and not (as in the *Odyssey*) just his enemies. The added complexity and instability of such irony are even less capable of suggesting a vision of a transformed reality. Indeed, when used most vigorously (for example, by Aristophanes and Pope), it needs the anchor of the author's own time and place.

As we shall see, in *Dead Souls* Gogol in some ways recapitulates this progression from pagan to Christian by moving from one type of descent to another. The mock-heroic condescension to the subject matter up through chapter 6 becomes the creator's descent into his creation to redeem it by incarnating himself — taking a voice, becoming a character, and thereby shouldering the burden of human frailty. The tones of persecution heard from the narrator at the end seem oddly uncalled for until we ponder the tradition of martyrdom and salvation from which he himself nervously descends.

To trace this movement, we must revert to the opening ironies of this self-declared and self-deflated "poèma" and to that other descent of the ironist, his literary genealogy, about which Gogol, like any good epic writer, solemn or playful, gives us abundant indication. Quite early we learn that it is not one but several forms of epic that *Dead Souls* at various times and in various ways fails to be. Even between the extremes evoked in "Taras Bulba" and "Rome," Gogol's posthumous "Textbook of Literature for Russian Youth" presents another category, "lesser epic," which accommodates *Dead Souls* next to *Orlando furioso* and *Don Quixote* at one remove from Homer and heading toward the novel.[29] In this form, an unremarkable and limited protagonist usefully symbolizes his age. This mixed form, narratively fantastic and psychologically acute, goes back at least as far as Ovid, whom

---

[29] Gogol, *Polnoe sobranie sochinenii*, 8:478-79. Only a sketch of Gogol's work remains. In it the author defines and compares several literary genres. The section that we quote, "malaya èpopeya," comes closest to his realization of *Dead Souls*, especially when Gogol writes, "In the modern era there originated a kind of narrative work that constitutes, as it were, a cross between a novel and an epic, the hero of which, although a private and unnoteworthy character, is significant nevertheless for the observer of human souls."

Gogol occasionally acknowledges ("such a transformation will overtake our Prometheus as even Ovid himself could never think of," p. 39)[30] and pervasively imitates. Operating in the shadow of the titanic Homer and Virgil, Ovid recast epic as a monumental form constantly mutating into brilliant, teasing particulars. His *Metamorphoses* presents a mythic landscape stripped of proportion, fixity, or stable grandeur, where one can rely only on the propensity of beings to turn into something else. As we discussed in chapter 1, one must not assume that such insouciance about epic *gloire* lacks an argument, for in fact the almost hidden path through Ovid's lush imagistic jungle does, convincingly or not, lead us from creation of the world to the glory of Rome in fifteen books.

Rus' is as much a telos of Gogol's tale as Rome is of Ovid's, and the landscape of the first half of *Dead Souls*, Part One, is itself constantly involved in similar metamorphoses. Chapter 1 begins with a doggedly close veristic description, then jars the sense of scale with an intrusion from a now defunct heroic world, a boot, in fact, "of such gigantic proportions that its equal was hardly to be found anywhere, especially in these times, when heroic bogatyrs are beginning to die out even in Russia" (p. 10). The image descends from the Homeric motif of rocks so heavy that three or four men of the current generation could not lift them (*Iliad* 12.445ff.). Among the playfully heroized ranks of children, animals, and boots, even bureaucrats can figure, as for example when one of them becomes in Chichikov's eyes "like ancient Zeus of Homer, who prolonged the days or sent quick-passing nights whenever the need arose either to bring to a close a martial contest between the heroes he liked or to permit them to fight to a finish" (p. 122).

In the *Metamorphoses*, Ovid, like Ariosto, Cervantes, and Sterne to follow, shrinks and refracts epic into endless variations, including the pastoral and mock-heroic forms that engage Gogol particularly in the *Mirgorod* cycle, sometimes from Ovidian sources, as we have seen. *Dead Souls* uses these various styles in its first half, though only long enough to suggest that something else is afoot. Manilov's absorption by the Epicurean virtues of tranquility, friendship, and pipe dreams recapitulates the amiable retirement from heroic engagement characteristic of the pastoral. He and

---

[30] Translations are by Bernard Guilbert Guerney, *Chichikov's Journeys: or, Home Life in Old Russia* (New York: The Readers Club, 1942). We have corrected any deficiencies against the original.

his wife enjoy a less fattening version of the courtly otherworldliness of Afanasii and Pulkheria in "Old World Landowners" (and Philemon and Baucis before them). Within this vegetal existence it is the children (as in "Viy") who embody the mock-heroic principle of disorder in assaulting each other and dismembering toy soldiers. Their very names trivialize heroic myth: "Alcides" is the patronymic of the voracious Hercules, perhaps a telling reflection of Manilov's own gluttony. Themistoclius bears a bungled Latinization of the Athenian statesman, hero, and (perhaps) turncoat Themistocles — a bad omen for Manilov's ambition that his son become a diplomat. Gogol's pervasive joke, as often Ovid's, is to provide an undignified good time in the guise of an "epic."

The mock-heroic joke starts on the title page. In response to the censors' relegation of the intended title to a subtitle under "Chichikov's Journeys" (to avert the oxymoronic blasphemy of implying that souls can die), Gogol buried both titles under the monumental label "poèma." As a complement to and reversal of Pushkin's "novel in verse," *Eugene Onegin*, labeling a prose narrative "poèma" may well declare indebtedness and independence in respect to Gogol's mentor, who had suggested the anecdotal plot. Above all, "poèma," especially for an audience gratified by "Taras Bulba," could only excite false expectations about the work to follow. Marching through the facade, one is surprised to find what looks at first like a rubbish heap. The narrator continues to present this bagatelle as something epochal, until in the second half it actually becomes so, if only by opening up voids into which consciousness can flood.

The Homeric similes that proved oppressively serious in "Taras Bulba" here return with splendid, deflating lunacy. At the outset Chichikov enters town society at the Governor's ball:

> Upon entering the main hall Chichikov was compelled to narrow his eye for a minute or so, since the brilliance of the candles and lamps and the ladies' gowns was terrific. Everything was flooded with light. Everywhere one looked black frock-coats flitted and darted by, singly and in clusters, as flies dart over a white, gleaming loaf of refined sugar in the summer season, on a sultry July day, as an aged housekeeper standing at an open window cleaves and divides the loaf into glittering, irregular lumps... (p. 7)

We are perhaps only an amusing half-step away from epic, for Virgil compares Dido's busy Carthaginians to bees when Aeneas first sees them (*Aeneid* 1.430-36), and in the opening scene of *War and Peace* Tolstoy will similarly capture the essence of Anna Scherer's soiree by the simile of a clockwork. Here, ominously, the squinting Chichikov and flitting frock-coats almost become insects before the simile begins, while the insects turn strangely human. To continue:

> all the children, having flocked together, are looking on, curiously watching the movements of her roughened hands as they lift up the maul, while the aerial squadrons of flies, held up by the buoyant air, fly in boldly, as if they owned the whole place and, taking advantage of the crone's purblindness and of the sun that bothers her eyes, bestrew the dainty morsels, in some places singly, in others in thick clusters. (p. 7)

Following the best Homeric practice, this simile has developed its own wayward story, and the physical point of comparison (the swarming of the groups) remains clear. But another group, the children, behave like the flies and also bear comparison to the socialites. The comparison becomes confusingly triangular. The crone's momentary blindness parallels Chichikov's. Are these somehow his impressions? With a curious mirroring, the flies to whom the socialites are likened themselves are compared to yet other human beings ("squadrons").

> Sated with the riches of summer, which spreads delectable repasts at every step even without such windfalls as this, they have flown in not at all in order to eat but merely to show themselves, to promenade to and fro over the mound of sugar, to rub either their hind- or their forelegs against each other, or scratch with them under their gossamer wings, or, having stretched out their forelegs, rub them over their heads, and then once more to turn around and fly away, and once more come flying back with new harassing squadrons. (p. 7)

Further precision now ruptures the network of similarities; flies do not merely promenade, especially on sugar; even the most muscoid socialites do not rub their legs on their heads. In the traditional epic simile, the realms of men and of animals define and reveal each other by discrete resemblances within larger dissimilarity. Here the two realms, by interpenetrating and confusing each other, lead us into the realm of the mock-heroic, and perhaps somewhat beyond. The socialites are not entirely diminished by the comparison to the flies, because the flies themselves begin to acquire human and even heroic purpose. The universe of the simile does have a thriving vitality that this tiresome provincial ball utterly lacks, for that universe is not just alive, but growing into a self-sustaining microcosm into which the reader might happily see the narrative escape. What interest the comparison confers on the ball is fleeting. More importantly, it serves to convey the mad, boundary-shattering energy of the narrator's imagination and his capacity to animate this moribund landscape by failing to report on it, dull and predictable as it is, with any steady competence. Every simile provided to mirror the object at hand tempts the narrator to step through the looking glass. In other words, what the simile chiefly tells us is that the one interesting person at the ball is the narrator himself, and we do not know to what degree he is or is not Chichikov. Even here one can begin to wonder how long this conspicuous but unidentified voice can confine his wayward imagination to the too easy job of deflating the puny present through evocations of lost heroic grandeur, or of replicating the now quaint heroic forms that once celebrated it.

Mock heroic also relies on the equal and opposite trick of aggrandizing the trivial. We have already seen a simile that makes a Zeus of a bureaucrat. The narrator, apparently bored with his ordinary subject matter, habitually interjects livelier narrative possibilities, and these comparisons, like the similes, have the potential to animate themselves into vignettes. Rather than delineate Nozdrev's fulminations, the narrator compares him to some desperate lieutenant rabidly urging his troops to suicide in battle (p. 74). Instead of dwelling on Korobochka's squalid life, he trades up to the better grade of squalor of Petersburg socialites (pp. 47-48). Partly, N — is being diminished by comparison to a larger world, partly, by comparison to the expansiveness of the narrator's imagination, erupting from within.

A final example of this device will locate it within the larger pattern of Gogol's texts: when a blonde maiden glides past our hero's coach, the narrator evokes the stunned response of some hypothetical twenty-year-old before dutifully detailing the middle-aged Chichikov's verbose and misogynistic reaction (pp. 7879). This is our first glimpse of the angelic type who later, as Ulinka, will play the Beatrice/Annunziata role in the uncompleted Part Two — yet another embodiment of that "sublime beauty" that will commence Gogol's survey of the world in *Selected Passages* (chapter 2: "Woman in the World"). Within the pattern of recurrence of such figures, Chichikov's cold reaction here signifies that his preoccupation with externals still blinds him to the emotional and imaginative forces that might be unleashed by this vision. The narrator, however, describes a reaction identical to that which ends "Rome," with the hypothetical twenty-year-old observer "grown oblivious of self, and of his work, and of the world, and of all the things that there are in the world." Even in this digression we are still in the heroic world, though much decayed, of works and deeds and external movement. In this world — as with Helen, Dido, and the fatal Polish beauty of "Taras Bulba" — one should steer clear of sirens. The narrator, however, is more inclined to linger.

Among the squirming bits of life in this comic first half of the narrative, the movement is all mutation, not development, so that much of the humor lies in eternal, mechanical repetition. Chichikov does not evolve in Part One and does not grow into any of the types of heroism that he, at moments, promises to embody. He is not finally an antihero, nor one of the pygmy heroes of mock epic, nor one of the dreamy cousins of heroes who look on from the pastoral pleasance. In his failure to develop, he ends up representing a featureless ordinariness: neither young nor old, rich nor poor, handsome nor repulsive, bright nor dull, loud nor reticent. Indeed, as Gogol characterizes him by elimination in the opening paragraph, we have the distinct impression of our hero's arriving at the equally featureless town of N — in an empty carriage. Along with his sundry valises and parcels, he seems not to have brought a personality. Neither learning nor changing, he seems content with the fitful progress of his swindle. The various episodes show facets of his character reflected in the various landowners,[31] as they could do equally well in any other order. Though ostensibly describing the grubby "now," the narrator can stitch together the various chapters, like the episodes of "Taras Bulba," as freely as a bard arranges his lays, since the stasis of the subject matter seems to leave it *in illo tempore*, in myth's endless cycles of lost time.

Yet for all the narrator's professed contentment with this stasis and inconsequence, he hides his own sweeping ambitions less and less successfully. His intrusions begin to reveal his impatience with a story that in its eternal circles is failing to accommodate his sense of calling. His emergence into the text makes the latter half almost a reversal of what precedes, even as the same characters file past again to expose Chichikov rather than to collude with him. Digressions still establish scale in the epic manner, but now they are less often similes than autobiographical

---

[31] See the discussion of Donald Fanger, *The Creation of Nikolai Gogol* (Cambridge, Mass.: Harvard University Press, 1979), 170.

reflections that advertise narrative subjectivity as clearly as the similes (falteringly) attest bardic distance. Imperceptibly, the surrounding universe changes character: the heroic age winding relentlessly down to vulgarity seems more and more like the coiled spring of Rus' (or at least of the narrator) ready to spring forward. Though we have not departed N — as the dead and deadening center of a turning universe, Gogol has shifted the epic coordinates on us.

An unsuspected virtue of the middleness of the setting, *nel mezzo del cammin di nostra vita* — the middle-aged Chichikov of moderate gifts and medium rank as he visits the midpoint between Petersburg and Moscow — is that the author can unobtrusively change his mind about what this is the middle *of*. As was noted in chapter 1, the middle distance functions variously in mock heroic and the pastoral. Here we might add Christian parables of Everyman. In the beginning of the narrative, as in *Mirgorod*, a grander age lies beyond, for the current generation lies halfway between their heroic ancestors and the animals to which the author so often compares them. By the end, however, it is the future of Rus' that overshadows the open plain — now less a wasteland than an empty stage awaiting the drama, a desert for the Chosen People to wander, a canvas empty enough to accommodate the narrator's national (or is it personal?) self-portrait. One may attach what meanings one will to these closing vistas, for what matters is no longer the place but the movement through it. The inconsequent "somewhere" of N — becomes an everywhere by virtue of the narrator's capacity to conceive hopes for it, while the tarnished "ordinary" in his subject matter grows into the instructively "typical," and provincial nonentities become normative Russians. Void is reperceived as freedom. The accommodating mediocrity of N — thereby allows a shift of project from forging deeds for serfs to forging the consciousness of the race. The very barrenness of the topography allows it to be transformed into the inner landscape of the soul, where time is not cyclical but developmental and progressive. And the narrator, who initially created this world only to join us in mocking it, finds himself trapped within it yet enabled to take us with him as he makes, or promises, his escape.

How this reorientation occurs is worth noting in detail. The sixth chapter brings the narrative to the midpoint of the eleven as the landowner Pliushkin brings Pushkin's anecdote to an end — and can the names be coincidental? As the full and final embodiment of death-in-life, the miser Pliushkin concludes the novel's opening movement, the picaresque tale of descent through the rogues' gallery. Pliushkin presents a Dantesque vision of the *privatio Boni* taken to an icy extreme.[32] He will be the single landowner not to show up at Chichikov's trial, where the president of the court inquires: "Is he still leading his frozen existence?" (p. 127)[33] Yet by its very placement, this low moment invokes a lofty heritage. For Chichikov's descent into the lifeless underworld falls at the same point as Aeneas's (in the sixth book of the *Aeneid*'s twelve). And even before this nadir is reached, the voice of the narrator begins liberating itself for higher strains. Up through chapter 5, the narrative has advanced steadily past the chapter beginnings without other flourishes of prelude or peroration. The end of chapter 5, however, takes a maximally incongruous moment (a muzhik's deleted expletive describing Pliushkin) as an occasion for celebrating Mother Russia: "The Russian people have a puissant way of expressing themselves!" (p. 94). The topic is suitably epic: the bestowing of epithets, their ineradicability, and, above all, their quintessential Russianness:

> That which is aptly uttered is tantamount to that which is written: there's no rooting it out, though you were to use an ax. And how very apt, of a certainty, is that which has come out of the very core of Russia, where there is no German, nor French, nor Finnish, nor any other sort of tribe, but the purest virgin gold, the living and lively Russian wit, that is never at a loss for a word, that doesn't brood over it, like a setting hen, but comes spang out with it, like a passport to be carried through all eternity, and there's no use your adding on later what sort of nose or lips you have: you are drawn, at a stroke, from head to foot!

The passage embodies the Russian wit that it celebrates by mixing the imagery associated with violence (ax), domesticity (mother hen), and diplomacy (passport) — all seen epically sub specie aeternitatis. The Gogolian perversity of celebrating the all-creating Russian Word in the

---

[32] This image is balanced at the very end of chapter 11, where Chichikov's damnation is figured similarly: "And perhaps, as in this very Chichikov, the passion that is drawing him on is not of his choosing, and in his chill existence is contained that which will cast man down into the dust and on his knees before the wisdom of the heavens" (p. 229).

[33] This is George Reavey's translation (Nikolai V. Gogol, *Dead Souls* [New York: W. W. Norton, 1971], 273), which contrasts with Guerney's rendition ("So is he still vegetating in this world?". Here the root *zyab* does indeed indicate vegetation, but on occasion it also suggests coldness or chilliness. Perhaps Gogol intended this association as well.

context of a censored epithet recapitulates the mock-heroic gestures of the title page as it thwarts the censors.

To an equal and opposite extent, the creating Word also evokes serious Christian reflections, which Gogol addresses with typically bizarre analogies and apparent enthusiasm in the chapter's final paragraph. As are the multitudes of churches in Russia, so are the numberless peoples of the earth. And each people has its word: the Englishman's, wise; the Frenchman's, flashy; the German's, ponderous: "But there is never a word which can be so sweeping, so boisterous, which would burst out so, from out of the very heart, which would seethe so and quiver and flutter so much like a living thing, as an aptly uttered Russian word!" This first celebration calls to mind, of course, the apostrophe of Russia in the troika scene that will end Part One. Both passages treat the Russian landscape as set apart from and above anything European, and lexically the passages coincide surprisingly. In both we find the words *Rus'* (Rus', Russia); *narod* (nation); *zemlya* (land); *vsyakii* (every); *sila* (strength); *Bog* (God); *boiko* (lively, adroitly). Perhaps also not coincidentally, chapter 5 had earlier introduced the fixtures of the final scene: "again there remained only the road, the light carriage, the troika of horses familiar to the reader, Seliphan, Chichikov, and the smooth and empty expanse of the surrounding fields" (p. 78). The Russian word giving birth to itself here, near the midpoint of Part One, announces a concept of literary autogenesis which, as we shall see, looms large in Gogol's later writing. It seems an almost inevitable gesture for a writer intent on launching a national tradition. Can it be coincidental that it comes just before the adieu to Pushkin/Pliushkin in chapter 6?

The first sign of a new narrative dimension is the narrator's emergence to self-consciousness rather than his earlier random blurting into the text. This emergent voice is a creation out of the void, even as the Russian word proclaims itself out of a deletion. For the narrative voice announces itself as stillborn, brooding over the sensations of youth now lost to it. That is, the bard of Chichikov's odyssey presents himself as a bored and incurious traveler: "Now I drive up apathetically to every unfamiliar village and look apathetically at its vulgar appearance; to my time-chilled gaze things seem bleak, and I am not amused, and that which in former years would have aroused an animated expression, laughter, and unceasing speeches, glides past me now and an impassive silence do my expressionless lips preserve. Oh, my youth! Oh, my fresh vigor" (p. 96). With characteristic paradox, the new bardic voice intrudes to announce itself with an apologia for its silence! The next words alert us to another curiosity that will persist: the narrator can speak for himself only when his hero is wool-gathering or sleeping. Chichikov had been inwardly chuckling over the deleted epithet, so it turns out that the narrator has only articulated what Chichikov was thinking. After the narrator makes his revelations, Chichikov wakes up. They exist in a reciprocity never quite explained to us, as if two sides of one personality.

The blurrings of identity continue. It is Pliushkin, not Chichikov, who more extremely suffers the spiritual death that the narrator diagnoses for himself with fearful hyperbole. Like all of the landowners, Pliushkin is a mirror for Chichikov, but the salient resemblance is to the narrator. Just as it is age that has eroded the latter's soul, so Pliushkin presents above all "the frigid, insensate features of inhuman old age" (p. 111). As if to point the moral for Chichikov and the narrator as travelers, Pliushkin's spiritual death is figured in the allegory of life as journey:

> Take along with you, then, on setting out upon your way, as you emerge from the gentle years of youth into stern, coarsening manhood, take along with you all the humane impulses, abandon them not on the road; you will never retrieve them after! Sinister, fearsome is the old age that will come upon you farther along the way, and it never releases aught nor ever aught returns! (p. 111)

Yet the parallel of the narrator with Pliushkin suggests even more by the way that it inevitably breaks down. Frozen in place, Pliushkin disappears from the tale; the narrator is just warming up. His profession of silence contradicts itself in the very act of being spoken. His blocked channels of perception are belied by the existence of the vivid tale that he conveys to us. Far from being static and moribund, he emerges into the text to become the most changeable, elusive, and lively figure in it. The narrator has, to be sure, classed himself among the dead souls who are his subjects, as well as with the traveler who is his hero. Yet by the logic of the self-creating word, this voice seems able to come to life by the very act of diagnosing its own death. In the beginning was the Word. And the Word said, "I am dead," and, lo, there was life. Such seems the destiny of the Russian Word.

For all the novelty and insouciance of this self-christening, it coincides with other important moments of literary emergence. The image of the journey recalls that the Russian novel had to this point launched itself quite literally into various journeys: *Eugene Onegin* commences with the hero's racing off to his uncle's deathbed and, in several unfinished chapters (usually placed after the conclusion of the work), recounts the disenchanted and directionless dandy's trip to Odessa and other points south. *A Hero of Our Time* opens with the narrator's account of his travels, shortly to focus on Pechorin himself, "the military man on the move," whose "road pass" represents a passport for excursions inside the psyche, a reason for the roving, questioning search to come. Further back, epic itself in its canonical Virgilian form radiates out from the wandering of Aeneas and the Trojans, as of Odysseus before them. Most suggestively, the allegorical overlay of Chichikov's journey as it figures the narrator's journeys (both in Russia and in writing) as they, in turn, figure the journey of life itself (as the above reflections of Pliushkin make explicit) calls to mind the distinctive allegories of Dante-poet, Dante-pilgrim, and the journey of this life. Lest the parallel escape the reader, Gogol notes of the collegiate registrar that he "served our friends even as Virgil on a time had served Dante" (p. 126). As the narrative voice creates itself from the void, it recalls *The Divine Comedy*'s vision of the new creating consciousness speaking itself into existence from the world of the dead.[34] Gogol will leave the moral allegory quite unconcealed by the end: "What twisted, god-forsaken, narrow, impassable by-paths that have diverted it far from the goal has not mankind chosen in its strivings to attain the eternal truth, when spreading right before it was an open way, like to a path that leads to a great fame, meant for a king's mansions" (p. 198) — a far remove from the nonreligious, almost existential point of view in the novels of Pushkin and Lermontov.

That Pliushkin should serve as the pivot for this transformation of plot and narrative style is something of a curiosity. Transparent to all and harmful chiefly to himself, he makes the least likely candidate for villain. Unlike the other landowners, he affects subsequent events only by his

---

[34] The earliest extended critical discussion of the relationship — real and proposed — between *Dead Souls* and *The Divine Comedy* is found in A. Veselovskii, "'Mertvye Dushi': Glava iz ètiuda o Gogole," *Vestnik Evropy* 3 (1891): 68-102, esp. 89-91. See, most recently, Yurii Mann, *Poètika Gogolya* (Moscow: Khudozhestvennaya Literatura. 1978), esp. 339-52; A. A. Asoyan, "Zametki o dantovskikh motivakh u Belinskogo i Gogolya," 104-19; and Marianne Shapiro, "Gogol and Dante," *Modern Language Studies* 17, no. 2 (Spring 1987): 37-54; reprinted in Michael and Marianne Shapiro, *Figuration in Verbal Art* (Princeton. N.J.: Princeton University Press, 1988), 191-211.

absence. Of the series, he is the most inert. So is Satan frozen into ice at the bottom of Dante's Inferno; he, too, without moving can support a large narrative shift. As noted above, already Homer and Virgil had assigned to the strengthless dead pivotal roles — indeed, right in the middle of the *Odyssey* and *Aeneid* — in the unfolding destinies of those who still live and act. To understand the structural shift in *Dead Souls* here at the middle we must look more closely at how Pliushkin epitomizes evil despite his self-limiting and harmless obsessiveness: he manifestly lacks the vivacity and mystery of wickedness, as well as its seductiveness. He comes closer to the medieval vision of the Devil as an ass. Within the featureless geography of *Dead Souls* he forms the middle point (narratively and morally) of a world paralyzed by "middleness," and therefore the extreme point of a world dangerously lacking in extremes. He exists, that is, in a mode of inert undifferentiation, chaos, the primal soup that preexists the discriminating fiats of the creating Word that set light and dark, land and sea apart from one another. His essence lies in the lack of essence, the deadening blurring of categories.

Pliushkin presents perceptual problems not hitherto encountered. Chichikov initially mistakes the master of this estate for a woman and a servant — naturally enough since Pliushkin, rich as he is, plays the beggar. For him, to administer is to imprison, with himself also as prisoner. Only here among Chichikov's purchases of souls do living runaways get mixed up with the dead serfs. This living embodiment of evil as moral absence is reprised in the registrar who figures in Chichikov's biography: "There was just nothing at all in him, either of wickedness or of goodness, and there was a manifestation of something fearful in this absence of everything" (p. 216). Chichikov's first view of Pliushkin's estate, luxury overlaid with squalor, testifies to the promiscuous erosion even of the categories of art and nature, man and what is not man:

Some of these aspens had branches broken but not completely severed, which dangled, their leaves all withered. In short, everything was as beautiful as neither Nature alone nor art alone can conceive, but only as when they come together, when over the labor of man, often heaped up without any sense, Nature will run her conclusive burin, will lighten the heavy masses, will do away with the coarsely palpable regularity and the beggar's rents, through which the unconcealed, naked plan peers through, and bestow a wondrous warmth to everything that had been created amid the frigidity of a measured purity and tidiness. (p. 98)

The long surrounding description of the decay and disorder of "this extinct place" parodies the encomium of the perfecting hand of time and moss among the ruins of "Rome." Like the Roman prince, Chichikov has become an observer, and he is being seduced by a garden suited to the perversity of his soul — not presided over by Calypso or Alcina, but a miser; not a Bower of Bliss, but the living death of uncommitted undifferentiation, a remaking of the Wood of the Suicides in *Inferno* 13.[35] Art and nature join together not to perfect one another but to cancel each other out and produce a warmth that is the warmth of rot.

Pliushkin therefore carries the confusions and blurred boundaries of this irredeemably ordinary land to an extreme, indeed to a point where he dislodges the narrator from his continuing search for the typical and the Russian to a diagnosis that Pliushkin can be the exception that proves the rule: "It must be said that one encounters such a phenomenon but rarely in Russia, where all things love to open up rather than to shrivel into a ball like a hedgehog" (p. 104).[36] As the final erosion of boundary and order, Pliushkin, this void, this "rent on the cloak of humanity" (p. 104), serves to offer standards for judging the rest. By comparison, Nozdrev's compulsive lies, which similarly obliterate distinction, retrospectively take on a certain vivacity, as for example in the delicious absurdity of marching the hungry Chichikov up to a boundary stone that divides what Nozdrev owns from (how can he resist the claim?) what he also owns on the other side (p. 62). That kind of imaginative confusing of things seems benign compared to the killing literalism of Pliushkin, who, very like a writer, shapes his private world into a microcosm but ends up with trash heaps rather than fictions because he collects things instead of words. As an odious embodiment of

---

[35] The allusion is discussed by Shapiro, "Gogol and Dante," 46-48 [=*Figuration*, 204-6]. Her astute comparison of Dante's shades and Gogol's landowners as symbol systems essentially ends with the visit to Pliushkin. We differ in seeing Gogol's allegory, like Dante's, as also dynamic. Pliushkin's garden, like that of the suicides, is not only a climactic symbol but the threshold of a yet steeper descent. While character does not develop in the landowners any more than among the shades, the concept of character does, for, as we shall argue, certain nimble human entities (Dante-pilgrim, Gogol's narrator) do escape these deadening realms.

[36] The image recurs in Chichikov's biography: "Anew he withdrew into himself, like a hedgehog..." (p. 225). In both cases Gogol uses the verb s"ezhit'sya, which means to shrivel or shrink, and which contains the word for hedgehog, *ezh*.

a kind of literalism, Pliushkin marks the point beyond which the reader can no longer read literally and must open up to the allegories that now begin to spin themselves out from the text.

Reading habits often mark the man in this narrative: Chichikov and Petrushka read without concern for content (the one, ripped-down posters; the other, any book that falls into his hands); Nozdrev has a study in which he keeps only guns. Pliushkin collects paper, but only for the purpose of keeping it blank. Ominously, he is the landowner most instantly in accord with Chichikov's scheme, and indeed even expands it to include runaways. The end of chapter 6 suggests that, as can happen in underworld journeys, Chichikov has come away from this visit infected with the disordering perspective that robbed Pliushkin of life. In a world where moral pathology centers on mediocrity and undifferentiation, the heart of darkness is twilight: "It was already dusk when they [Chichikov and Seliphan] drove up to town. Light and shadow had become thoroughly intermingled and, it seemed, all objects had also become intermingled among themselves" (p. 114). In the remainder of Part One, Chichikov, as increasingly fantastic tales gather around him, will not know whether the townspeople are mad or he is mad, or perhaps stuck in a nightmare. In escaping Pliushkin's estate, Chichikov does not escape the moral vacuum that it represents.

As Fanger[37] notes, it is with Pliushkin that time enters the narrative. As in other ways, the old miser dispatches his structural role rather paradoxically, for the new temporal dynamic in the narrative is inspired by this most static of the characters, the one decisively eroded beyond all change. His character is epitomized by the broken pocket-watch that he contemplates giving to Chichikov (and does not). But broken timepieces imply the existence of those that still work, just as Pliushkin does the existence of people still alive. The narrative to follow will proceed against the background of a ticking clock, a doom waiting to descend on Chichikov (and possibly the narrator), as well as a heightened sense of history — a reminder that these are the years after 1812 and perhaps, therefore, a moment for Russia to be going somewhere. The very lifelessness of Pliushkin calls into question the life that made him thus; he alone among the landowners has a biography. As we have seen, the narrator introduces this episode by his own autobiographical reflections. Here begins the movement that will culminate in Chichikov's

[37] Fanger, *Creation of Nikolai Gogol*, 189.

biography at the end of Part One, as well as the narrator's reflections, following the Public Prosecutor's death, on the proper relationship among the generations of human beings, that is, on the claims of tradition. In all, the visit to Pliushkin, as underworld visitations are wont to do, has worked dialectically: the step out of time enables progress; departing the bounds of human morality creates terms for discrimination. This structural motif repeats itself at the end of Part One, when Chichikov's final liberation follows from an encounter with the Public Prosecutor's funeral cortege. As Seliphan notes, "That's a good thing, though, meeting this funeral; they say meeting a dead man is an omen of good luck" (p. 207).

Among the discriminations precipitated by Pliushkin's moral inertness is that of the narrator from his narrative. He becomes sufficiently aware of his own consciousness and problems (the audience, eternally the audience) that he can discuss them separately from the narrative, which, not coincidentally, at this crucial point begins to complicate and advance itself rather than just accreting vignettes. As noted above, the narrator's descent into the text generates vertical dimensions, relations between creator and created, that compound the allegorical meanings of the text. From the first, one has been able to read literally and with amusement. Yet now, thinking back over the various landowners, one begins to sense that these comic "types" may also serve a more profound moral allegory — not, to be sure, of murderers, traitors, and simonists, but of those who are neither hot nor cold. As Marianne Shapiro points out, the landowners, with their lack of moral commitment, could all fit comfortably into Dante's Limbo.[38] That suspended, excluded state of the moral neutrals — neither in Hell nor quite out of it — becomes another way of conceiving the middleness and mediocrity out of which Gogol has built N — . And beyond this allegory, confirmed by the narrator's discussion of the symbolism of the road, comes a third level (to use Dante's schema), the moral, as the narrator introduces himself with his preoccupations about the well-being of his soul and of the text that expresses it.

This narrator, as we shall see, will stand in a variety of relationships with the protagonist: sometimes coextensive with his consciousness, sometimes as a foil, sometimes entirely separate. Doubtless this relationship is kept problematic not only for the purposes of comedy but because it implies

---

[38] Shapiro, "Gogol and Dante," 45-48 [=*Figuration* 203-7].

so much about the most dangerous relationship of all, that of the narrator to Gogol himself. In other words, an analogy inevitably suggests itself between the authorial "voice" in the text (narrator: Chichikov) and the author himself (Gogol: narrator). By calling his pilgrim "Dante," Dante sets up an identity among protagonist, narrator, and author. By contrast, Gogol prevents Chichikov from seeming simply a projection of the narrator's own identity and thereby keeps the narrator from seeming simply a hypostasis of himself, that is, some unfictionalized record of his own voice. By the same token, the sporadic interpenetration of the consciousness of Chichikov and the narrator implicates Gogol himself, again fragmentarily but tantalizingly, in his nervous narrator.

The blurring of allegory prepares for a climactic evasion, for it is in the troika scene that we are left with no way of telling whether this is a vision or a joke. The narrator has an expansive sense of Russian destiny. Chichikov has none, so far as we know. What, then, of Gogol? Does he write more of himself into his patriotic, overwrought narrator or his cynical protagonist? He leaves us with the sense that he, personally, may have the vision or lack it or sustain both propositions by the ironic sense that all visions are jokes, as the creating Russian Word, born of its own deletion, might lead us to expect. As noted at the outset, this irony is a complex development from the essentially mock-heroic humor of the opening narrative, for it directly assaults the basis of that irony — namely, the ability of author and audience to stand securely superior to what is being described. The status of the author and, as we shall see, of the audience, has become acutely problematic, and the ironies of the creating, uncreating Russian Word do not generate mocking distance from the text but implosion, a sense of unleashed energies that are at once redemptive and nihilistic, generative and self-canceling, saccharine and sacrificial, and that thereby witness to the impossibility of reducing the Russian spirit to any single philosophical, religious, or political principle.

The plot of *Dead Souls* does not so much resolve and seal itself off as shift its coordinates to another temporal dimension, another pattern of narration, within which narrative resolution would have no meaning, a dimension with no more closure than the evanescent "now" of experienced time. The plot, insignificant as the narrator claims it is, means little. The shift means everything, and it is also the watershed in Gogol's career. Like the *Mirgorod* cycle (and every Greek tragedy), the narrative is framed by entrances and exits: Chichikov comes to town; Chichikov leaves town. The bachelor carriage is the same; the servants are the same; and Chichikov thinks he is the same. But the very fact that we know this unremarkable last item makes all the difference, for in the interval we have crawled inside Chichikov's head. The carriage is the same; the road is the same; it is the audience that is not the same.

Through its first half, *Dead Souls* proceeds so episodically that, like *Mirgorod*, it could as well be separate tales. As the link element, the hollow Chichikov could just as well be given a variety of names and identities. In fact he is, when his victims variously describe him as a counterfeiter, a spy, Napoleon, the abductor of the Governor's daughter, or Kopeikin. They themselves end with no strong sense of all having been in the same story; indeed, they end up spinning out stories (Nozdrev's fantasies, the Postmaster's tale of Captain Kopeikin) in the vignette style of the first six chapters — aggrandized, psychologically flat, pointless. They are doing what the narrator used to do, while he has moved on to something else. For the great advance in Gogol's artistry shows itself in the wake of Pliushkin, as the parts cohere and interact ever more closely into a single action. Our distracted narrator still afflicts us with gaps and discontinuities, but now they are less the interstices between vignettes strung out in a row (Chichikov's various visits) than leaps to different levels of a concerted action, levels that communicate with one another along some unexplained but constantly rattling chain of being. Initially, narrator and audience sat in Olympian amusement over the pomps and alarums of this pygmy village, while the stasis of the characters and simple linking of one episode to another evoked the sense of cyclic, nonprogressive time found in "Taras Bulba" and classical epic, a harmlessly remote "then." In the last six chapters, however, autobiography and biography bring instead a notion of time as experienced from within — that is, as developmental, linear, and subsumed into the continuing "now." This is the temporal continuum of "Rome" as it follows in the wake of the grand scheme bequeathed to epic by Dante, that is, the vision of pilgrimages not sealed off *in illo tempore*, but leading ultimately to the writer and the reader, the infinitely deferred closure of a lost, yet unlosable and still beckoning paradise. The bard buys that dream at the price of his anonymity and in descending from his perch confers new vertical dimensions on his creation, dimensions that need not be solemn to be real.

So it is that our slightly haunted narrator loses his detachment from the text, as episodes mesh into orchestrated movements — he senses conspiracy — that attest to a narrator strongly in control of, though also strongly controlled by, his text. As the narrator discloses his own inner life, he confers such a dimension upon his characters. He even anticipates it in his audience, thereby eroding the anonymity and ironic distance with which he began the tale. It was initially the sophisticated narrator who tarted up the grubby tale with epic flourishes for the delectation of his sophisticated audience. But by the end it is the Postmaster and Nozdrev who have expropriated the overblown style. The tale of the brigand Kopeikin comes to us with a filigree of allusions to Scheherazade, Semiramis, Lethe, "a whole epic, in a sort of way," claims the Postmaster (p. 185). And it is no more the narrator's sophisticated audience but the erstwhile pygmies of N — who, with vast credit to their own intelligence, do the dismissing. That is, the initial mock-heroic ironies of *Dead Souls*, the interaction of narrator and audience, have been absorbed into the text itself, so that we see a reflection — crude, but unmistakable — of the skeptical and self-congratulatory audience that we have lately been.

In the Christian confessional mode of epic, it is of course the writer's own spiritual development that is ultimately called to account. In contrast to the narrative freedom, almost randomness, of the first half, after Pliushkin there comes an increasing feeling of things *following*:[39] as the townspeople close in on Chichikov and as the narrator senses his audience closing in on him, claustrophobia and causation develop in tandem, so that increasingly one thing narratively has to follow upon another. Herein lurks the seamless vision of "Rome" or of the *Paradiso* turned into nightmare. The deadening obsession with acquisition that in the first half freezes the characters into stasis now gives way to an eruptive and illimitable growth of consciousness, which closes in on narrator and protagonist as it threatens almost literally to waken the dead, or the audience.

The narrator and protagonist at moments coincide to such a degree that, for example, when Chichikov risks contamination by Pliushkin, it is the

---

[39] Fanger notes this quality of Gogol's novel when he claims that "If *Dead Souls* seems colder in its brilliance than any of the previous writings, it is because there alone the values of childhood and free fantasy have virtually no place. An informing nostalgia for the past had yielded to an anxious concern for the future" (*Creation of Nikolai Gogol*, 246).

narrator who feels impelled to profess his own immunity to the epidemic loss of perspective, as he does at the beginning of the next chapter. Here begins the self-defense that evolves throughout the rest of the narrative by means of protracted reflection on the writer's lot figured in terms of a journey. Indeed, it is the integrating image of the journey, the road rather than the stops along it, that signals the narrative shift toward continuity. The narrator's celebration of his vocation, mixed with self-mockery and self-defense, may parallel those epic writers (for example, Apollonius Rhodius, Virgil [i.e., *Aeneid* 7.37-45], and Milton) who commence the latter halves of their works with new invocations of the Muses. Indeed, the narrator admits to the help of a similar "wondrous power" (p. 117), if not quite the traditional sisterhood, in composing his tale. To be sure, his intent is not to espouse but to decline the calling to heroic song. The *recusatio* of the high style, the solemn refusal of the epic vocation, is a fixture of classical rhetoric, a way of evading the pretensions of patrons. Yet within the allegories generated by the Christian, spiritual reading of such acts, *recusatio* can function nobly as renunciation; self-abasement becomes self-fulfillment; the ordinary becomes the redemptively humble; what in secular terms is the lower calling becomes a spiritually true vocation.

A single statement, therefore, can be both an abashed apology for foregone heroics and a triumphant proclamation of spiritual allegory in the text:

> happy the writer who has picked out only the few exceptions from the great slough of everyday figures revolving around him; the writer who has not changed even once the lofty strain of his lyre, has never descended from his aerie to his poor, insignificant brethren, and who, without touching the common earth, has devoted himself wholly to his images and forms, far removed from that earth and enlarged to heroic size....
>
> But not such is the lot and different is the fate of the writer who has dared to bring out all the things that are before man's eyes at every minute, yet which his unheeding eyes see not — all that fearsome, overwhelming slimy morass of minutiae that have bogged down our life, all that lurks deep within the cold, broken, workaday characters with which our earthly path, at times woeful and dreary, swarms. (p. 116)

On one, more literal level, the narrator, in an apologia that is as old as Aristophanes, begs only that we not confuse him with his ignoble subject matter or, perhaps more gravely, suspect that he shares the fatal lack of discrimination that has reduced Pliushkin from man to thing and to which

Chichikov shows himself susceptible. After the countless proemia in which some poet claims to sing a higher strain (*paulo maiora canamus*), here the writer openly sings of his vocation to the low road. However, by a more allegorical and Christian reading, the absorption with "poor, insignificant brethren" is not frailty but evangelism, and the true Muses are evoked not on the slopes of Helicon but in the confessional.

The narrator has begun Pliushkin's chapter with a confession that he suffers the same erosion of sensitivity by time already infecting Chichikov (who saw nothing in the lovely blonde but a potential dowry) and which has entirely robbed Pliushkin of human emotion. The account of Pliushkin is sufficiently appalling that to balance the personal confession introducing it (at the beginning of chapter 6) there needs to be literary self-defense to conclude and isolate it. And the narrator does insist on the point that this low road is where life actually thrives and swarms — a truth deducible already from the vivacious flies and dull socialites of the opening soiree, but now affirmed in the mode of authorial self-reflection rather than epic simile. Author and audience looked down mockingly on the flies on that sugarloaf; increasingly, they will find themselves squirming there below.

Luckily, before the narrator gets lost entirely in his brooding self-reflections, he lets Chichikov wake up: "Let us plunge suddenly and head first into life, with all its inaudible blather and jingle-bells, and see what Chichikov is up to" (p. 117). Thus the narrative of the second part of the novel begins with the image of plunging ahead with which it will end, though here it is the narrator and readers who do the plunging, as later Chichikov will do when we have reached our stopping point. Awakening proves to be the dominant theme of the rest of Part One, as Chichikov quite unintentionally stirs the townspeople first into frenzied admiration and then into rampaging speculation about his identity and purposes. Their lackluster sameness of values and habits gives way to the brilliant particularity of their convictions about the man, as these fantasies variously derive from fear, jealousy, desire, and a total lack of proportion. The gray, faceless populace now begins to differentiate itself: men and women harbor quite diverse suspicions about the mysterious stranger, as do servants and masters. As we have noted, the range of their accounts, from the grotesque and almost folkloric to the heroic (Chichikov is Napoleon) reflects what has been the narrator's own range of styles. The creating Russian Word seems to be working its strange magic, if only in the form of gossip (but the narrator has made no loftier claims for it). In fact, by the time we come to the Postmaster's tale of Captain Kopeikin, the villagers would seem to have reached the state where they themselves could have written the first chapters of *Dead Souls* and thereby force the audience, as noted above, to self-reflection about how they themselves read those chapters.

It is perhaps here in the text that Gogol's ironies reach most deeply into tales within tales and frauds within fictions when the narrator gives us the Postmaster spinning an overblown and underplotted tale of the nonentity Kopeikin (so like the nonentity Chichikov), as he fabricates a heroic, indeed redemptive, identity for himself (and, like Chichikov, carefully gives his victims receipts). Here we see the interaction of author and audience replicated simultaneously at various levels. At the bottom of this vortex of ironic self-reflection we find Gogol's eerie insight into his own potential, virtually a map of his career. For Kopeikin calls to mind that single, multileveled entity Chichikov-narrator-Gogol. However, Kopeikin's progress from pointless wandering to success as a brigand and organizer neatly reverses Chichikov's career in N — , for Chichikov does bring the villagers together — but to his own cost. The narrator (and implicitly Gogol) ends by claiming that galvanizing effect for himself.

It is, however, with Kopeikin's next step that the parallels become compelling, for he leaves Russia and then redeems it by writing letters back to it, to which the czar himself proves receptive — precisely what Gogol was to do with *Selected Passages from Correspondence with Friends*. At the very core of this embedded text, of fictions compounding themselves, we hit on a stratum of fact. The telos of this account of deceitful bureaucrats who turn the innocent Kopeikin himself to brigandage and trickery is the writing of letters to the czar that reveal an important and unacknowledged truth. It was serious business for Gogol to bring the czar into the text, whatever the degree of distance through narrative framing. He does so in the context of the increasingly apparent project of saving Russia. The Postmaster does not know the end of the tale. Having disseminated his great truth, Kopeikin may have returned to Russia and to his earlier fictions by coming back to Russia disguised as Chichikov. Unless the maimed Kopeikin has also grown a leg and an arm, the Postmaster's audience remains unconvinced. But in perhaps the most framed, distanced, and ironic point in the text, Kopeikin presents a paradigm of fiction turning itself inside out into truth, a paradigm that generalizes itself to Chichikov and the narrator and, better than he knew, to Gogol himself, who was to live out his last years as if plotted from this fiction.

Meanwhile, the narrator, with a bit more deliberation than Chichikov, has set about waking up his audience, as his earlier cringing courtesy gives way to exhortation, baiting, and vociferous self-defense — a homiletic function basic to Christian epic and unknown to classical. Having descended fully into his own creation to assume a voice and a function, the narrator takes his prophetic function seriously. His audience, like the citizens of N — , should come to feel themselves as a group. This summoning of the reader from obedient passivity is itself a creation, a calling from nothing into consciousness. And, as the first lecture on the subject established, the creating Russian Word can just as well be a servant's curse as anything else. Basic to the narrator's message is that his readership feel themselves to be Russians and members of their generation, with responsibilities to those earlier and those yet to come. Like Chichikov and the narrator, the audience acquires origins and posterity — indeed, in heightened terms of apocalypse that address it as fully an epic audience:

> The present generation sees everything clearly now; it wonders at the delusions and laughs at the lack of comprehension of its ancestors, not perceiving that this chronicle is written over with heavenly fire, that every letter therein is calling out to it, that from every direction a piercing forefinger is pointed at it, at it and none other than it, the present generation. But the present generation laughs and, self-reliantly, proudly launches a new succession of delusions, over which it, descendants will laugh in their turn, even as the present generation is laughing now.
>
> Chichikov was utterly unaware of what was going on. As ill-luck would have it, he had contracted a slight cold at this time.... (p. 198)

The juxtaposition of the oblivious Chichikov to the now prophetic narrator indicates how far the two have grown apart, even though both have come to a point where they confront a mob of critics. Like the most pessimistic and demonic of the early fictions ("A Terrible Vengeance" and "The Portrait"), Part One resolves itself into a day of reckoning, a final moment of exposure. That moment involves the narrator vis-à-vis his audience as fully as it does Chichikov before the citizens of N — . Indeed, since the latter meets his downfall when the townspeople start paying attention to him instead of his fictions, one wonders if the self-absorbed and self-proclaiming narrator is not courting the same disaster.

Chichikov will stumble forward in his eternal present, having learned nothing. The readership, however, no longer has that option, as the narrator turns the joke on them. Yes, to plunge from lofty abstractions to Chichikov's head cold is still amusing. But the long temporal dimension here presented sub specie aeternitatis changes the mode of the satire and retroactively causes the reader's condescending laughter to ring hollow. As we have laughed at these vain and dead souls, so will later men laugh at us — if we even have the luck to receive the kind of memorial that the citizens of N — have received in this text. Whether this chronicle is written over with heavenly fire or, as the audience may suspect, with provincial fireflies, matters less than their realization of their own vantage point, both infinitely distant and subjectively trapped within the fiction itself. The extrinsic perspective, the long view of epic, forces the audience to the paradoxical recognition that these figures are themselves. From this view point, the readers must confront the prospect that by insisting (as the narrator anticipates we will) on subjects nobler than these for "epics," we leave ourselves without the chance of a memorial. Merely raising the issue further ruptures the closure of the narrative, for beyond the time of composition lies the time of reading, which, barring apocalypse, even the audience cannot finally define and limit.

To be sure, the contradictions in which the narrator mires himself only grow as he progresses. The more he insists on a higher consciousness — in morality, in national identity, in a sense of tradition and destiny — the odder seems his commitment to low subject matter. The very essence of the Russianness that he is trying to distill in this epic is a vitality that cannot be captured in writing: "And lifeless will seem beside them [noble Russians] all the virtuous people of other tribes, even as a book is lifeless before the living word!" (p. 210). The spirit animates; the word kills. We are forced by the compounding contradictions before us to read at a higher, allegorical level. No more than for Dante is comedy excluded thereby: if the narrator's highest use, like Chichikov's, is to be a provocateur, to wheedle, abuse, or cheat people into consciousness, then logical consistency would only weigh him down, as ethics would Chichikov (or scrutability would Socrates). The ultimate hero of the piece is neither the protagonist nor the narrator, but Russia — that is, the readership, the completers and creators of the allegorical decipherment that transmutes this commedia into an instructive parable. To make either Chichikov or his narrating double estimable or even finally comprehensible would risk the act of erecting a false idol.

The narrator ends his tale with more force than control, more speed than direction, and a question rather than a denouement. The final epiphanic moment in *Dead Souls* may reveal more than the narrator can quite keep reins on. He amplifies Chichikov's current uncertainties into a question of national destiny. The tone may verge on the inflated and mock-heroic, but the question gets asked nonetheless: Whither Russia? The narrator, having thoroughly abused his patient readership and provided no proper resolution for his plot, seems fully as much in flight as Chichikov and, in retrospect, about as trustworthy. He need not label or explain his final moment. It is sufficient that he return us to the same carriage, same Chichikov, same road, so that we may realize the degree to which we see them now with different eyes.

Suddenly, with these new consciousnesses, the large surrounding shell of the "poèma" is not so empty; or, to put the matter differently, a new and nobler reading is placed on the emptiness. The bare landscape presents, finally, no obstacles to the narrator in imposing heroic expectations, if not heroic value, on this fictive universe. For the sense of absence is seen as coinciding with the challenging emptiness and openness of the Russian landscape. A stagnant backwater comes to seem more and more like the void in which a Second Creation can happen. Whereas the society of N — had proved frustrating to the narrator, complete absence leaves the imagination free. As seen initially in mock-heroic terms, the mediocrity of protagonist and locale stood as an Iron Age degenerated from some Golden Age. With the new set of coordinates, middleness becomes centrality, a midpoint in a new creation, the birth of consciousness — an organizing topic in Christian epic.

As we have seen already in numerous ways, the very notion of an epic journey in pursuit of dead souls brings to mind Dante's infernal descent. As the wellspring of Italian literature, Dante would recommend himself to the project of promoting Russian literature to world attention. For Gogol, eternally split between memorializing Russia and abandoning it, the figure of Dante would also provide a welcome model of how a national identity might be captured only from exile. How convenient for someone of Gogol's bent that Dante had demonstrated how the road to high and redemptive seriousness may begin through irony and satire, through sinking into the filth of human weakness and insignificance! One needs only the barest of plots; a pageant of rogues will carry the narrative. The national life can easily insinuate itself into the delicious descent.

In its character portrayal, as well as in the dynamics of tone and voice, *Dead Souls* derives much from Dante's *Inferno*. As has long been appreciated, both works reveal how the living are really dead, sorted out by their characteristic sins and eternally fixed in the landscape. Chichikov himself, especially in the early chapters, functions largely as a reflection of what goes on around him, a foil for the various types he meets; they, in turn, serve as crystallizations of his own nature. In the *Inferno*, Dante-pilgrim proceeds in much the same way, seeing sides of his own nature reflected in the denizens of the various rings. How the various types perceive Chichikov is as indexical of their real natures as are the devils' misperceptions of Dante-pilgrim. As Fanger[40] notes, each of Chichikov's encounters occurs in a landscape conceived to reflect the character of the proprietor; the rings of Hell are emblematic in the same way. The deformative life-force of the Gogolian landscape, nature perceived as rot and overthrow, in its own modest way often calls to mind the antinature of Dante's Hell. Having surveyed many human failings, both the *Inferno* and *Dead Souls* save betrayal for the end (as Chichikov is turned upon and driven out by his erstwhile friends). Both end with a landscape that is the very embodiment of absence: the featureless Russian plain and the lifeless ice that entombs Satan along with the treacherous threesome of Judas, Brutus, and Cassius. Stasis in the latter case and unbounded freedom in Chichikov's prospects seem equal, though opposite, symbols of the lack of meaningful possibility. Perhaps, also, Gogol's bounding, directionless troika is, on a much reduced scale, an inversion of the Trinity in the way that Judas and company are.

Both narratives conclude with the sense of having hit bottom. As Part One ends, the double sense of a final plunge into the abyss yet also of a redemptive surge recalls the turning point between the *Inferno* and the *Purgatorio*, a terrifying fall downward that pivots at the earth's (and Satan's) center to become an ascent. At the end of Part One, Gogol announces that "there are still two long parts ahead of us" (p. 232), and the critic

---

[40] Fanger, ibid., 174.

Vyazemsky[41] tells us that he directly regarded this first part of his proposed trilogy as the equivalent of the *Inferno*. That plunge seems strangely familiar when we take it, for the nadir was already indicated firmly enough with Pliushkin in chapter 6, and in equally Dantesque terms, though without any sense of release or uplift. Characters in Part Two will keep slipping downward to despond, and in 1847 *Selected Passages* gave voice, a bit more autobiographically, to the same sense of having only just hit bottom. Herein we can see a reason why Gogol's adaptations of Dante remain always large in promise and inchoate. Though invoking Dante's whole spiritual cycle as a program for his work, Gogol felt powerfully only certain moments within it, particularly the final drop to the bottom, which he seemed constantly to be reexperiencing. *Facilis descensus Averno*. The way up again proved harder to find.

This chapter began with the double descent of the ironist, and perhaps now we are in a position to appreciate its source. The descents of mock heroic — of author and audience together condescending to the hollow pomposities of the world depicted — give way in the latter half of *Dead Souls* to the redemptive descent of the creator into his work, even as the paranoid but well-meaning, and perhaps genuinely visionary, narrator recapitulates a movement from within the *Inferno*, the movement from pagan to Christian. Virgil-guide can descend into the pit largely as a satirist, to see and mock. He can instruct others but cannot, like a pilgrim, see to his own redemption. We are particularly aware of his role in the early cantos and in our own first readings of the text. Further descent and deeper familiarity with the text draw out the antecedents that will ultimately be of more importance to Dante-pilgrim: the infernal visits of Saint Paul and of Christ. Their descents involve a shouldering of responsibility, ultimately martyrdom, that is simultaneously an awakening. The final ambiguity of both Gogol's troika (advancing or escaping?) and Dante's satanic trinity (the nadir that is the pivot upward) captures the paradoxical spiritual energies here at work.

[41] See Simon Karlinsky, *The Sexual Labyrinth of Nikolai Gogol* (Cambridge, Mass.: Harvard University Press, 1976), 239.

Dead Souls, Part Two

Gogol, notoriously, spent the rest of his life failing to answer either "Whither Rus'?" or "Whither Gogol?". He labored, rather, to establish that they were the same question. Though Dante-pilgrim is similarly reduced at the end of his infernal descent to a state of helplessness, incrimination, and infantilism, he has a miracle and a guide to rescue and lead him to purgation. Gogol seemed not to have been able to find either. He reversed his promising strategy of going to Rome to reinvent Russia into a disastrous attempt to import Rome to Russia. The sequel did get written — and mostly burned (as the dying Virgil and exiled Ovid had ineffectually directed their epics to be). In 1847 *Selected Passages* appeared to offer a troubled Russia counsel and advice until the Second Coming that the sequel's publication would be. The requisite miracles were prophesied, but Gogol still seemed hard-pressed to suggest a Virgil other than himself.

The surviving fragments of Part Two of *Dead Souls* and Gogol's outlines nevertheless show gropings toward a tale of purgation and redemption. The opening landscape, like that of *Purgatorio*, is of a mountain sloping down to the shore. The first character encountered, the landowner Tentetnikov, shows potential for being saved, though, like the procrastinators of Ante-Purgatory, also a tendency to waste time. Like the penitents of Dante's second canticle, he is "simply a fellow crawling between earth and heaven" (p. 239).[42] His biography boasts figures comparable to those that Dante found redemptive: a Virgil in the charismatic teacher Alexander Petrovich, as well as an unmistakable Beatrice, Ulinka. He is thirty-three, that important year in life when Gogol himself finally released *Dead Souls* and reissued "Taras Bulba" and the very age at which Christ died, as a later Russian writer, Joseph Brodsky, reminds us, musing on his own advancement to this stage:

> Thirty-three, the age of the Perfect Man, the age of Christ…Christ lived for thirty-three years, and all the time he was following a script. It was

---

[42] Gogol's expression is *koptitel' neba*, an idiom that means to idle one's life away, to live aimlessly. Reavey renders the phrase as "sky-gazer," thereby including the sense of *nebo*, which means sky or heavens. The literal meaning of the phrase is "to besmirch the sky with soot."

all written, but only for the space of thirty-three years. At thirty-three only one thing can begin: Resurrection. Christ did not escape repetition. You can find this "blasphemy" in Kierkegaard. The Resurrection is the repetition of the process. All life is in a sense repetition. This is the lesson of Christ.[43]

Tentetnikov now directly embodies the conflict between writing and doing, words and the world, that had bothered Gogol all along, though now that conflict increasingly expresses itself in the ancient Christian debate about the merits of faith versus works, the *vita contemplativa* versus the *vita activa*, which figures so largely in the *Purgatorio*.

Apart from the opening, Gogol has not inserted the talkative narrator of Part One. In Part Two, the distance between the characters, on the one hand, and the author and his audience, on the other, has narrowed greatly, so that Gogol may either have had trouble finding space in the narrative for this mediating, confessional, self-advertising voice or may have abandoned it so as to let his characters, especially Tentetnikov, stand in some ambiguous but unmistakable autobiographical relationship to himself. The anomie and paralysis that afflict Tentetnikov when he loses his teacher may reflect something of Gogol's reaction to the loss of Pushkin, who had, after all, suggested the idea of Part One and might now be sorely needed to give direction to the sequel. Stirred variously by the challenges of being a gentleman farmer or Ulinka's suitor, Tentetnikov glimpses redemption in forsaking words for action: "Fate meant me to be the owner of an earthly paradise, a prince, but I conspired to make myself a burrower among dead papers" (p. 248). At other moments he reverts to the oblivion of writing "a great work on Russia" (p. 252)[44] to save the nation with words when he despairs of doing so with deeds.

The great redemptive Russian book that is taken up and abandoned replicates the admonitory letters attributed to Captain Kopeikin and anticipates what *Selected Passages* will actually attempt. When we get to

---

[43] Rosette C. Lamont, "Joseph Brodsky: A Poet's Classroom," *The Massachusetts Review* 15, no. 4 (Autumn 1974): 553-77.

[44] Further evidence supporting the autobiographical relationship between Gogol and Tentetnikov may be found in the author's letter to Zhukovsky of December 29, 1847, in which he also uses the expression "bol'shoe sochinenie," a great or major vvork. See *Sobranie sochinenii v semi tomakh*, 7:361.

the core of Tentetnikov's malaise, we find that it is above all a reaction to the spiritual extravagances that conclude Part One. For it is Tentetnikov who inherits the crisis of the bounding troika — momentum without direction — which is implicitly the narrator's, Gogol's, and Russia's. Tentetnikov experiences his crisis in just these terms:

> What did these sobs mean? Did his ailing soul reveal thereby the grievous secret of its ailment — that the exalted inner being which had begun to rise up within him had not succeeded in taking shape and growing strong; that, not having been put to the test in his youth by a struggle against fiascoes, he had not attained to the high ability of rising higher and becoming stronger by overcoming barriers and obstacles; that, having become molten like metal at great heat, the rich reserve of great emotions within him had failed to receive its final tempering; and now, unresilient, his will was impotent; that the extraordinary preceptor had died too prematurely to benefit him, and that there no longer was anybody in the whole world who had the power to raise up anew the forces shaken by eternal vacillations and the impotent will deprived of its resiliency, who could have called out to his soul as an awakening call that heartening word "Onward!" which the Russian thirsts after everywhere, no matter what rung of the ladder he may be standing on, of whatever station, calling, and pursuit he may be? (p. 252)

This passage gives a fair sense of the conceptual evolution of the text thus far. Part One had moved from static vignettes to a sense of biographical and autobiographical time. Here the perspective moves beyond clock time altogether into a nonlinear dimension of spiritual or psychological time. Tentetnikov's (or Gogol's or Russia's) inability to advance results from no current circumstance, no lack of opportunity or resources, but from a developmental failure, the missed chance of being tempered, challenged, and hardened at the right time.

The phrasing of the next paragraph moves beyond the fictional context altogether into a meditation on what has emerged as the central evangelical project of *Dead Souls*: "Where is he, then, who would be able to tell our Russian soul in its native tongue this omnipotent word 'Onward!' — he who, knowing all the forces and abilities and all the profundity of our nature, could with a single thaumaturgic wave of his hand set us streaming toward the exalted life?" (p. 252). Parts of this allegory are stereotypical: this dark moment of despair over the lost preceptor and the resulting life of error leads directly to the emergence of the redemptive Ulinka — a shift from Virgil-guide to Beatrice, from the past to a vital present — for Ulinka is "alive as life itself" (p. 253). One suspects as well a more deeply felt lament for Pushkin at this point, and perhaps a dark sense that his passing is something that Gogol can never overcome, a moment that he will never psychologically grow beyond. The style of the valediction is such as to suggest that it can never quite be finished so as to liberate the author for other concerns — and in this it violates the standard allegories of spiritual pilgrimage. It is on the basis of their limitations that the ghosts of such parent/guide figures (for example, Virgil's Anchises or Dante's Virgil) can be laid to rest. The lost preceptor here is less limited, less forgivable, and less forgettable. For in passing prematurely he failed to save his pupil from easy success, failed to be there, as it were, to apply the reins.

The narrative provides little explanation of how this circumstance might still afflict Tentetnikov; its applicability to Gogol is evident, and we shall still be hearing it in *Selected Passages from Correspondence with Friends*. Since Part One as an exercise in provocation predicated its impact on being rejected by the audience, its popular success has presumably undermined its message. A prophet honored in his own country loses credibility, and Gogol in *Selected Passages* will go to considerable lengths to rescind that honor. One senses that Pushkin cannot be forgiven or forgotten for failing to limit and restrain the disconcerting experience of literary success, or perhaps even for suggesting the good idea that led to that affliction in the first place, especially when he is not present to suggest another to redeem the situation.

Whatever the mixture of tribute and defiance directed toward Pushkin amid the necromancy of Part One, it apparently has neither conjured up nor exorcised his ghost, and he casts his shadow over Part Two in the way of an unshakable influence, an unpayable debt. From the outset, the bounding energies of the troika are felt to be compromised by unresolved issues from the past. As in "Rome," Gogol falters once the moment comes to shift the focus to an Annunziata or an Ulinka. This blockage may result not just from the undeveloped symbolism of the feminine for Gogol but also from the unresolved business of cutting loose from fathers and mentors. To the degree that *Selected Passages* manages to map out, if not to dramatize, spiritual progress, it is by positing a stringently patriarchal world of czars, Hebrew fathers, and male authors into which women are invited only for the honor of being given advice.

Gogol's outline suggests that Tentetnikov was to make a final purgatorial leap into the world of affairs through a secret political society, which would lead to exile in Siberia, where Ulinka was to follow.[45] In liberating himself from his own words into redemptive suffering and perhaps finally to earthly paradise, Tentetnikov traces something like the same arc as Dante-pilgrim, who is held back in Ante-Purgatory by the enchantment of hearing his own poetry sung by his friend Casella, then advances through voluntary suffering to the Eden on the mountain top, drawn by Beatrice, as Tentetnikov will be by Ulinka.

When Chichikov rejoins the narrative in chapter 2 he seems little changed. Gradually, however, his picaresque wandering transforms itself into pilgrimage. He experiences his visit to the extraordinary estate of the wonder-working Kostanzhoglo as something of a homecoming, as if "he had come into everything he had desired and had cast aside his wanderer's staff, saying 'Enough!'" (p. 308). In his own terms, he begins to contemplate resurrection: "he determined, right then and there, to acquire with the money he would derive from mortgaging his fantastic souls a country seat that would by no means be fantastic" (p. 310). His desire to escape his own fictions parallels Tentetnikov's flight from his own words; he, too, now dreams of a life-mate.

Apparently some salvation was in the cards for characters like Khlobuev, Pliushkin, and Chichikov himself, if only in the trilogy's final canticle.[46] How they were to be saved is a difficult and apparently unsolved question. The characters of Part Two are at least not static and fixed in their damnation, as the characters of Part One initially are. Collectively, they seem very much like the late-repentant waiting in Dante's Ante-Purgatory, destined for purgation but not yet launched. The "prodigal son" Khlobuev (as Chichikov calls him, p. 323) may represent one of Dante's four categories in Ante-Purgatory, the lethargic. His idleness involves him in depressing situations. "But he was saved by a religious streak that in some strange way existed within him side by side with his shiftless way of life" (p. 323). One way or another God always does provide for him. "Reverently, gratefully, would he acknowledge at such a time the unencompassable mercy of Providence, have a mass of thanksgiving said — and begin his shiftless mode of life

[45] See Gippius, *Gogol*, 170.

[46] See ibid., 175.

all over again" (p. 323). As an antithesis to Khlobuev, Gogol portrays the hyperactive but melancholic Kostanzhoglo, perhaps an incarnation of the fourth group in Ante-Purgatory — the preoccupied, mostly princes, who were too busy running the world to save their own souls; Gogol also sees Kostanzhoglo in royal terms ("like a king on the day of his triumphant coronation," p. 307). In this contrast of the wonder-working Kostanzhoglo to the ineffectual Khlobuev, the preoccupied to the lethargic, lurks the opposition of the *vita activa* and the *vita contemplativa*, a subject for Dante as well, as in Dante-pilgrim's dream of Rachel and Leah (canto 27), though Gogol has wittily reversed their respective fecundity (the contemplative figure, unlike Rachel, has six children; the activist Kostanzhoglo, only one).[47]

In one particular, Part Two does come unmistakably close to Dante's vision of purgation: the pursuit of a redeemed vision of art that can parallel the redeemed vision of man. The axis of metamorphosis is not so much, as in Part One, between the human and the bestial or the dead as it is between nature and art. Indeed, any person who stops moving for an instant risks being turned into a representation. Ulinka enters the narrative as "a living figurine" with "a pure, noble facial outline [that] could not have been found anywhere save perhaps on ancient, small cameos.... And if one were to translate her, with all the drapes of the dress that clung to her, into marble, she would have been considered the work of some sculptor of genius" (p. 268). Landscapes take on such detail and animation that they begin to look back, forcing the reader into an active relationship with what they depict, as Gogol elsewhere claimed should be the artist's goal. As he wrote to Annenkov:

> If I were an artist, I would depict a special kind of scene. What trees and landscapes are now painted! Everything is clear, sorted out, determined

---

[47] Marianne Shapiro sees instead a scheme based on the Gregorian seven cardinal vices distributed throughout all of Purgatory: "Each character newly presented in this volume adheres more clearly than his counterpart in the first to a specific vice by which he is defined. Tentetnikov (whose name is based on *ten'*, 'shadow, shade'), has a biography but is particularized for sloth, the grounding sin which together with greed (materiality) guarantees petrification. Kostanzhoglo virtually stands for anger; General Betrishchev, for pride; Khlobuyev for prodigality, Koshkarev, for gluttony. As in Dante's *Purgatorio*, sloth (*acedia*) is the preambular vice that introduces the others." "Gogol and Dante," 48 [= *Figuration*, 207].

by the master himself, with the spectator able to follow it quite logically. I would bunch the trees all up, confuse the branches, throw light where no one would expect it — those are the kind of landscapes that need to be painted.[48]

Thoughts begin spontaneously to express themselves in pictures: when the enamoured Tentetnikov doodles, pictures of Ulinka automatically appear on the page. The connections between things and words still lurk in the background; traveling through Russia becomes a journey through a "living book" (p. 293). But now even the mock-heroic touches are translated into visual terms: "Platon Mikhalych was Achilles and Paris rolled into one: a graceful build, a painter's ideal in height, fresh vigor — he combined all these" (p. 282). By the continuing comparison of the Mount of Purgatory to a cathedral, as well as to objets d'art like the vivacious bas-reliefs along the way (cantos 10 and 12), Dante likewise posed the question of what kind of art can embody and instruct about the ideal without itself competing with and thereby obscuring the Creator's own handiwork. How can the artist celebrate divine perfection through the materials of a fallen world? The answer lies in an art that reveals and deflates its own illusions. As an ironist, Gogol should have been particularly well suited for such instructive self-contradiction, but it remains to be seen how much his sense of irony survived the religious intensities of his final years.

The importance of this issue had emerged already in chapter 1, which begins as if continuing the authorial apologies of the end of Part One:

> But why depict mankind's poverty, and more poverty, and the imperfectibility of our life, digging up types from the backwoods, from the god-forsaken nooks and crannies of our realm?…And so we once more find ourselves in the backwoods, once more have we stumbled upon a nook. But then, what backwoods and what a nook! (p. 237)

There follows one of Gogol's most elaborate landscapes, indeed, almost heroic in its presentation: "Like the titanic rampart of some unending fortress, with corner turrets and embrasures, the mountain heights stretched along windingly for hundreds upon hundreds of miles" (p. 237). This descriptive tour de force complexly recalls Gogol's earlier ways of starting and ending narratives. From the barren, symbolically malleable plain at the

---

[48] Quoted in P. V. Annenkov, "N. V. Gogol' v Rime letom 1841 goda," in *Gogol' v vospominaniyakh sovremennikov*, ed. S. Mashinskii (Moscow, 1952), 283.

end of Part One we have moved to a cluttered landscape, yet the feeling of motion, almost flight, continues as the description focuses from this vast topography into a single manor house. Like Part One, the text begins with an entrance — ours, for here "we stumble upon a nook." The large prospects, stratified into layers of historical symbolism, that concluded "Rome" and "Taras Bulba" are reworked here, even to the detail of the reflecting river. Where we had been brought in as the spectators, it turns out that the scene itself, "tree-tops, roofs, and crosses pointing down," in the river "seemed for all the world to be scrutinizing this wondrous image" (p. 238). From the mirroring image the landscape looks back at itself, and what is seen is itself a point of observation, indeed a better one: "The view was very fine, but the inverted view, from the superstructure in the distance, was still finer." This landscape that is an observer is lulled by a musical silence: "All this was enveloped in imperturbable stillness, which was not disturbed even by the echoes of the ethereal singers, lost in ethereal vastnesses — echoes that barely reached one's ears" (p. 238). A noninvocation of nonexistent Muses? What is announced here programmatically at the start is a tendency to turn the tables on the readers, to present them with a pretty scene that then looks back out at them.

Gogol is always given to such reversals, but they had at the start of Part One chiefly concerned matters of proportion and dignity, as the puny became pompous and great phonies tripped over themselves. Here the confusions between observer and observed, the creator and his artifact, which the intrusion of the narrator brought to Part One are built into the order of nature itself. One of the clearest indices we have for the various characters lies in what they manage to see, or fail to see, in what surrounds them. Of Tentetnikov in his spiritual paralysis we learn that "a view which no visitor could observe with indifference, was to all intents and purposes non-existent for the very master of that village" (p. 241). When he then seeks remedy in the *vita activa* without sufficient spiritual grounding and soon loses interest, his ineffectuality stems from perceptual problems, confusions of the great and the small, very like those of the slightly dizzy narrator of Part One: "if the rustic labors were being carried on near at hand, his eyes would be fixed on some point as remote as possible; if the work was going on at a distance, his eyes would seek out objects as near as possible... (pp. 250-51). His temporary delusion that his estate is actually "an earthly paradise" delays his true pursuit of same. And Chichikov himself must be warned off his own newfound aesthetic sense: "'Oh, so you're a lover of views, are you!' said Skudronzhoglo,[49] suddenly looking at him severely… Look for utility and not beauty. Beauty will come of itself…" (p. 315).

These continuing references to matters of perception show the self-consciousness of Part One raised to a more abstract level: not a narrator calling attention to himself, but art calling into question the bases of its own operation to serve the larger moral allegory. Moral growth is compared with estate management, and indeed Chichikov, once again leaving town in a carriage, inspires the comparison of redemption to architecture:

> One might have compared the inner state of his soul with that of a structure that had been pulled down, but only for the purpose of putting up a new building from its materials; the new building had not been started yet, because a definite plan had not yet come through from the architect, and the builders are left without knowing what to do. (p. 365)

To pick up Gogol's metaphor, the architectonic pretensions of Part Two are clear from the start: the text as Dantesque trilogy, as cathedral, as icon of the evolving soul. But from start to finish, one waits for the plans to arrive. The ambitious scheme to use art to puncture the illusions of human artifice and thereby reveal the artistry of the divine turns out to be a dead end, perhaps because Gogol's new pieties were eroding the very irony required to make such a scheme succeed.

Selected Passages from Correspondence with Friends

Dead Souls, Part Two, cannot finally provide the answers to which it aspires, and *Selected Passages* (1847) largely concerns itself with that failure.[50] Among the letters' detailed prescriptions to Russians at large,

---

[49] Kostanzhoglo and Skudronzhoglo are the same person.

[50] A recent student of Gogol's last published work, Jesse Zeldin, argues that it represents the ideas upon which the author proposed to base at least the second part of his trilogy, if not the third as well, and that it "points the way to a regeneration of the 'dead souls' whom he finds in Part One, in much the way that Dante's *Purgatorio* shows the way of salvation for sinners — not a contradiction of *Inferno*, but a part of the same structure in which *Inferno*, *Purgatorio*, and *Paradiso* all have a definite place." Introduction to his translation of Gogol's *Selected Passages from Correspondence with Friends*. xv. Andrei Sinyavsky (Abram Terz) makes some excellent comments on this topic

over half the text concerns itself with literature, much of it Gogol's own writing. Here the spiritual and prophetic side of the author, seen before in *Annunziata*, comes clearly to view, and the terms are still recognizably Dantesque. In *Annunziata* the protagonist/narrator attains vision finally through the casting out of all voices but disembodied prophecy. In *Selected Passages* the even larger vision of Gogol's (and Russia's) own spiritual development echoes through an even more perfect soliloquy. With its preface, *Selected Passages* has thirty-three parts and begins and ends with the theme of pilgrimage toward which Part Two of *Dead Souls* moves. In his last letter, "Easter Sunday," Gogol unmistakably replicates Dante's own moment of emergence from the Inferno. As strongly as in the *Divine Comedy*, national destiny is seen to hinge on individual redemption; conversely, human art may be forgiven its imperfections until the Second Coming perfects the world that it depicts. As in the *Purgatorio* and in *Dead Souls*, Part Two, the artist becomes emblematic of the rhythms of salvation. Various artists (the starving engraver of "Testament," the painter Ivanov, Gogol himself, even the blind Homer) must suffer through to their reward. Gogol argues that delay itself can be formative, and we may be reminded of the souls learning patience on the ledges of the Mount of Purgatory. Redemption comes from loss:

> The second part of *Dead Souls* was burned because it was necessary. "Lest the seed die, it will not live again," says the Apostle. It is first necessary to die in order to be resurrected...Immediately that the flame had carried away the last pages of my book, its content suddenly was resurrected in a purified and lucid form, like the Phoenix from the pyre, and I suddenly saw in what disorder was what I had considered ordered and harmonious. (pp. 108-9)[51]

Though the burning of epics was a classical practice (Virgil, Ovid), the sacrifice is here presented entirely in terms of Christian immolation and transfiguration.

One sees in *Selected Passages* explicit if not always convincing resolutions of problems that the second part of *Dead Souls* has not yet brought under control. The pervasive uncertainties about the relationship of art and life underlie Gogol's encomium of the painter Ivanov, who has (like Gogol in

in his book *V teni Gogolya* (London: Collins, 1975), esp. 204-7.

[51] Translations are by Zeldin, *Selected Passages*.

Rome) been sacrificing his career and his life to complete a masterpiece showing the movement of man to Christ, a canvas he cannot complete until that movement finally happens. Gogol draws a parallel at once to himself: "My works are strangely connected to my soul and to my inner education. For more than six years I could do no work for the world. All my work was done within myself and for myself alone" (p. 152). The great strength of Ivanov's work (and implicitly of Gogol's) lies in its directness as spiritual expression; the question of a fit audience may be postponed. Earlier, in talking about the public criticism of *Dead Souls*, he similarly admitted that "my heroes are close to the soul because they come from the soul; all my last works are the story of my own soul" (p. 103). Indeed, the one passage of the novel to which he explicitly refers is that moment of lyrical reflection, discussed above, where Chichikov's consciousness and that of the narrator seem to merge. Gogol now sits himself down in Chichikov's carriage: "I have never been able to bear the doleful, lacerating sounds of our songs which rush across all of the boundless Russian space. These sounds eat into my heart, and I marvel that everyone is not aware of the same thing" (p. 99).

The autobiographical substratum of *Dead Souls* now comes clearly and undeniably to view, confirming Michael Holquist's claim that "the specific quality of Gogol's personal experience...which is at the center of his life and work, is a radical ontological rendering of self (*Zerrissenheit*)."[52] Gogol seems now to be experiencing in all seriousness the process, parodied at the end of *Dead Souls*, of losing track of the boundary between one's own fictions and the phenomenal world from which they derive. It is no longer literary form but salvation history that imposes limits on the utterance, for the text that can redeem society cannot appear, any more than can Ivanov's canvas, until there is a redeemed society to describe.

These rantings of the spiritual and prophetic Gogol reveal a writer who has thoroughly painted himself into a corner. Having admitted now to purely autobiographical fiction, as well as to ineffable spiritual purity, how is the writer ever to tell an interesting story? Yet he claims that he burned the sequel because it was too panegyrical: "To describe some fine characters who are supposed to demonstrate the nobility of our race would lead to nothing. It would only arouse empty pride and vanity" (p. 109).

---

[52] James M. Holquist. "The Burden of Prophecy: Gogol's Conception of Russia," *Review of National Literatures* 3, no. 1 (Spring 1972): 41.

Although a logical extension of the Dantesque turn of the end of *Dead Souls*, Part One, *Selected Passages* works as much to seal off that inner world of subjectivity and confession as to explore it. For the letters pursue the autobiographical mode to such an extreme that the voice talking about the voice talking about the voice becomes entirely disembodied. Having taken up the option offered by Christian confessional literature of presenting oneself as an Everyman, Gogol exaggerated it to the point where no particular personality at all shows through, no vivid scene of conversion, no delicious history of sins, no confession of continuing and individuating mortal weaknesses (apart from writer's block) such as Saint Augustine, Dante, and others made compelling. Given the confusions of text and world, the writer who creates the text asserts no more individuality than the Creator, whom he simultaneously expresses and assists. The letters, in fact, sound like nothing so much as the epistles of Saint Paul, also written from abroad, trying to promote faith and support temporal authority until the Second Coming, which in the closed universe of *Selected Passages* seems to be the advent of the sequel to *Dead Souls*.[53] Just as Gogol had to leave Russia in order to write about it, so he seems to confront the task of self-examination as virtually an exile from the self. Like Narcissus, he has vanished into his own reflection, having finally decided that it may be easier to issue a new Gogol than a new *Dead Souls*. The search for the third Rome gradually gives way to a search for a third Gogol, after what are now seen to be the false starts as storywriter and novelist.

Gogol has also found a way to keep his captious audience at bay by casting them in a kind of closet drama for which he writes all the lines. His fear of the audience had always surpassed that of most writers, often causing him to leave town when a new work appeared. The readers closing in on the narrator at the end of Part One of *Dead Souls*, even as the townspeople close in on Chichikov, are still a humorous fiction. But those earlier joking justifications of his scurrilous characters, such as we have cited above, are now repeated in dead earnest: "My heroes are not at all villains… But the banality of all of them frightened my readers… The Russian is more frightened of his insignificance than of all his vices and shortcomings… None of my readers knew that while laughing at my heroes he was laughing

---

[53] Holquist (ibid., 51) extends the list of possible messianic or prophetic models recalled in Gogol's letters to include John the Baptist and, perhaps, Christ himself.

at me" (pp. 103-4). Gogol has reversed the comedic stance taken at the end of Part One of *Dead Souls* — "Don't confuse me with my nasty characters!" — into a demand that readers make precisely that identification.

While *Dead Souls*, Part One, halts the action only occasionally (though increasingly) to address the audience, the whole of *Selected Passages* is an address to the readers — conceived of as individual recipients, or as social categories, or as Russia — to the exclusion of the fiction. The invented reader becomes the work's protagonist. However, Gogol's very stance of direct address unmediated by fiction and unclouded by pride shows careful rhetorical calculation: one would be caddish to criticize a writer who shows himself easily shattered by criticism. Self-criticism itself preempts outsiders' opinions. In taking what were in some cases letters that his perplexed, even angry, correspondents had received and presenting these messages as exemplary, working them into a pattern, arraying the now anonymous recipients into his own vision of a redeemed Russia — his own City of God — and by comparing, then finally confusing, their spiritual destiny with his own progress as a writer, Gogol manages to translate the audience from real (that is, the original recipients) to hypothetical.

The epistles of Saint Paul, when published, had a comparable effect in helping to translate a scattered collection of communions into an enduring ideal of Christendom. In recasting his troublesome audience into his own version of true (that is, Russian) Christendom, Gogol puts them on their best behavior. A communication from writer to reader so ritualized, so immersed in the matrix of religious language and obligatory charity, renders both parties ideal, innocuous, predictable. So inevitable is the Christian scenario, of course, that Gogol can supply everyone's lines — not only those for painters and writers, but even those for wives of provincial governors. In Part One of *Dead Souls*, Gogol had unexpectedly trapped the readers and the writer himself among the company of dead souls — a wicked but rather winning joke. *Selected Passages* implicates the reader in resurrection, a strategy equally fraught with contradictions without, however, the irony that held in suspension the contradictions of *Dead Souls*. The running joke of Captain Kopeikin's letters to the czar and Tentetnikov's grand and soon abandoned blueprint for the Russian nation now realizes itself in earnest. Gogol, while extolling humility, seems in fact to be replicating the animating act of the primal Ventriloquist who brought His creation to life by projecting His Word into it.

With the translation of self and audience into the controllable realm of the ideal comes the eradication of fiction. What Ivanov is painting is directly the Truth, mimetic to an extent that it cannot be completed until its subject matter (namely, redeemed humanity) completes itself. Gogol's feelings about his own involvement in belles lettres, in particular epic, can perhaps be read from "*The Odyssey* in Zhukovsky's Translation." The claims made for Homer's epic here fall little short of those for the Second Coming of *Dead Souls*, and in writing to Zhukovsky (December 14, 1849) Gogol observed, "At times it seems to me that the second volume of *Dead Souls* could serve for the Russian reader as a kind of step toward reading Homer."[54] Though pagan, the *Odyssey* comes to play a central role in salvation history, having been "Christianized, Gogolized and moralized into a conscious social blueprint," as Fanger observes.[55] The *Iliad*, the model for "Taras Bulba," now seems to Gogol just "an episode" (*Selected Passages*, p. 32). The *Odyssey*, by contrast, presents all of life. Like Christian revelation itself, it languished misunderstood in Europe, waiting for Russia to discover its ultimate riches. Now, in Zhukovsky's version, it is not just translated but reborn, reincarnated in "*the living word*" that even its first author did not hear, so that "all Russia might accept as its own... a miracle... a re-creation, a restoration, a resurrection of Homer" (p. 33).

Homer's purpose was not only to affirm "all the bewitching beauty of poetry" but also "to remind man that there is something better and holier in him." Gogol borrows from Dante and other Christian classicists not a few of the prophetic claims for pagan literature as parallel to and almost an extension of the Old Testament when he talks of how Homer could write "a living and complete book infused by law at a time when there was still neither law nor founders of order" (p. 36). But in seeing the *Odyssey* as the perfect and instructive model of patriarchal society, Gogol virtually manages to unmake it as a fiction. Although his own earlier tale of a traveling trickster descended from that very *Odyssey*, Gogol now looks squarely at the epic prototype and manages to unsee the fictive, playful, finally skeptical outlook that the reader finds in Homer's epic as much as in *Dead Souls*, Part One. Gogol's way of escaping from the dilemmas of his

---

[54] Quoted by Terz. *V teni Gogolya*, 295.

[55] Fanger, *Creation of Nikolai Gogol*, 214.

own fiction is to deny that fiction exists or, even back to the time of Homer, has ever existed. There is only scripture. Though celebrating the triumph of the life force, Gogol has, in the largely imaginary recipients of these unsent letters, found himself yet another set of dead souls.

Dead Souls, Part Two, implicitly diagnoses its own paralysis: Tentetnikov waits for another fit preceptor to appear; Chichikov waits for some blueprint for rebuilding his soul; Gogol waits for a plan to complete the immense cathedral of letters for which Part One can serve as cellar.[56] The solution here proposed is not to find another fit guide — the perfect critic that Pushkin should have lived to become — nor even to proceed without a guide, but for Gogol to become the critic himself and perhaps not proceed at all. In the pivotal eighteenth chapter, "Four Letters to Divers Persons Apropos *Dead Souls*," more or less at the midpoint of the book, Gogol scrutinizes both Part One and its critics, indeed even applies the allegories of the text to its misguided reception: "And if but one soul had begun to speak out in public! It was exactly as though everything had died out, as though Russia in fact was inhabited not by living but by *Dead Souls*" (pp. 97-98). His critics have taken his writing too literally, especially the "lyric digressions" of the intruding narrator, and have accused him of pride for the expansive assertions made. But he bears the responsibility for having issued an ill-made book prematurely, for relying on ironies that were misconstrued.

Pushkin plays an innocent role in this misadventure:

> It is enough for me to tell you when I began to read the first chapters of *Dead Souls* to Pushkin, in the form in which they formerly were, Pushkin, who always laughed at my readings (he loved laughter), slowly became gloomier and gloomier, and finally he was completely somber. When the reading was finished, he uttered in an anguished voice: "God, how sad is our Russia!" This amazed me. Pushkin, who knew Russia so well, had not noticed that it was all a caricature and my own invention!... From this time forward I began to think only of how to mitigate the painful impression which *Dead Souls* had produced. (p. 105)

The surrounding discussion suggests that in heightening the ironies and moving the characters closer to the banal, Gogol threatened to irritate the

---

[56] "...after having read the whole book [Part One], it seems exactly as though he [the reader] were emerging from some stifling cellar into God's light." Gogol, *Selected Passages*, 104.

Russian audience all the more. Alone among mortals, Pushkin perceived Gogol's "principal essence," rivaled by no other writer: "the gift of representing the banality of life so clearly, of knowing how to depict the banality of a banal man with such force that all the *petty details* which escape the eyes *gleam large* in the eyes" (p. 103). For all Pushkin's insight, his death kept him from seeing everything: "Only afterwards was it [Gogol's gift for the banal] deepened in me by its union with some spiritual circumstance. But I was in no condition to reveal it then, even to Pushkin."[57] Gogol speaks here as the perfect critic of his own work, of his critics, even of Pushkin's wondrous critical insight. He has become the guide that Pushkin did not live to be.

Even as his reading of the *Odyssey* implies that fiction does not exist nor ever has, Gogol's retrospective profile of himself as fiction writer presents that entity as little more than a result of the audience's and his own confusions. When he thought he was inventing fictions, he was actually stumbling upon the great truth about Russia. It is his clumsiness, and his clumsiness alone, that has upset people; but the Russian truth writes itself without the imagination as an intermediary. In proof of this thesis and in answer to the criticism of the troika scene at the end of Part One, he simply rewrites that vision as fact:

> In Russia, now, it is possible to make oneself a hero at every step. Every rank and place demands heroism... I perceive that great vocation which is not now possible for any other people, which is possible for the Russians alone, because before them alone is there such scope and their soul alone is acquainted with heroism — that is why that exclamation was wrenched out of me, and it was taken for vainglory and presumption! (p. 102)

To be sure, there is such a thing as literary craftsmanship, and Gogol has nothing good to say about his own, even though critics overlooked his careless stitching together of materials and indecent rush into print. What they have criticized is beyond criticism, for the Russian destiny announces

---

[57] One wonders, of course, how Pushkin would have reacted to his newly evangelical friend. Gogol has dealt with this problem retroactively in chapter 14, "On the Theater," by refuting imputations of deism to Pushkin and by rehabilitating him as a Christian. Even Pushkin's 1830 "When out of sport or idle boredom" becomes Christian with the omission of its first stanza (pp. 82-83). One is reminded of the posthumous conversion that Dante wished for Virgil.

itself, and his own recognition of it was simply wrenched out of him, "an awkward expression of a real feeling" (p. 99).

Literary criticism has produced few experiences odder than hearing this unsurpassed ironist test and reject his work on the touchstone of sincerity and monolithic truth. "My personal thoughts, simple, unpuzzling thoughts, I did not know how to transmit, and I myself gave grounds for these misinterpretations, and on the harmful rather than the useful side" (p. 101). Part One "is still no more than a prematurely born child" (p. 106). Gogol does not see his work as an artifact, but rather as something brought out from within, about which the author can at most decide the moment of delivery. Though any creative mind can feel itself transparent — as inspired, seized upon, spoken through — that passivity sounds strangest coming from an ironist whose effects depend on obvious calculation. Though the intruding narrator and the resultant voices within voices of Part One raise introspection to the level of comedy, we dare not assume that the eternal jokester who can mime and mock such tones of desperate sincerity as we hear in the "lyrical digressions" is not himself, at some level beneath and beyond the giddy play of his levels and levels of irony, desperately sincere. What is most exhilarating about the authorial self of Part One as it radiates concentric and contradictory rings around itself — the narrator, Chichikov, Russia, Christendom, all clumsily allegorizing and bruising one another — is the deducible sense that here for once is a mind liberated, as ours cannot be, from the killing literalism of introspection. Here is a mind capable of leaping from ledge to ledge of its own abyss and looking back at itself without, like the rest of us, being sentenced always to experience consciousness on one flat, literal plain, without perspective and without proportion.

Selected Passages deflates that happy myth. Gogol discusses irony purely as a matter of communication, not introspection. His accounts of his relations with Pushkin and the Russian audience center on questions of irony. His observations about himself here, as in his earlier letters and in the half-fictionalization of those letters in "Rome," all proceed in the mode of unrelieved literalism. And indeed, the faltering of fiction in Part Two and the virtual exorcism of it in Selected Passages bring us back to the solemn, fragmented worlds of "Rome" and "Taras Bulba," the worlds, as we have seen, of Gogol narrating without irony. In its own labored and doctrinal terms, the self-abnegation of *Selected Passages* works toward the rapt passivity, the absorption into a perceived grandeur, of the ending of "Rome." The onerousness of the Russian identity in *Selected Passages* and its momentary absence in "Rome" commonly leave the artist with little to do with his illusion-making: in the latter case he lacks subjects; in *Selected Passages*, Russia's cooperatively manifest destiny has already done his work for him. In neither work is the reader constantly on the defensive, as in *Dead Souls*, lest pious affirmations suddenly be overthrown by abrupt shifts of perspective. The stringent hierarchies of *Selected Passages* recall the patriarchal and nationalist world of "Taras Bulba," again without fear of a shift to mockery. So ferocious is the authoritarianism of this Russia, both Cossack and Christian, that it threatens even to obliterate personality. In *Selected Passages* the polarity between the pagan and confessional modes of monumental literature, "Taras Bulba" and "Rome," collapses under the weight of heroic and impersonal solemnity. If anything, the bardic anonymity of "Taras Bulba" shows more warmth and emotion than the inhuman dispassion (for all the pretense to confessional fervor) of the perfect critic who writes the letters, no longer Gogol but the daimon who has watched over his shoulder through misspent decades and now flies free to tell the tale or, as Gogol explains it, the "simple, unpuzzling thoughts" (p. 101) that have always lurked beneath his gifts for irony and illusion — gifts for which he now quite credibly claims to have found a cure.

Bakhtin's category of the "polyphonic" usefully illumines the evolution, or we might say attenuation, of the quality of voice in Gogol's writings in his last decade. The voices that begin *Dead Souls* are legion: earthy, pompous, rude, above all contentious, as they torture Russian prose into a particular brilliance. The emergent narrator asserts a more consistent literary discourse, and this discourse prevails, largely to the exclusion of dissonance and variety, in the long descriptive stretches of Part Two, fragments without drama because there are not enough voices to play it. *Selected Passages* marks the triumph of the monotone, the rejection of polyphony, as of irony and the world. As we have argued, this straitening into solemnity and consistency does not constitute a movement from the novelistic to the epic, but rather the sacrificing of the epic fiction's range and treachery, its evocation of many struggling voices so that one may impressively prevail. Gogol's faceless, official discourse might satisfy the theoreticians as epic but in fact mimes the voicelessness of scripture.

In a letter of December 29, 1847, Gogol described to Zhukovsky his literary impasse:

> For a long time I have been occupied by the thought of writing a *great* work in which I would present all that is good and all that is bad in [the] Russian man and thereby uncover before us the most obvious *quality* of our Russian nature. Though I have seen and grasped separately many of [its] parts, the plan of the whole has just not unfolded itself to me or taken shape in the form needed for me to begin writing it.[58]

In describing these uncooperative ideas and structures, he gives no indication that he is waiting for a story to jell or characters to evolve. We seem to be still among the ethical preachments of *Selected Passages*. "At every turn I have felt that I am lacking much, that I still can't tie and untie events, and that I need to learn the structure of the great masters. I've taken them up, starting with our beloved Homer." Bakhtin rightly observes that Gogol undid himself in trying to write a dead literary form but repeats Gogol's error in calling that form "epic."

Gogol's final drift to literal-minded prophecy, his renunciation of his narratives for some higher, more purely religious and confessional form of artistic expression, anticipates an apparent syndrome that was to recur, if never again so acutely, among masters of Russian monumental literature. Propelled by the momentum of his own large creation, Tolstoy rejected *Anna Karenina* (and no doubt *War and Peace* as well) when he insisted to his friend V. V. Strakhov: "I assure you that this abomination does not exist for me and that I am only vexed that there should be people who have need of it."[59] "What Is Art?" — Tolstoy's iconoclastic repudiation of the goals and methods of modern fiction in the name of a simpler, more edifying, and universally accessible aesthetic — could follow only after a statement such as this, much as *Selected Passages* could issue forth only after Gogol claimed in 1845: "I have no love for what I have written and published up to now, and especially *Dead Souls*."[60] What André Gide observed about Dostoevsky

---

[58] *Sobranie sochinenii v semi tomakh*, 7:427.

[59] Letter of May 1, 1881, quoted in N. N. Gusev, *Letopis' zhizni i tvorchestva L'va Nikolaevicha Tolstogo* (Moscow, 1958), 535.

[60] Letter of July 13 to A. O. Smirnova in *Polnoe sobranie sochinenii*, 12:504.

applies to other giants of Russian prose: "The literary creator who seeks himself runs a great risk — the risk of finding himself. From then onwards he writes coldly, deliberately, in keeping with the self that he has found. He imitates himself."[1] Gogol was only the first Russian novelist to find himself in that frozen, infernal rut, but also the first to show how monumental can be the journey that leads to it. Even in failing to arrive at his heroic goal, he opened the way for a tradition of Russian prose that adapts and extends the classical and Christian modes of epic perhaps more successfully than any other modern literature. Of the innumerable transmitters of Homer through the ages, Gogol seems among the least likely, but it is in this role that Dostoevsky cast him when he, too, took up the question of Whither Rus'? at the end of his career. We turn now to *The Brothers Karamazov* as another address to Gogol's great, unfinished project.

---

[1] André Gide, *Dostoevsky* (New York: New Directions, 1961), 50. Originally published as *Dostoïevsky: articles et causeries* (Paris: Plon, 1923).

3. Dostoevsky's
The Brothers Karamazov

> *For books continue each other, in spite of*
> *our habit of judging them separately.*
> — **Virginia Woolf,**
> ***A Room of One's Own***

Like *Dead Souls*, *The Brothers Karamazov* was envisaged by its author as the first canticle of a Russian *Divine Comedy*. Both novels were conceived as multivolumed works about the life and spiritual rebirth of their sinner-heroes, Chichikov and Alyosha. Shortly before he began *The Brothers Karamazov*, Dostoevsky abandoned his idea for a master novel in five parts, entitled *The Life of a Great Sinner* (*Zhitie velikogo greshnika*), which, recalling Gogol, he later termed a "real *poèma*." "It will be my last novel, about the size of *War and Peace*," Dostoevsky wrote to A. N. Maykov. And further: "The main question which will run through all its parts is the very one I have struggled with consciously or unconsciously all my life — the existence of God."[2]

Although the project was conceived as early as 1869 and abandoned shortly thereafter, its fundamental theme remained with Dostoevsky until his death, partly surfacing in *The Devils* (1872) and even more so in *The Brothers Karamazov* (1880). "Fyodor Mikhailovich had great faith in this projected novel and considered it the culmination of his literary career," asserts Dostoevsky's widow in her reminiscences. "His pre-vision proved correct, since many of the characters of this novel figured later in *The Brothers Karamazov*."[3] To Strakhov, Dostoevsky wrote about his grand

[2] Letter to A. N. Maykov, Dresden, March 25, 1870, in Fyodor M. Dostoevsky, *The Brothers Karamazov*, trans. Constance Garnett and Ralph Matlaw, ed. Ralph Matlaw (New York: W. W. Norton and Company, 1976), 752-53.

[3] Anna Dostoevsky, *Dostoevsky-Reminiscences*, trans. and ed. Beatrice Stillman (New

scheme much as Gogol had written about *Dead Souls*: "I consider this novel to be the last work in my literary career."[4] And in his October 9 letter of the same year to Maykov, the writer admits, as Gogol had earlier confessed to Zhukovsky: "Being more a poet than an artist, I have chosen themes which are beyond my strength."[5] Of the applicability of Gogol's subtitle *poèma* not only to Dostoevsky's projected *The Life of a Great Sinner*, but to any of his late novels, Donald Fanger has recently noted: "One can hardly doubt the source of this term or the peculiar significance of the fact that Gogol's successor — not the author of *Poor Folk*, but of *Crime and Punishment, The Idiot, The Possessed, The Brothers Karamazov* — chose consistently to identify himself as a poet rather than a novelist."[6] Finally, both writers used the texts themselves to announce their projected sequels. Gogol announces in *Dead Souls*, Part One, that "there are still two long parts ahead of us" (p. 232), while Dostoevsky informs the reader in his preface to *The Brothers Karamazov* that it is the first part of a larger work, with Part Two, "the main novel," to follow shortly.[7] As we know, he did not live to complete the project.

As in Gogol, the sin, suffering, and redemption of the central character would bind together the different parts. In 1933, Pavel Bitsilli viewed Dostoevsky's sinner as an Everyman and, by placing *The Brothers*

York: Liveright, 1975), 158. Originally published as *Vospominaniya* (Moscow, 1925).

[4] Letter to N. N. Strakhov, December 2, 1870, in *F. M. Dostoevskii-Pisma*, ed. A. S. Dolinin (Moscow-Leningrad, 1930), 2:298.

[5] Ibid., 290. In his famous letter to Zhukovsky of December 29, 1847, Gogol also distinguishes between poet and artist, implying that the continuation of *Dead Souls* required more the talents of a poet than of an artist: "But in general one should focus not on censuring others but on *contemplating* one's own self. If the creation of the poet does not contain within it this quality, then it is merely…the fruit of the temporary state of the artist." See N. V. Gogol, *Sobranie sochinenii v semi tomakh* (Moscow, 1966-67), 7:363.

[6] Donald Fanger, "Influence and Tradition in the Russian Novel," in John Garrard, ed., *The Russian Novel from Pushkin to Pasternak* (New Haven and London: Yale University Press, 1983), 48.

[7] For a discussion of *The Brothers Karamazov* as an exposition of the "main novel," see Maximilian Braun, "*The Brothers Karamazov* as an Expository Novel," *Canadian-American Slavic Studies* 6 (1972): 199-208. For a contrary opinion that interprets the "projected" continuation to the novel as a literary device of Dostoevsky's narrator, see Robert Belknap, *The Structure of* The Brothers Karamazov (The Hague: Mouton, 1967; rpt., Evanston, Ill.: Northwestern University Press, 1989), esp. 107-8.

Karamazov in the tradition of Dante's epic, invited comparison to Gogol's fictively rendered inferno as well.[8] The German scholar N. Hofmann quotes Dostoevsky's widow regarding the plot for the unwritten sequel: "It was the author's plan for Alyosha… to take upon himself [the world's] suffering and its guilt…After a stormy period of moral straying, doubt, and negation, Alyosha, left alone, returns to the monastery once more. There he surrounds himself with children and dedicates all the rest of his life to them, loves them truly, teaches and guides them."[9] As Fanger has argued but few have explored: "If Gogol's significance for the young Dostoevsky is a matter of record, the later record is no less indicative."[10] Not only did his predecessor's Petersburg "nightmares," such as "The Nose" and "The Overcoat," influence Dostoevsky's earliest prose narratives, but it was Gogol's later, larger vision of Rus' that would inspire and challenge him at the very end.

Quite in the Gogolian tradition, *The Brothers Karamazov* is evasive about its literary legacy. Dostoevsky holds overt allusion to classical models to virtually only one strand: the continuing preoccupation of Alyosha's boys with the founders of Troy. In a novel where names are often significant to the point of punning, the unremarkable scene where Kolya's classmate Dardanelov can only vaguely answer the question "Who founded Troy?" may arrest the reader's attention, since Dardanelov, had he done his homework, should have identified Dardanus (along with Tros and Ilus) as being among the various generations of Trojan founders. On first reading one scarcely knows whether or not to take this as one of the series of parables of characters' failing to recognize their own identities, just as, for example, Dmitri fails to account for the etymological link of his name to Demeter in the myth of this goddess and her daughter that he rehearses to Alyosha in "The Confession of an Ardent Heart." Concerning the founders of Troy, even ingenious Kolya is to be preempted by Kartashov, who figures thereafter as "the boy who discovered about Troy" (p. 731).[11]

---

[8] See Pavel M. Bitsilli, "Pochemu Dostoevskii ne napisal *Zhitie velikogo greshnika*," in *O Dostoevskom. Sbornik statei*, ed. A. L. Bem (Paris: AMGA Editions, 1986),149-54.

[9] Cited by Beatrice Stillman in her notes to Anna Dostoevsky, *Dostoevsky-Reminiscences*, 410.

[10] Fanger, "Influence and Tradition," 47.

[11] All citations from the text are from the Garnett-Matlaw translation of the Norton Critical Edition (above, n. 1).

This preoccupation with epic history seems a peripheral element of the childhood subplot until it becomes, in the last chapter, the matrix within which the novel ends. As we shall see, it may be a telling indication of where Dostoevsky located himself in the epic cycle.

To investigate how *The Brothers Karamazov* presents itself within the monumental tradition and as an extension of Gogol's epic vision, we might first examine the reading habits that help to discriminate one Karamazov from another. To some degree, they are what they read as well as what they write. On the first page of the novel, the narrator senses that Dmitri's mother went astray, like many another would-be Ophelia, as a result of reading European novels; bovarism thus emerges as the first threat to Russian identity. Her son, like Fyodor, shows himself much influenced by Schiller, whom he misreads. He sobs about the ode to Ceres (= the Greek Demeter) and Proserpina as if the focus (and an analogue for himself) were the poor, martyred daughter (just another Ophelia), and not in fact the grieving mother. As we shall see, his destiny is finally to see himself more in terms of his namesake, Demeter, and to recognize, as he fails to do in his effusion to Alyosha, that this is a myth not just of fall, but of resurrection. The Madonna and Sodom, between which Dmitri feels himself fatally trapped, have long since been reconciled in the redemption of Mary Magdalene, which Grushenka will embody to him. Like his mother, Dmitri begins by reading romantic literature, and reading it badly.

Ivan's devil has much to say about his reading habits, which are predictably broad and slanted toward rationalists and ironists, or so we gather when his demon finally divulges the sources of this not-so-original young intellectual: Voltaire, Heine, Pushkin, Tolstoy, and, above all, Ivan Karamazov. Of course, his demon derives less from the sins of these writers than from the way that Ivan has misappropriated them. His torment lies in being misquoted, twisted, and misused by his own muse, turned demonic, in precisely the ways that he himself has perfected. Whereas Dmitri and his mother misread to warrant misbehaving as they please, Ivan has used these texts as a justification for not acting at all. They reduce his interaction with people to "plotting," a mode of authorship that fails to engage Alyosha, who declines to play the role proposed to him by Ivan in "The Grand Inquisitor," but one that succeeds unwittingly and all too well with Smerdyakov.

With a demon like Ivan's, who has so much to say about his own literary origins, we miss Dante in the rogues' gallery beside Voltaire, Pushkin, and the others, although Gogol figures briefly by allusion when the demon refers to himself as a "Khlestakov" grown old (p. 608). Ivan had taken Dante as the literary context for his poem about the Grand Inquisitor, but his absence from the climactic delirium is telling, for he is the author best at recognizing devils as such, while Ivan's torment consists in his inability to define and excise his own demonic side. Of authors cited by Dostoevsky, Gogol receives a second honor in a demonic context: it was his *Evenings on a Farm near Dikanka* that Fyodor, in a wicked and witty gesture, gave to Smerdyakov to stir his interest in books (p. 113).[12] Smerdyakov naturally failed to see the humor. Though putting himself in the Dantesque tradition as he fictionalizes his own darker side in "The Grand Inquisitor," Ivan similarly fails to see the humor, fails to recognize that the devil is an ass, despite all the years Fyodor has spent demonstrating that it is so. Ivan goes fatally wrong in conferring tragic solemnity on such petty and pathetic figures (the Inquisitor, Fyodor, and himself). Dmitri, who can laugh as well as cry, finds a less pernicious fantasy in the absurdity of seeing the Karamazovs as insects rather than tragic heroes.

The insect world of Dmitri, Ivan's denial of demons, and the humor that Smerdyakov fails to grasp all point in the direction of Gogol, whom Dostoevsky began his career by parodying in his short novels, starting with *Poor Folk* (1845) and *The Double* (1846).[13] He begins and ends his masterpiece, *The Brothers Karamazov*, with the various Gogolian questions posed at the various Gogolian levels. The novel takes its epigraph from John

[12] Given the importance of symbolic foreshadowing in *The Brothers Karamazov*, it is probably not accidental that Gogol's earliest short stories constitute Smerdyakov's first and ostensibly exclusive experience in reading fiction. Though filled with lovely scenes, exuberant village life, and local Ukrainian color, the tales are permeated with peasant superstitions and the presence of the devil. The latter two traits are particularly suitable to Smerdyakov (and to Ivan's other devil, the one in his nightmare), insofar as Dostoevsky, like Gogol, derisively treats these "devils" as fools.

[13] See Priscilla Meyer and Stephen Rudy, eds., *Dostoevsky and Gogol* (Ann Arbor, Mich.: Ardis, 1979). Nina Perlina's contention that Pushkin's is the most authoritative secular voice in *The Brothers Karamazov* (for which, see *Varieties of Poetic Utterance: Quotations in* The Brothers Karamazov [Lanham, Md.: University Press of America, 1985], 25) seems uncontestable. We do not subscribe to Victor Terras's claim that "[w]hile Dostoevsky loved and admired Pushkin, he never developed a similar deep feeling for Gogol" (Victor Terras, *A Karamazov Companion* [Madison: University of Wisconsin Press. 1981], 18). As we are arguing, Gogol is, after Pushkin, the strongest Russian literary presence in the novel.

12:24, "except a corn of wheat fall into the ground and die, it abideth alone; but if it die, it bringeth forth much fruit," the scriptural base of *Selected Passages from Correspondence with Friends*. Better than he knew, Gogol had thereby aptly characterized the fertile death of his own narrative gifts — fertile, that is, for his followers. By the end, *The Brothers Karamazov* can rightly claim to take its birth from the deliquescence of Gogol's storytelling: the Public Prosecutor climaxes his case against Dmitri, sarcastically, with Gogol's image of the troika and the question, "Whither Rus'?". Yet the narrative undercuts the Prosecutor's irony:[14] the troika — adumbrated in *Dead Souls* as possibly the Holy Trinity, possibly Dante's Satan, Brutus, and Cassius — has become flesh and dwelt among us in the persons of Dmitri, Ivan, and Alyosha; and the question of "Whither Rus'?" has been posed seriously by the trial. Though answers had in the interval been found on the Tolstoyan scale of war and peace, Dostoevsky pointedly returns to the Gogolian scene of the crime. In both works we are confronted with a nondescript provincial town, a rustic aristocracy, and a toy version of a Russia that can turn in on itself in search of a central enigma — Who was Chichikov? Who killed Fyodor? — and instructively sort itself out for us by failing to grasp the core of the answer: "ourselves."

That the reader should read *The Brothers Karamazov* in the context of *Dead Souls* becomes clear also in the pivot of the action, Dmitri's fatal rampage in Book 8, where his weird journey recalls Chichikov's. For the moment, Dmitri becomes a confidence man, trying to hock his patrimony, a scam scarcely less dishonest or less macabre than Chichikov's acquisition of dead souls. This midpoint and pivot of the plot, like Chichikov's crucial visit to Pliushkin in *Dead Souls*, centers on the question of time as embodied in a broken watch (hocked by Dmitri, offered up as a gift by Pliushkin). Dmitri's visits to various proprietary figures (Samsonov, Mme. Khoklakova, Lyagavy) provide an array of dead souls to figure Russia in its various modes of materialistic folly. At Mokroe, the question is squarely posed whether the buffoon Maximov is the same as that in *Dead Souls*. In both novels, the second half devotes itself to conspiracy against and

---

[14] Here we agree with Terras's intelligent observation: "The prosecutor is referring to the concluding passage of Gogol's *Dead Souls* (1842). He misquotes it (of course Gogol's passage does not say 'respectfully') and thus makes a travesty of it." Terras, *Karamazov Companion*, 18.

prosecution of the harmless rogues that we know Chichikov and Dmitri to be. Both plots revolve, as we have indicated, around riddles of identity: "Who is Chichikov?" (a veiled posing of the central question. "Who are these dead souls?"); "Who killed Fyodor?" And the surrounding groups, separated out by class, sex, and sophistication, reveal the stratifications and respective delusions of Russian society as they instructively fail to see their own responsibility. The similarity of these structures underscores the diametrical differences of the topics at hand. In *The Brothers Karamazov* we have, not a scam, but a real murder; not just a pretense to mortgage the dead as if living, but a serious preoccupation with resurrection; not just a comic embodiment of Russianness, but a publicized and influential test of Russian justice. Yet the mystical significances that Dostoevsky finds underlying Gogol's basic structure are precisely those that Gogol himself looked back to and found after 1842.

To be sure, the ramification of allegory in *The Brothers Karamazov* has little enough to do with Gogol even in his later mystagogic phase. With an elaboration worthy of Dante himself, the troika, the holy and unholy trinity, becomes not just the three brothers and their respective women, but eventually three confessions, three temptations, three lacerations, three torments, three visits to Smerdyakov. Yet in explaining his system of symbols, the relating of large and small that allows the individual to figure Russia and thereby figure Christendom, Dostoevsky allies himself with Gogol in opposition to Tolstoy. That trenchant but tendentious literary critic, Ivan's devil, presents himself as Tolstoy's muse — that is, whatever combination of delirium and dyspepsia allows a brilliant mind to grasp both the large and small without grasping their organic link:

> Listen, in dreams and especially in nightmares, from indigestion or anything, a man sometimes sees such artistic visions, such complex and real actuality, such events, even a whole world of events, woven into such a plot, with such unexpected details from the most exalted matters to the last button on a cuff, as I swear Leo Tolstoy could not create…. (p. 606)

The demonic characters in the novel uniformly mark themselves out as literalists who fail to grasp the metaphoric and developmental connections that can exist between large and small, microcosm and macrocosm. Smerdyakov, in the midst of his dinner-table casuistries, centrally distorts the terms in which the mustard seed and the mountain are meant. Ivan, rescued by Alyosha from his devil, indicates how a better grounded but not less pernicious physicalism has enthroned itself in science, in his delirious jumbling of seraphim and molecules: "Dmitri calls you a cherub! Cherub!…the thunderous howl of the seraphim. What are the seraphim? Perhaps a whole constellation. But perhaps that constellation is only a chemical molecule" (p. 618).

Ivan's devil also recalls the dialectic of destruction and rebirth announced in the novel's epigraph from John 12:24. Even in parodying the Christian sense of miracle, the devil articulates an alternative to the dissociating visions of science and intellectualism: "I shall sow in you [Ivan] only a tiny grain of faith and it will grow into an oak tree…" (p. 612). The small and the large can be related, then, not just by scientists with microscopes and telescopes or by authors like Tolstoy with notebooks to catalogue and organize buttons and battalions, but by the germinal powers of the childlike, the latent, the absurd, and the believed. As a symbol of redemption, Grushenka's onion also provides an image for symbolic structure, the rings-within-rings of signification within the narrative, as within the mind and the nation. Whether it is faith or irony that grows one layer from another resists explanation; the oak and the acorn stand in as absurd a relationship as that of the mountain and the mustard seed. Yet Dostoevsky more than hints that, if it were left to Tolstoyan objectivity, molecules could never grow into constellations nor families into nations. For nations and constellations are more than accumulations, as Zosima can perceive even in the ocean: "for all is like an ocean, all is flowing and blending; a touch in one place sets up a movement at the other end of the earth" (p. 299). As the epigraph reminds us, without dirty work there is no growth for seeds, nor unsoiled lives or literal understandings. In stark contrast to Tolstoy's immaculate version of history, what came out from under Gogol's overcoat to riot through Skotoprigonevsk was legion.

Before considering the implications of Dostoevsky's use of *Dead Souls* for the structure of *The Brothers Karamazov*, let us recall Gogol's bestiary, and in particular the possibility that the insect world — the teeming, squirming mites that draw Dostoevsky's eye as they do Gogol's[15] — has its own direct link to the monumental tradition. As we saw with the opening

---

[15] On the possible sexual latencies of the insect imagery in both writers, see Ralph E. Matlaw, "Recurrent Imagery in Dostoevskij," *Harvard Slavic Studies* 3 (1956): 201-25.

simile of *Dead Souls*, the comparison of the socialites at the governor's ball to flies promenading over a sugar loaf, it is the most irreverent narrative jabs that turn out to convey heroic force most directly. With Gogol's flies and Dostoevsky's Karamazov insects we would seem to be at a polar remove from the high style that Homer initiated. Rather than seeing provincial dignity (Gogol) or degradation (Dostoevsky) in terms of creepy crawlies, Homer famously confers dignity and lyricism even on carnage. In *Iliad* 16, Sarpedon, the son of Zeus, falls mightily and, as the potter Euphronius recalls, Sleep and Death fly him from the fray at the bidding of his bereaved father. "Good night, sweet prince, and flights of angels sing thee to thy rest." Yet in the Homeric imagination, Sleep and Death were not the only winged creatures in this grand, sad moment:

> No longer
> could a man, even a knowing one, have made out the godlike
> Sarpedon, since he was piled from head to ends of feet under
> a mass of weapons, the blood and the dust, while others about him
> kept forever swarming over his dead body, as flies
> through a sheepfold thunder about the pails overspilling
> milk, in the season of spring when the milk splashes in the buckets
> So they swarmed over the dead man....
>
> (*Iliad* 16.637-44)[16]

Homer's and Gogol's swarming flies are not entirely different. On the windy, odorless plain of Troy, where bodies tear and burst but do not putrefy, and fall prey to the clean excarnation of dogs, birds, and fishes (and that only in baleful warnings, never in depicted scenes), the image of flies swarming over a corpse is daringly potent as the reality most familiar to the audience and best suppressed by this poem. What darkens and enriches the fantasy of Sarpedon preserved incorruptible, as if turned into a statue, and carried off by Sleep and Death is the simile of flies on a corpse. Death is death, and even for the sons of gods admits of only insignificant variations. Some of the most powerful effects of the high style, even in the definitive Homer, issue from low subjects.

To persist a moment with the millennial history of the Entomological Sublime, which in monumental literature may be argued to culminate in

---

[16] The translations from the *Iliad* are by Richmond Lattimore (Chicago and London: The University of Chicago Press, 1951).

Dostoevsky, the simile of the swarming flies in *Iliad* 16 serves centrally to widen perspective from the duel of Sarpedon and Patroclus to the much larger canvas of the battle over the corpse. A wasp simile had been used earlier to describe the numbers and fury of Achilles' men when they are finally allowed to resume fighting:

> The Myrmidons came streaming out like wasps at the wayside
> when little boys have got into the habit of making them angry
> by always teasing them as they live in their house by the roadside;
> silly boys, they do something that hurts many people;
> and if some man who travels on the road happens to pass them
> and stirs them unintentionally, they in heart of fury
> come swarming out each one from his place to fight for their children.
> In heart and in fury like these Myrmidons streaming
> came out of their ships....

(*Iliad* 16.259-67)

Implicit in Homer's image of the very small, the wasps, is the notion of the very large. The audience's memory of having seen and felt the pure horror of such tiny, ferocious swarms makes the army of Myrmidons seem incomprehensibly larger.

Parallels abound. The biggest single percussion in the epic is that of Apollo knocking over the Greek wall as easily as a boy kicks down a sand castle (*Iliad* 15.362-64). What better referents have we for imagining the scale and freedom of gods on earth, their wantonly enormous advantages over human striving, than children and their toys? The breaching of the wall marks a climax, made all the grander by the contrast to the inconsequent world of youth. More's the horror that this is anything but child's play, that walls serve finally for the casting down of Hector's son and other conquered children. But the poet leaves all such reactions to contrast. Enormity must be deduced from child's play, as oppositely elsewhere from hugeness — similes of oceans, forest fires, tumbling boulders. Such are the familiar eccentricities of an epic whose unrivaled Achilles sometimes compares himself to a wolf or lion, sometimes to a mother bird. The *Iliad* looms so large in memory, not because it makes any steady use of bigness or smallness, but because we never know quite what to expect. In all seriousness the *Iliad* can present Athene in Book 17 (570ff.) as possessing "the persistent daring of that mosquito / who though it is driven away from a man's skin, even / so, for the taste of human blood, persists in biting him."

Of course, ounce for ounce, mosquitoes suffer no comparison in ferocity to lions and wolves. And if one asks what is the epic animal par excellence, though the Hellenist would automatically propose Homer's silent lions, it is the insects which inherit the epic earth, because they above all pose the questions of scale and energy that have to preoccupy the heroic poet. We recall, in *War and Peace*, Tolstoy's comparison of Moscow to a queenless and doomed hive, a simile that derives ultimately from Virgil's comparison of the Carthaginians to bees when Aeneas first arrives and from Dido's perception of the departing Trojans as ants. Between Virgil and Tolstoy, Milton, in the first book of *Paradise Lost*, shrinks Satan from the shiplike Leviathan on the fiery lake to the insect-sized being who can fit with myriads of peers into Pandemonium. Here is the locus classicus of demonism as literalism, for the swarming devils are not just compared to bees but in the process actually become bee-sized. From medieval notions of Beelzebub to Dmitri's Karamazov vermin, somehow insects manage to say more about what is perverse in man or his world than do lions and boars: quoth Gloucester, "As flies to wanton boys are we to th' gods / They kill us for their sport" (*King Lear* IV.i. 36-37).

Dostoevsky, like Gogol, forces us to distinguish monumentality from grandeur and to recall that the big impact of epic relies not on the bigness of what is described but on the paradoxes of finding the immense in the minuscule, the sublime in insects, evil in insignificance. What is not to be relied on, apart from the aggrandizing distortions of retrospect, is any quantifiable weight of words, or the cast of thousands, or days and days of hacking. Epic focuses much more on the active contrasting of big and small, of grand and inconsequential, which tends not to be an axis of central importance to novelistic fiction. As a low-grade romantic and a sloppy reader of Schiller, Dmitri fits comfortably in the world of the novel. But his imaginative range, not just along the axes of good and bad (the Madonna and Sodom) but of the grand and the slight (Mother Earth and the insect), reaches also into the monumental tradition.

We have seen Gogol's concluding fumble to be the most telling narrative gesture, the inability at the end of a volume either to stop the tale conclusively or to continue on to volume 2 in a way consistent with the assumptions of what precedes. The concluding question of *Dead Souls*,

Part One, much as it would seem to open the way to a sequel, provides unexpectedly inviolable closure, to be reopened, if at all, through criticism, theory, or apology, but not story telling. When we come to *The Brothers Karamozov* as yet another first canticle of some Russian *Divine Comedy*, we may well ask the following: along with the Gogolian questions and the Gogolian subject matter, did Dostoevsky not also inherit from *Dead Souls* the tendency for a certain open-ended view of experience to seal itself off narratively beyond hope of continuation? Does the novel not end with beginnings, as did Dante in the circular structure that leads from the end of the *Paradiso* to the beginning of the *Inferno*? Dostoevsky's concluding questions may in fact provide closure as final as Gogol's.

To end with the childhood theme, as Dostoevsky does, suggests such circularity. As we have argued with reference to Tolstoy and Pasternak, the orderly and classicizing monumentalists in the Russian tradition inherit classical epic's usual inability to find a single ending faithful both to the public and to the private concerns between which it presumes to discriminate.[17] Reunion with Penelope is one sort of ending; pacifying Ithaca, quite another. With the same awkwardness, *War and Peace* ends once with Natasha and Pierre, then again and again with historical epilogues. Ivan's devil reminds us that Tolstoy can so magisterially get buttons and battalions onto the same canvas only through rigid assumptions about the bigness of the big and smallness of the small, the constellation and the molecule. Much as Tolstoy would like to reassign values between big and small, Napoleon and his head cold, of Russian stylists he is the least inclined to tamper with proportions. The more phantasmagorical and oneiric imaginations of Gogol and Dostoevsky jumble scale, let the public be swallowed up by the private, the private by the mind, and the mind by the universal (for Russia is spirit) — the universal itself being subsumed back into the public in this coiled reality always swallowing its own tail. By virtue of the dense network of sympathies, emanations, and ghosts that bind together their little nowhere/everywhere worlds, Gogol and Dostoevsky are therefore the more capable — and more capable than they may quite have liked — of finding a closing chord in which all that precedes can resonate. We shall end with Dostoevsky's ending.

[17] See Chapter 4 of this volume.

Before proceeding with the comparison of Dostoevsky to Gogol, however, we must also recognize that one of Dostoevsky's most un-Gogolian aspects is the extent to which he has completed the Gogolian project. He has gone further than his predecessor in reconciling the satiric and the redemptive and in finally working fiction into salvation history in a way that mends the rupture between *Dead Souls*, Part One, and *Selected Passages*. We do not, as with Gogol, have a brilliant, crazy tale followed by years of exegesis, but rather the unfolding of both modes together. Mostly from the mouths of the brothers themselves, we have our lectures as we go along. It is a received truth of literary history that Gogol's breakthrough to psychological analysis is brought to an unrivaled consummation by Dostoevsky. Not just Maximov, but all the other dead souls have found a new home in Skotoprigonevsk.[18]

Looking at Dostoevsky's use of Gogol in more detail, we shall find that he has in some ways reversed the arc of Gogol's career, moving from autobiography back to myth,[19] from linear to cyclical time. Where Gogol

---

[18] Dostoevsky, as we know, began his career by "re-reading" seminal works of Gogol, by refashioning Gogol's Akakii Akakievich ("The Overcoat") and Major Kovalev ("The Nose") into the more emotionally complex characters of Makar Devushkin (*Poor Folk*) and Yakov Petrovich Golyadkin (*The Double*). Nor are we surprised to find other standard Gogolian techniques throughout all of Dostoevsky's work, especially name symbolism. The very name of Dostoevsky's fictitious town "Skotoprigonevsk" ("Cattle Corral") has an absurdly Gogolian ring to it.

[19] One of the most cogent and insightful statements regarding the mythic quality of *The Brothers Karamazov* is found in Proust's novel *The Captive*, from *Remembrance of Things Past*:

> But what a simple, sculptural notion it is, worthy of the most classical art, a frieze interrupted and resumed in which the theme of vengeance and expiation is unfolded in the crime of old Karamazov getting the poor simpleton with child, the mysterious, animal, unexplained impulse whereby the mother, herself unconsciously the instrument of an avenging destiny, a combination of resentment and physical gratitude towards her violator, comes to give birth to her child in old Karamazov's garden. This is the first episode, mysterious and grandiose, august, like the Creation of Woman in one of the sculptures of Orvieto. And as counterpart, the second episode more than twenty years later, the murder of old Karamazov, the infamy committed against the Karamazov family by the madwoman's son, Smerdiakov, followed shortly afterwards by another act as mysteriously sculpturesque and unexplained, of a beauty as obscure and natural as the childbirth in old Karamazov's garden, Smerdiakov hanging himself, his crime accomplished.

Marcel Proust, *Remembrance of Things Past*, vol. 3, *The Captive*, trans. C. K. Scott Moncrieff and Terence Kilmartin, and by Andreas Mayor (New York: Random House, 1981), 387. Originally published as *A la recherche du temps perdu*, vol. 6, *La Prisonnière*

announced emergent nationhood in the concluding "Whither Rus'?" Dostoevsky submerges that chauvinism back into a larger meditation on nationhood that leads back simultaneously to the Sermon on the Mount and the founding of Troy — that is, in the latter case, to the beginning of the epic cycle here being concluded yet again. We shall need to follow in some detail that shift in narrative time.

In *Dead Souls*, Part One, as we have seen, a narrative that starts in the cyclic time of myth moves toward the stronger lines of causation of autobiography. The various landowners could be reshuffled in the narrative, decimated, or augmented without disrupting the flow; the plots can be encountered in any order in this provincial cemetery. With Pliushkin, time enters the narrative, Chichikov gains a biography, and the narrator emerges into self-consciousness and moves toward autobiography. The first six books of *The Brothers Karamazov* mark a clear movement along this Gogolian axis, beginning with the capsule biographies of the brothers. These factual and detached sketches largely leave the Karamazovs' motives, as well as their interrelationships, to be established, as happens in the early scenes. The centripetal, psychologizing, inward-looking values of the final movement of *Dead Souls* form, then, the first narrative movement, though the emergent narrator is conspicuously absent. The psychological filling-out does not affect all characters equally. As we see in the monastery scene, the traitors (here Rakitin, as later Ivan) reveal themselves fully, while the redeemers (Zosima, and in his wake Alyosha) reveal only more and more of their enigmatic natures. The climax of this opening movement, as Dostoevsky himself indicated[20] is reached in Book 5, with Ivan's poem about the Grand Inquisitor and its answer in the Life of Zosima. The outlook and style of the opening narrative culminate in Ivan, whose psychologizing supplants faith. As a creator of fictions and poser of unanswerable questions — why must children suffer? — he embodies the powers of Dostoevsky himself as narrator.

The questions posed by Ivan in the one style are answered in quite another by Alyosha, whose literary style in itself does not concede Ivan's basic assumptions. The saint's life, wherein the meaning of Zosima's

(Paris: Editions Gallimard, 1923).

[20] Letter to N. A. Lyubimov, August 7, 1879, in *The Brothers Karamazov* (above, n. 1), 760.

experience is distilled by Alyosha, does not proceed in the historical time of the narrative, where every moment is to be accounted for (even, as in Part Four of this novel, accounted for repeatedly in explaining Fyodor's murder), and where the causal link of one event to another is decisive. Hagiography presents instead moments when the divine intersects with the human; and these moments, far from being links in a chain, need not be recounted in chronological order or as a causal succession among themselves. For each such moment testifies independently to a higher truth, so that even a partial catalogue of them, like Alyosha's unfinished Life of Zosima, is fully meaningful. Nor is there any need for a full account of human psychology, as is apparent in Alyosha's telling of the high points of Zosima's experience: Markel's death, Zosima's duel, his mysterious stranger. As a text encapsulating the character of its author, Alyosha's Life of Zosima follows in the wake of Dmitri's ardent confessions, Smerdyakov's casuistries, and Ivan's "poem" of the Grand Inquisitor as Alyosha's central self-identification. Each of the brothers is an author in his characteristic way: Dmitri with drunken spontaneity, Smerdyakov with lethal calculation, Ivan with calculated vulnerability. For his part, Alyosha, like the Christ who does not speak to the Grand Inquisitor and like the gospel writers who assume no persona in their own narratives, eludes attention as much as his brothers seek it. His anonymous detachment, his redemptive passivity in relation to the narration, marks a polar opposite to Ivan's thinly disguised self-fictionalization in the Grand Inquisitor and his inability to provide allegories of anything but himself, leading to the final claustrophobia of his inability to produce a devil that is other than a mirror. Well before Ivan meets this other self, Alyosha has articulated and controlled his own alter ego in the hagiography of Zosima.

In the movement from psychological biography to saint's life, Dostoevsky reverses the movement of *Dead Souls*, Part One, from the flattened, atemporal perspective of its first half to a self-revealing narrator who, like Ivan, projects his own torments onto the tale. Gogol, as we have seen, had to depart fiction altogether to continue with the project of self-examination and self-justification. *Selected Passages* went on to break down and answer, area by area, the question of "Whither Rus'?" in the mode of confession. Moving from Ivan to Alyosha, Dostoevsky can address the large national issues still within the form of his novel. He recasts Gogol's homiletics as saint's life to capture Russia's future through the lens of its literary origins.[21] In the contrast of narrative styles between Ivan and the self-effacing Alyosha lies a justification for the problematic elusiveness of the narrator of the novel's events of thirteen years before.

Characteristic of both *Dead Souls*, Part One, and *The Brothers Karamazov* is that the narrative splits at the center, though in rather opposite ways. As we have seen, the central point of *Dead Souls* leads to the intrusion of a narrator, as the succession of landowners comes to an end with Pliushkin. In the reminiscently Gogolian Book 8, Dmitri's capture and delirious dream initiates what might be called an angelic counterplot, for which "The Russian Monk" has provided a sort of scriptural basis. This other, increasingly independent plot concerns children. Dmitri in his dream of the babe spiritually gives his proxy to Alyosha. Fixed and immobile as he is, Dmitri forfeits the ability to mediate in action between the faith of Alyosha and the rationality of Ivan. The narrative movements that were drawing Alyosha closer into the plot (chiefly at the end of Book 4, with the series of lacerations around him) fail to develop, and his ministry to the children proceeds as a largely unconnected narrative foil — or, at least, unconnected in comparison to the increasingly densely woven narrative strands within the crime and punishment plot.

Two strands in the narrative proceed for the most part separately. On the one hand, we have the implicit continuation of the Life of Zosima, now centered on Alyosha; and, on the other, we have the enactment of Ivan's scenario for the Grand Inquisitor — not just in the temptations of Smerdyakov to which Ivan immediately and unwittingly falls prey, but in the whole courtroom full of inquisitors who ask the wrong questions. The latter crime and punishment plot develops like a noose tightening around Dmitri: the facts are ferreted out until the truth becomes irrecoverable. Ivan's understandings close in until they collapse onto themselves. For those who insist on rational causality, and the law does so insist, the explanations become so dense as to be indecipherable or unbearable. But such, in the

---

[21] Some have suggested a parallel between Dostoevsky's "confessional" and (largely) nonfictional *Diary of a Writer* and Gogol's similarly utopian *Selected Passages from Correspondence with Friends*. "In many respects Dostoevsky's word was as poisoned as Gogol's," claims Alex de Jonge. "The appalling jingoistic chauvinism of *Diary of a Writer* is his version of Gogol's *Selected Passages from Correspondence with Friends*." See Alex de Jonge, *Dostoevsky and the Age of Intensity* (New York: St. Martin's Press, 1975), 217.

Christian view, has always been the limit of the law in contrast to the workings of grace, and the childhood theme speaks powerfully, though it is constantly interrupted and lacks central narrative links. The loose ends are not a structural flaw but a tribute to the paratactic style of saint's life, early epic, and myth, forms of discourse in which events placed one after (but not because of) the other gain eloquence from the power of shared cultural values, the common agreement about the benign gods, or the tragic mortal limits that shape all experience.

The responsibility, the legal or novelistic "Who did it?" for Ilyusha's death is never worked out as it is for Fyodor's, since causation must yield to meaning, and meaning is clear. Like Alyosha in writing Zosima's life, the narrator is anonymous within this strand, while he is increasingly self-revealing in his report of the trial: we know he was there; he tells us directly what he sees and does not see and what he knows now with the advantage of thirteen years of hindsight. Were he to provide such hindsight for Alyosha's boys, that information would have incomparably greater impact, for those years of maturation would dispel the ambiguities of their young natures. Alyosha organizes his homily on memory around the theme of "whatever happens to us in later life," that is, on the uncertain prospects of whether they will turn out well or ill and perhaps not even meet again for twenty years. That uncertain prospect is left as pointedly unresolved as Gogol's concluding "Whither Rus'?" Otherwise the youths' mysterious potential would evaporate, and the final implications of Kolya's precocity would explain themselves. This strand of narrative, the childhood plot in the wake of hagiography, does not concern itself with results of that sort. Such information is all that matters to Ivan and the various other inquisitors in the crime and punishment plot, for lives cannot be measured otherwise. Boys matter only by virtue of the men they become. From the nonhierarchical standpoint of Zosima, such eventualities matter little: the boys are not less themselves as youths than they will be as adults; the boy Kolya has an identity beyond the consuming question of whether he will turn into a saint or a monster.

The two plots, then, articulate different views of the world in contrasted styles and proceed with different rhythms. The trial brings the rationalizing and psychologizing narrative to implosion. Knowledge is destroyed, the characters succumb one by one to paralysis, and Russia becomes less herself. In its plotlessness, the childhood plot is, to an equal and opposite degree, expansive and liberating. Whereas the centripetal pressures of the trial and of Ivan's introverted rationality reveal the dark, anarchic centers of Dmitri, Ivan, and contemporary Russia, Alyosha suffers no such explanation because, in his current angelic mode, his center is everywhere. By the final chapter we have come back to the subject of the first chapter: the lives of boys — once the three Karamazovs, now these other twelve. The empty frame that we have seen filled, unacceptably, by psychologizing and rational analysis, is now seen as filled again by collective spirit and suprarational participation in timeless realities, the replication through Alyosha and the twelve boys of both the Sermon on the Mount and, as we shall see, the rituals of heroic memory.

To look now at the conclusion, *The Brothers Karamazov* ends on a double note, as is typical of monumental structures. Looking to the epic tradition, we might first be inclined to diagnose the opposition as being between public and private: the inquisitors and the children, the world of Ivan and the world of Alyosha. Yet the distinction is not between public and private, and therefore finally beyond resolving, but between adults and children, fathers and sons. The reuniting of fathers and sons that resolves Homer's plots and resonates throughout the subsequent tradition may figure equally in the distinctive concerns of the modern novel. Indeed, Michael Holquist sees filiation as the theme through which *The Brothers Karamazov* resolves the dilemmas of Dostoevsky's earlier novels:

> in his last novel he was to go beyond the unbridgeable antitheses of such models [*imitatio* of *Geist* or *imitatio Christi*], to find a way out of the narrative dilemma defined by the absolute hegemony of self (*The Idiot*), the absolute hegemony of the others (*The Possessed*), or the absolute hegemony of the Completely Other (*Crime and Punishment*). A man cannot become a God, absolute ego cannot become another, but a son may become a father, which is the progression of *The Brothers Karamazov*.[22]

The adult world has incriminated itself, has choked on its own overabundant answers, on too many plots. The inheritors, however, need no narrative development. Alyosha never finished his Life of Zosima, but we can scarcely tell where it leaves off, nor do we much regret the loss. That life

---

[22] [James] Michael Holquist, *Dostoevsky and the Novel* (Princeton, N.J.: Princeton University Press, 1977; rpt., Evanston, Ill.: Northwestern University Press, 1986), 175.

is not in need of added chapters because its pattern is clear. To the degree that it is scriptural, it bids not to be ended but to be lived. That "life" is the incorporeal and unstinking remains of Zosima, reincarnated in Alyosha and in any others who enact its truths. It is finally independent of narrative time because, as the source of life — the Logos that was in the beginning — rather than its memorial, it is not ultimately narrative. It does not need further plot any more than the acorn needs an instruction booklet. With the relationship of large and small, the relationship of the one and the many may be taken as understood: having come to understand the acorn and the oak, we have little need to wait around to watch a bushel turn into a forest.

Because of its brief and intermittent nature, we may be tempted to label the childhood theme as the counterplot. Yet that purely diagnostic literary judgment embodies precisely the kind of literalism that Dostoevsky is teaching us to avoid. The childhood theme is not a foil for the murder story, but rather the matrix within which it exists. For in this case the children, Alyosha and the twelve, are the fathers of the men, and the realities encountered among them are prior and causal. They provide explanation when the judicial inquiry voids itself. Each plot centers on a death that may be read as sacrifice, but they inspire different questions: *Who* killed Fyodor? *Why* did Ilyusha die? As we see in the long and erroneous working out of the official investigation, the question of "who?" encourages deductive thinking that succeeds only in concealing its own fallaciousness. Seekers of causation are baffled by the fact that too many causes can be found. Finger pointers go wrong in failing to realize that quite a number of people are responsible for Fyodor's murder, including themselves. For Ilyusha's death, however, a worthy interpreter is to be found in Alyosha, who does not deductively sort out causes but celebrates the meaning of what has happened in a formalized ritual of memory that reenacts the origins of literature, as of religion. Memory, seen serving Ivan demonically for delusion and escape, can also be the act of taking responsibility. This final scene of foundation, far more than resolving just this particular tale, leaps to an explanation of why such tales are told or ever have been told.

Along with the two plots and the two narrative styles, two explanations of the origins of culture compete in the tale. As Michael Holquist has observed, the killing of Fyodor partakes of that primal killing of the father that, in other terms, Freud in *Totem and Taboo* took to be the origins of culture, a sacrifice lately analyzed in religious terms by René Girard.[23] Yet the cultural yield of this death is purely negative: it reveals the brothers' respective failures to take responsibility and lures rationalists into a search for causes that are doomed to endless confusion among the intertwined, redundant, and indecipherable strands of responsibility. Yet Fyodor's death poses strangely few questions about the mysteries of human life: everyone is better off with him dead. The very respect for fatherhood, as for brotherhood, that has to be affirmed by the brothers' process of taking responsibility condemns Fyodor more tellingly than his resentful sons ever managed to do. In and of itself, his death manifests a just and cooperative universe; the vipers consume each other. For the death of Ilyusha, by contrast, one cannot even begin to sort out the causes, for the loss can never be explained or justified either rationally or emotionally. This loss does not allow the universe to be sorted out into familiar and reassuring hierarchies. Among other things, in this case the child can see and bear the meanings far more than can his deformed parents. Ilyusha's death belongs to a different category of sacrifice, that of sons rather than fathers, which rivals the actions of Freud's primal horde as an explanation of culture.[24]

Two cultural traditions center on this sacrifice, the biblical and the classical heroic, and Dostoevsky invokes both to round out the novel — or, rather, to leave the ending monumentally open and generative. To trace out his use of biblical paradigm we must return to "The Russian Monk" and its relationship to the subsequent narrative. Holquist has aptly compared Alyosha's biography to a frame without a picture, a field waiting to be filled. Among its omissions is Zosima's particularly fragmentary representation of Job, a Job whose endurance, along with God's rewards for that endurance, is omitted. The plot provides two enactments of Job's role to explain the omission. The one is the disconsolate Snegiryov, as distraught and destroyed by the death of children as is Ivan. Ivan, in "The Grand Inquisitor," invokes

---

[23] See René Girard, *Violence and the Sacred*, trans. Patrick Gregory (Baltimore: The Johns Hopkins University Press, 1977). Originally published as *Violence et le sacré* (Paris: B. Grasset, 1972).

[24] A recent and insightful article that discusses Dostoevsky's novel as a story about the death of sons, wherein the father becomes the active agent and the child the recipient of his punishment, is Neil Bruss's "The Sons Karamazov: Dostoevsky's Characters as Freudian Transformations," *The Massachusetts Review* 26, no. 1 (Spring 1986): 40-67.

insoluble questions like Job's about why he must suffer. Job turns out to be at the bottom of the eternal grudge borne by Ivan's devil: "How many souls have had to be ruined and how many honorable reputations destroyed for the sake of that one righteous man, Job, over whom they made such a fool of me in old days" (p. 615). The other enactment of Job's role is Alyosha, who has assumed the surrogate paternity of the boys that Zosima assumed for him. His ability to confer meaning on the death of Ilyusha in the absence of an explanation recalls the New Testament answer to Job through a Creator who has lost his own son. Here the most characteristic and least welcome aspects of the mortal condition — anguish, loss, and the chilliest insights into the void of explanations — assimilate suffering mortals to the very experience of the divine. The god in this case has set the pattern for human suffering at the cost of his own son, that is, not so much by imposing sacrifice, as long ago in the testing of Abraham and Job, as by experiencing it himself and bequeathing it. The dignity of gods and men is commonly achieved.

Within the theology of the novel, taking responsibility for the death of the father is not the final step. Ivan and Dmitri have both done so but remain confused and desolate. Such responsibility does lead to a rebirth of fraternity, yet the perception that we are our brothers' keepers remains still within the enlightened legalism of Genesis — that is, still literalistic, partial, and unredeemed. Alyosha has proceeded to the new dispensation by taking responsibility for the death of the son, the step whereby sons become fathers and the step whereby the New Testament sets itself apart from the Old. The essence of madness and torment for Ivan is to be confronted with offspring (for instance, his ideas, Smerdyakov) that he will neither acknowledge nor take responsibility for. Like Lucifer (also incensed by the ambiguities of his Creator), they rise up against their maker. Ivan remains fixed and tormented in a stance that is reactive and filial. The beginnings of salvation for Dmitri lie in perceiving in different terms the myth of his namesake, Demeter (Ceres), and Proserpina that he once presented to Alyosha as the key to his identity in "The Confession of an Ardent Heart." In his self-absorption and longing for annihilation, Dmitri identified himself then with the lost daughter, Proserpina. In the dream of the child, he now progresses to the sorrowful vision of the mother.

In showing Alyosha with the boys, the last chapter of the novel, then, is not just a sentimental set piece, but an unprecedented act in what turns out to be the privileged (because explanatory) plot in the novel. Alyosha takes responsibility for Ilyusha's death by shouldering the burden of explaining its meaning (but, emphatically, not its causes) and enacts that meaning in ceremonial remembrance. What derives from Ilyusha's death, as not from Fyodor's, is worship rather than deductive explanation and a ritual of memory predicated on praise and blame rather than on analysis. It is not just the possibilities of Christ among the apostles that Alyosha renews among his own twelve, for the scene has Homeric antecedents as well. The ritual spontaneously regenerated here lies behind the earliest traditions of heroic verse. Herein the recurring references to the founders of Troy and the name of Dardanelov (recalling the Trojan founder, Dardanus) explain themselves. In these scenes among the consolidating youths are inherent not only the origins of Russia, but also the origins of Europe in Troy. And Alyosha's cult of memory is also the origin of heroic poetry, the *klea andrōn*, the "glories of men," that lie behind the monumental tradition, here flowering yet again.

If psychological explanation is one of the characterizing modes of the novel, then in taking psychology beyond itself in *The Brothers Karamazov* Dostoevsky has also taken the novel beyond itself, back to the prototype of heroic poetry from which it ultimately derives. In significant ways, the boys exist outside of the bourgeois society that is the source and subject of the novel as a modern form. As an all-male and not yet sexually active group, they exist before and outside of questions of sexual difference, domestic obligations, and rivalry over women. Their gregariousness is only now being challenged by disputes over property and class (the dog Perezvon, Ilyusha's poverty) but may still withstand the threat. Though youth can narratively serve the definition of middle-class manners and values by depicting the process of their absorption, such is not the direction in which these boys are being led by Alyosha as chief educator and authority figure. As a gang they still have the capacity for collective feeling and action that comes to be perceived as a fatal absence in adult society.

The boys, then, form a group apart from the typical concerns of the novel, even beyond its central explanatory use of individual psychology. Attacking Ilyusha, they embody the primal horde that the Karamazov brothers symbolize only at an allegorical remove. Along with their comparative freedom from the preoccupations of property, class, and manners, the boys exist in a mode of time that novels normally cannot accommodate. With the benign inexperience of youth, they think themselves immortal; as a horde, they *are* immortal, for the gang will eternally replicate itself with new faces and eternally fail to learn the error of its ways. Dostoevsky has isolated that part of any society, Russian or other, in which the primordial questions of myth can be confronted without the distractions of politics, decorum, or philosophical self-seeking. For the boys, the death of Ilyusha is Death itself coming into the world, as Markel's was for Zosima; for them, Alyosha's preaching is the definitive experience of the Messiah, as his own memory of his mother before the icon contains the very experience of the Madonna. The narrative issues are confronted with the distillation and immediacy of heroic poetry. Such is the single-sex, fraternally bonded, primally vicious, and primally charitable cohort of boys, as of fraternal warriors.

This final scene of unrelated individuals constituting themselves as a family by virtue of accepting responsibility as fathers and sons echoes precisely the last note of the *Iliad*, where Priam and Achilles come to accept each other in their recognition of the primacy of family roles. That famous encounter from *Iliad* 24 has just been evoked through unusually close allusion in the visit that Snegiryov receives from Alyosha, a scene in which a grieving father, like Priam, receives one of those responsible. Those who received Hector's body in Troy are also represented: the distraught mother, Hecuba, finds a parallel in Snegiryov's "crazy weeping wife." Like the clairvoyant, doomed Cassandra, the crippled Nina is the only family member who sees clearly. The contrast of participants is as marked as in Homer: like the abject Priam, who has been rolling in the dung, Snegiryov is destitute, crazed, and sentimental. Though angelic rather than heroic, Alyosha, like Achilles, is the figure of youthful glory: composed, sober, eloquent, emotionally generous. Snegiryov has lost a son, Alyosha a father, even as Priam and Achilles grieve for son and father, respectively. Both Achilles and Alyosha, though from the "enemy camp," come forth to acknowledge the harm that they have done to the grieving fathers. Both Ilyusha and Hector died fighting for the honor of their fathers. Consoling gestures deepen and complicate the character of both young men: the brutal, volatile, and selfish Achilles speaks compassionately and with almost philosophical detachment. Alyosha's gesture reminds us that, saintly as he is, he bears his own responsibility for Ilyusha's death, for he shares that part of Karamazov — the *kar* — that is (certainly in Dmitri) capable of destructiveness and baseness. In both scenes we see the anointed bodies of dead sons wrapped in shrouds and laid on coffin or couch. As Achilles finally bids Priam to put an end to grieving, so to Snegiryov does Alyosha offer the equivalent Christian solace: let us not weep for Ilyusha but cherish the memory of his presence when he was among us — and hope and live for the (positive) future. Achilles speaks in the resigned tones of one who has lived through it all: consider Peleus, my father, thought to be the luckiest of men. He married a goddess. But he had only a single son, who does not comfort his old age. With these words, he plays father to Priam.

Having experienced such a reversal of old and young with Snegiryov, Alyosha in the final scene assumes a paternal role with the twelve lads. In recommending food to the grieving survivors, he directly recalls Achilles' advice to Priam not to weep forever over Hector. Even Niobe, bereft of nine sons and nine daughters, took food and was comforted (*Iliad* 24.599-620). Such is Alyosha's final laughing advice to the twelve as well: "Don't be put out at our eating pancakes — it's a very old custom and there's something nice in that!" (p. 735). That funeral dinner is a Russian ritual that predates Christianity, a trace of the human origins of the eucharist itself.[25] The "unholy-stone" (*poganyi kamen* — literally, "pagan, heathen") beside which the speech is given similarly combines Christian and pre-Christian associations. In this scene of foundation, it may represent the rock on which Jesus founded his church (Matthew 16:18) or the rock rolled from the tomb, the first sign of the victory over death.

Yet this pagan rock where Ilyusha wanted to be buried may also recall the only human landmark on the Trojan plain, the tomb of Ilus. The foundation myth of the death of Ilyusha unifies and invigorates this band even as the death of the founder Ilus stands behind Ilium.[26] As Ilus's tomb stands midway between the warring camps, so Ilyusha's tomb marks the center of Dostoevsky's moral geography. In this sense, Alyosha's boys have

---

[25] See Terras, *Karamazov Companion*, 443.

[26] Dostoevsky's novel is not the only text to arrive finally at the beginning of the *Iliad*. The now lost *Cypria*, composed not long after the *Iliad*, did so to fill out the cycle of myths of the Trojan War. Apollonius Rhodius's *Argonautica* ends with the Argonauts sailing past Aulis, where their sons will launch the next great expedition. Jean Giraudoux's *La Guerre de Troie n'aura pas lieu* reimagines the preliminaries to the war as a critique of militarism.

discovered the founders of Troy by becoming them. In the light of this final *Ilus-Ilyusha* etymology, it becomes less surprising that Zosima, as the locus of Christian authority, should have a name so reminiscent of Zeus; for Alyosha's memorialization of Ilyusha, his *Iliad*, though quintessentially Christian, presents itself as a prolegomenon to the opening note of the European tradition: the Homeric tale of wrath, of revenge, and of fathers and sons as they finally come to recognize each other. Alyosha's advice that there is nothing higher or more wholesome in life than a good memory renews that of Zosima, for of course Fyodor does not define the kind of father Alyosha is to be.

In this final moment, then, we have evocations equally of sacred and heroic poetry, of scripture and the *Iliad*, the horde and the twelve apostles. The gesture stands out all the more in an author who, unlike Gogol, is not given to such allusiveness. Both public and personal motives suggest themselves. Having taken on the role of prophet, Dostoevsky may have felt the pressures of tradition here at the end. Since *Dead Souls* attaches itself to the cycle of tales that started from Troy, *The Brothers Karamazov* cannot afford to do less, if only in its final moments, for it is by such linkages that the monumental tradition identifies itself. By ending his masterpiece with the "founders of Troy" allusively arrayed beside the founders of the Church, Dostoevsky invokes the secular and sacred traditions of the West from their origins and provides a genealogy for his work.

Another explanation comes from the formidably well-read Dostoevsky that one sees in his letters, a connoisseur of the classical texts that he does not invoke in his fiction. Two instances may be cited, separated by some fourteen years. The later one comes upon his release from prison in Siberia, before his return to civilian life. On February 22, 1854, he wrote asking his brother Mikhail to send books, namely, ancient and modern historians.[27] Here Vico leads the list. The Italian critic Attila Fáj has recently argued that the cyclical view of history in *The Brothers Karamazov* derives from Dostoevsky's reading of Vico's theories.[28] Fyodor and his sons are taken

---

[27] Letter to M. M. Dostoevsky, February 22, 1854, in *Dostoevskii-Pisma*, 1:138-39.

[28] Attila Fáj, *I Karamazov tra Poe e Vico: Genere poliziesco e concezione ciclica della storia nell'ultimo Dostoevskij*. Studi vichiani, vol. 16 (Naples: Guida editori, 1984). The allegory is summarized on pp. 97-101. Fáj discusses Dostoevsky's view of a final *ricorso* without reference to the final scenes (pp. 184-90).

to represent the various phases of historical possibility as they all reassert themselves in the final decline: Fyodor represents prehistoric barbarism; Alyosha, the age of gods; Dmitri, the age of heroes; Ivan, the human period; Smerdyakov, renewed barbarism. If in fact Vico did fill the gap left by the now rejected Fourier and the utopians, then Dostoevsky, like Gogol with Dante, used Italian mysticism to free himself from French rationalism.

The typology of the brothers has, to be sure, been well explained in numerous other ways, and the Hesiodic-Platonic myth of the ages could have come to Dostoevsky through many channels other than Vico. Yet one can say that the final band of youths in a universe made newly poetic does come remarkably close to dramatizing the *ricorso* of Vico, the return to the rough, vital, and concretely sensual era that spawned the Achilleses, and later the Homers and the Dantes. Dostoevsky may in some measure have been led back to Homer by the same Neapolitan guide who later led Joyce.

The end of *The Brothers Karamazov* may constitute a *ricorso* of another and more personal sort. Amid the reflections on youth and age that end the tale, Dostoevsky obviously engages his own youth on many levels. Here, at the pinnacle of his achievement, we may perhaps see him confess to the formative impressions that inspired his ambitions and stayed with him throughout his life — to wit, his reverence for the two prophets of the West, Christ and Homer. To Mikhail, the eighteen-year-old Fyodor wrote, attributing an almost scriptural role to the *Iliad* very like that conferred on the *Odyssey* by Gogol in *Selected Passages*:

> As to Homer and Victor Hugo, it seems that you have deliberately chosen not to understand me. This is what I am saying: Homer (a legendary person who was perhaps incarnated and sent to us by God, as Christ was) can be compared only with Christ and not Goethe. Look through Homer, read the *Iliad* carefully and understand its meaning (admit, you haven't read it). In the *Iliad* Homer gave the whole ancient world the same organization in spiritual and earthly life that Christ gave to the new world.[29]

[29] Letter to M. M. Dostoevsky, January 1, 1840, in F. M. Dostoevskii, *Polnoe sobranie sochinenii v 30 tomakh*, vol. 28, pt. 1 (Leningrad: Nauka, 1985), 69.

The Brothers Karamazov is not an epic. In formal and thematic terms, it continues that tradition much less than does *Dead Souls*. Rather, Dostoevsky created within the form of the novel a monumental surpassing of the novel that leaves off where the epic tradition takes up, as if — somehow — Chichikov, bounding directionless across the Russian steppe, were finally to draw near to a lofty city that might be Jerusalem, or might be windy Troy.

4. TOLSTOY AND HOMER

Even Tolstoy's fiercest critics allow that *War and Peace* is Russia's great book. Other nations have waited in vain for a Great War to issue in the national epic. Milton searched all the way back to Arthur before abandoning the project for the War in Heaven, and as recently as 1941 the young Norman Mailer was debating whether to stalk the Great American Novel in the Pacific theater or the European.[1] For much of the nation, of course, the Civil War and *Gone with the Wind* had already ended the quest.[2] Things are a good deal simpler for the Russians, since the victory of 1812 and the seven years preceding are the great moment in their military history and Tolstoy their great storyteller. So much was evident to them within a generation of the book's appearance, as when Strakhov hailed *War and Peace* as "a truly unheard-of phenomenon, an epic in a contemporary form of art."[3] Early in this century Tolstoy himself relieved Gorky of any doubts about the matter: "Without false modesty, *War and Peace* is like the *Iliad*."[4]

But is it just one book? While Homer had perfected "unity of plot" (Aristotle, *Poetics* 8), the Tolstoyan *Iliad* is notoriously several books at once and for some readers none of them convincingly: historical saga, romance, philosophical tract. Henry James included it among Tolstoy's "loose baggy monsters";[5] Percy Lubbock diagnosed therein "a confusion of two designs";[6]

---

[1] Norman Mailer, *Advertisements for Myself* (New York: Putnam, 1959), p. 28.

[2] See Leslie A. Fiedler, *The Inadvertent Epic* (New York: Simon and Schuster, 1979), 59-70.

[3] Nikolai Strakhov, "The Russian Idea in *War and Peace*," in *War and Peace*, ed. George Gibian, trans. Louise Maude, Aylmer Maude, and George Gibian, (New York: W.W. Norton & Co., 1966), 1387.

[4] Quoted in Maxim Gorky, *Reminiscences of Tolstoy, Chekhov and Andreyev*, trans. Katherine Mansfield, S.S. Koteliansky, and Leonard Woolf (London: Hogarth Press, 1948), 57.

[5] Percy Lubbock, preface to *The Tragic Muse*, by Henry James (New York: Charles Scribner's Sons, 1908), p. x.

[6] Percy Lubbock, *The Craft of Fiction* (New York: Viking, 1957), 39. Lubbock further

R. F. Christian declared the text "not a finished work."[7] In the eyes of many other critics as well, Tolstoy has failed to learn what Aristotle prescribed that storytellers first learn, and learn from Homer, the art of narrating "a single action." The *Iliad* says what needs saying about the Trojan War by recounting forty days or so in the last year of the siege, as Tolstoy well knew. In 1857 he called the epic a "marvel." In 1864 he listed it with the *Odyssey* among the ten books which had influenced him most. By 1871, when he had come to realize that "one cannot be educated" without knowing Greek, his wife's diary shows him "terribly excited" to be reading Homer in the original.[8] Yet in this period Homeric standards of unity seem to have slipped further and further from his grasp. Just as Homer had focused on a single emotion of a single character, the wrath of Achilles, Tolstoy began writing with no hero but the intense and contradictory Prince Andrei, whose career follows the same tragic rhythm. As the story progresses, however, Andrei is crowded off center stage.[9] Midway through his quest for some absolute, he drops out of the final text, to be replaced by the lovable and unlikely Pierre, whom we are meant to have been watching all along. Or is the hero finally that voice from the whirlwind which arrests the narrative increasingly toward the end to prophesy about the meaning of History? Beyond his original seven years of narrative, Tolstoy could not resist later adding another eight as an afterthought (Epilogue One) or a final stab at larger issues (Epilogue Two),

claims that the book has "no centre, and Tolstoy is so clearly unconcerned by the lack that one must conclude that he never perceived it."

[7] R.F. Christian, *Tolstoy's War and Peace* (Oxford: Clarendon Press, 1962), 124.

[8] See in general N. N. Gusev, *Letopis' zhizni i tvorchestva L'va Nikalaevicha Tolstogo* (Moscow: Gosudarstvennoe izdatelstvo khudozhestvennoi literatury, 1958), and more briefly Chauncy E. Finch, "Tolstoy as a Student of the Classics," *The Classical Journal*, 47 (1952): 205-10. In 1879 Tolstoy compiled a second list, this time of the eight books that had influenced him between the ages of thirty-five and fifty. Only the *Iliad* and the *Odyssey* recur from the 1864 list.

[9] As Tolstoy recounts the process: "I had abandoned what I had started not because it was necessary for me to describe the earliest days of my hero's [Andrei's] youth but, on the contrary, because among the half-historical, half-social, half-invented great characters of the great era, the personality of my hero was being pushed into the background, and the foreground was being occupied, with an equal interest for me, by old and young people and by men and women of that time." Leo Tolstoy, "Draft for an Introduction to *War and Peace*," in *War and Peace*, ed. George Gibian, trans. Louise Maude, Aylmer Maude, and George Gibian, (New York: W.W. Norton & Co., 1966), 1364.

and ended with plans for a sequel to subject Pierre to the more advanced stages of "family happiness" and the Decembrist uprising of 1825. These plans issued in the Levin of *Anna Karenina*, which presents in a still more extreme form that merging of two disparate tales about nearly antithetical protagonists which Tolstoy explained as almost an accident of composition in *War and Peace*. Whatever Tolstoy was learning from Homer, it was not those lessons about narrative unity which the Greeks found primary. *War and Peace* in its final form lacks a center, divides itself between two heroes and an increasingly intrusive narrator, and has trouble ending on either a heroic or an individual note, with either war or peace.[10]

Even apart from Homer, literary antecedents have so far done little to account for the structural problems of *War and Peace*. In a more complicated world, epic inclusiveness had become a more complicated matter. Homer's descendants, like Dante and Ariosto, relied all the more strongly on the single protagonist who can witness the proliferation of new concerns. The novel itself is, to be sure, a form designed to accommodate discursiveness. Yet the novels that influenced *War and Peace* show nothing like its centrifugal tendencies: Thackeray's *Vanity Fair* as "a novel without a hero" proves far less troublesome than Tolstoy's novel with two largely antithetical heroes, nor will the instructive bad example be found in Stendhal. Tolstoy himself disclaimed the influence of novelistic form because even it was too unified: "We Russians do not know how to write novels in the sense in which this genre is understood in Europe. This work of mine is not a tale. No idea is being put forward in it; nothing is being proved; no single event is described in it. Still, it cannot be called a novel — with a plot that has growing complexity, intrigue, and a happy or unhappy denouement, at which point interest in the narration ceases."[11] Nor, finally, is the promotion of novel to epic scale necessarily the source of narrative inconcinnity: Proust's *Remembrance of Things Past* and Joyce's *Ulysses* gather up and hold together their proliferation of references and cross-references through the integrating consciousnesses of Swann and Bloom.

---

[10] On the intellectual and moral consequences of the book's lack of a central character, see Käte Hamburger, *Leo Tolstoi, Gestalt und Problem* (Bern: A. Francke, 1950).

[11] Tolstoy, "Draft for an Introduction," p. 1363. See also, James M. Holquist, "Did Tolstoj Write Novels?" in *American Contributions to the Eighth International Congress of Slavists*, vol. 2, ed. Victor Terras (Columbus, Ohio: Slavica Publishers, 1978), 272-79.

We must not, of course, forget the man: Tolstoy lived and wrote with a spectacular and unwelcome freedom from that hobgoblin of little minds, consistency. He may be (to use Isaiah Berlin's famous gloss on Archilochus[12]) a knower of many truths, a "fox," trying to become a "hedgehog," the knower of one (but important) truth, and in the process sounding like several foxes at once. His constant scurrying to cover his tracks betrays him all the more clearly: *War and Peace*'s two epilogues can be taken as attempts after the fact to prove that the tale had been unified all along, that is to establish a broader concluding perspective which can integrate the text's diverse concerns. As the sequel evolved steadily into a double tale, the title alternated between *Two Marriages* and *Two Couples* and was fixed at *Anna Karenina*. As he had with Andrei, Tolstoy began with Anna as a single protagonist in a world moving steadily toward tragedy; as had Pierre, the valiantly durable Levin claimed more and more attention in successive drafts, to the point that he embodies a second and opposite mode of heroism, one capable of withstanding the crucible of Tolstoyan domestic bliss. Yet the odd architecture of the piece worried Tolstoy sufficiently that he suppressed its doubleness in his final title, then in the often quoted letter to Rachinsky protested a bit too earnestly that the tales of Anna and Levin really do converge at the end.[13] Readers as philosophical as Tolstoy hoped to make them would indeed accept Anna's fatal self-gratification and Levin's painful but rewarding progress to sublimation as useful halves of a single sermon about the city's wickedness and redemptive family happiness in the Russian countryside. Those more numerous readers who tend to forget that Anna is fictitious may be only briefly satisfied with the narrative accommodation of the two tales. Grief for Anna can upset the elegant moral calculus of Tolstoy's conclusion. If the book had epilogues like *War and Peace*, the final sense of balance would surely disintegrate. By the end the reader may suspect that Tolstoy, like Milton, has dutifully signed up on the side of the angels while his imagination is really lingering

[12] Isaiah Berlin, *The Hedgehog and the Fox* (New York: Simon and Schuster, 1966).

[13] Letter of January 27, 1878, in Leo Tolstoy, *Polnoe sobranie sochinenija*, vol. 62, ed. V.G. Chertkova (Moscow: Gosudarstvennoe izdatelstvo khudozhestvennoi literatury, 1928-1964), 377, on which see Elisabeth Stenbock-Fermor, *The Architecture of* Anna Karenina (Lisse: Peter de Ridder Press, 1975) and Joan Delaney Grossman, "Tolstoy's Portrait of Anna: Keystone in the Arch," *Criticism*, 18 (1976): 1-14.

in the Satanic camp. Anna is not so easily silenced. Similarly, at the end of the first epilogue of *War and Peace*, when Pierre and Natasha, Nicholas and Mary have bored the reader into submission to the felicities that Levin will later affirm, we find ourselves rooting instead for Andrei's orphaned son — in some ways as driven, fragile, and death-devoted as his father. In the midst of this Edenic and slightly fattening bliss, young Nicholas must be the snake — a principle of turmoil — to suggest that what will ultimately grow out of the hard-won achievement of peace and family happiness will be a renewed intoxication with war and a rebirth of heroic solipsism. The essence of Tolstoyan visions seems to be the revisions. The man cannot make up his mind.

Now, novelists probably should. But bards need not, and Tolstoy's epic antecedents, if we consider them in their entirety, did sanction and perhaps inspire the bipolarity that so conspicuously characterizes *War and Peace*, starting with its title. Among the Greeks single epics may have narrated single actions, but they were also from the first inextricably bound into a mythic cycle that reached with total comprehensiveness and vigorous inconsistency from the creation of the world to the death of Odysseus.[14] Even the few brilliant remains that we have from this cycle — only two intact epics — demonstrate the complexity of the larger structure. Homer's epic of war leads into an epic of peace, the *Odyssey* — just as tightly unified, though in a completely different format. The two read as forty-eight continuous books of narrative. The possibility that the larger structure might derive from two or many "Homers" had no impact on the European literary tradition. What was influential was the yoking of two nearly antithetical heroes, Achilles and Odysseus, and the shift of scene and values from the plains of Ilium, where even the gods look on, to a hero's own backyard in Ithaca. The talents worthy of reacceptance by a Penelope may finally rival those once needed to conquer Hector, just as much as Pierre's conquest of domestic tranquility proves no less painful and frustrating than Andrei's martial pursuit of *gloire*. Though these two quite different views of the world would later crystallize into tragedy and comedy, the larger unity of Homer's forty-eight books was received as a fact of nature, and when Virgil reduced the format to twelve books he drew equally on both epics.

---

[14] For a brief introduction to the Greek epic cycle, as well as Odysseus' role in it, see W. B. Stanford, *The Ulysses Theme*, 2nd ed. (New York: Blackwell, 1963), pp. 81-89.

His programmatic introduction to the *Aeneid*, *arma virumque cano*, comes very close to labeling the work "War and Peace," "arms and the man," *Iliad* and *Odyssey*. The two halves of the *Aeneid*, six books of travel and six of civil war, reflect that bipolar vision in a way that becomes definitive for the epics to follow. The large innovation Virgil made — readers have, on the whole, not been happy with it — was to conflate Achillean and Odyssean heroism into the single evolving figure of Aeneas, whom moderns variously find enticingly ambiguous or maybe just mad. He serves successively as good soldier and bereaved husband at Troy, caddish lover of Dido, staunch and remorseful leader of the pilgrimage to Italy, then champion of an invasion which we are meant to take also as a homecoming. As the epic modulates from Odyssean travel to Iliadic combat, Aeneas must (in the opposite direction) learn to tame his Trojan furor (the direct equivalent of Achilles' wrath) into Roman pietas, a more altruistic version of Odyssean self-control. Finally the oil and water of the combination will not set, and perhaps the gloomy Virgil never intended that they should. Aeneas grows remote and lifeless, then in the poem's last lines breaks down abruptly into the rage which he was meant to have unlearned long since. What Virgil does establish definitively is the necessity of imitating both the *Iliad* and the *Odyssey*, as well as the impossibility of doing so gracefully or in a way that can lead to a single convincing resolution.

Virgil's follower Statius formulated a polarity of *sapientia* and *fortitudo* in heroic character which remained axiomatic throughout the Middle Ages with Odysseus and Achilles as the respective archetypes.[15] In Christian writers, of course, it is the diverting mischances of the risk takers which prove the greater wisdom of being wise. Though Dante conceives character far more complexly, the progress from *Inferno* to *Paradiso* simply takes bipolar structure to its logical extreme, along with an ample amount of mediation in *Purgatorio*. Yes, it is from the beginning to the end the same poet speaking the same vernacular, but now turning it to the high style instead of the low and shaping his pilgrimage around Beatrice instead of Virgil. Again, the journey moves past tragic defiance frozen into ice and on to universal and comedic reunion in the City of God. *Paradise Lost* takes roughly the same two Dantesque steps from damnation to salvation in moving our attention

---

[15] See Ernst Robert Curtius, *European Literature and the Latin Middle Ages*, trans. Willard R. Truk (Princeton, N.J.: Princeton University Press, 1973), 167-82.

from Satan to Adam to Christ, even though the memory of Satan survives disconcertingly well. Joyce advertised only the *Odyssey* as a model, as is largely true for *Ulysses*. But Joyce is quite obviously writing a narrative cycle which has good claims to being a modern equivalent of the epic cycle, as the French translator of *A Portrait of the Artist as a Young Man* indicated in retitling the work *Daedalus*. Even if Stephen Dedalus becomes mainly a Telemachus in *Ulysses*, in *A Portrait* he has been something of an Achilles manqué — earnest, infantile, in quest of absolutes — as the title of the aborted *Stephen Hero* suggests. From *A Portrait* to *Ulysses* we move from a world where only tragic actions are awaited to a world where comedy lurks and *may* possibly prevail. That Tolstoy had in mind the doubleness of the Homeric model emerges from his diary when he notes that he was shaping *War and Peace* to present "a picture of manners and customs based on the historical event: the *Odyssey*, the *Iliad*, 1805."[16] Like his many predecessors who affirmed one epic mode of heroism by equipping their tales with some rival and opposite type, Tolstoy ran the risk that the wrong side might win or neither side. After all, it is primarily the fierce energies of the Bad Old Days — the Achillean firebrands — that win the hearts of readers: the passionate Aeneas of Troy and Carthage, Francesca and Ulysses, Milton's Satan, Roland more than Charlemagne, Heathcliff and not Hareton.

Of the innumerable influences on *War and Peace* Tolstoy openly invited comparison only to Homer, with whom consideration of the work as an epic structure must therefore begin.[17] Some of the parallels may, of course, be fortuitous; some may be subconscious; at least some must be pointed and deliberate. We might begin by noting the gross movements of Homer's and Tolstoy's pairs of heroes as they leave and reenter society. Achilles begins the *Iliad* as the consummate insider: the best warrior at Troy, a better fighter than Agamemnon is a king and politically not much less powerful,

---

[16] Entry of September 30, 1865, quoted in Gusev, p. 315.

[17] Formal parallels between Homer and Tolstoy are briefly outlined by Rosemarie R. Ulis, "Has the Historical Novel Replaced the Epic?" *Classical Bulletin*, 40 (1964): 50-52, and George Steiner comments on thematic and philosophical similarities throughout *Tolstoy or Dostoevsky* (New York: Knopf, 1959), esp. pp. 71-83. Two recent works deal with *War and Peace* as epic, although without any detailed attention to structure: Harry J. Mooney Jr., *Tolstoy's Epic Vision: A Study of War and Peace and Anna Karenina* (Tulsa, Okla.: University of Tulsa Press, 1968); and Laura Jepsen, *From Achilles to Christ: The Myth of the Hero in Tolstoy's War and Peace* (n.p., 1978).

son of a goddess and therefore entitled to prerogatives not granted to other mortals. Feeling insufficiently rewarded for his valor, he abandons the Greek siege of Troy and dooms it to failure by his absence as well as by the gods' connivance. The mirror of this tragic tale of withdrawal is the myth of return: Odysseus' decade lost in fairyland shows him to an equal and opposite extent the outsider trying only to get home, and even in Ithaca he must reenter society slowly and from the margins dressed as a beggar to dupe and destroy the far more numerous suitors of his wife. At Anna Scherer's soirée at the start of *War and Peace*, Prince Andrei is the supreme insider who only wants out. Scornful, aloof, remote, he is an Achillean malcontent holding a teacup. He, too, will hear the growing claims of inward and private concerns and, like Achilles, confuse them with some call to cosmic and glorious attainment. At the same party, Pierre, a great clumsy bear of a man "like a child in a toy shop" (p. 10),[18] is making his debut in that same society. Like Odysseus, his final destiny will be the family happiness from which Andrei is in flight. While Achilles and Andrei in their wild swings between paralytic self-involvement and cosmic assertion rarely pause in between, Odysseus and Pierre show more profound connections with earth and with life as it is lived moment by moment. They are comfortable in the human community. Pierre, despite his foreign name, proves the very embodiment of Russianness, while Andrei spends much of the end of his life in voluntary withdrawal (for health, to be sure) in Switzerland. That Pierre marries Andrei's fiancée and beguiles his orphaned son is only the most concrete symbol of the extent to which the two men have exchanged places in the course of the narrative as the outsider gravitates to the center. Achilles and Odysseus embody a parallel contrast of self-immolation and homecoming.

Homer, no more than Tolstoy, cannot negotiate this radical turning without an element of contradiction, as emerges most disconcertingly when the *Iliad*'s heroes reappear as somewhat different characters in the *Odyssey*. The sympathetic Helen of the *Iliad* seems unmistakably witchy in her later years (*Odyssey*, Book IV), and the same Achilles who in the *Iliad* threw away his life without a second thought now reports from Hades (Book XI) that life is worth clinging to at any price. But, then, it is not

---

[18] The translations of War and Peace are those of Louise and Aylmer Maude as printed in the Norton Critical Edition (see n. 3).

really the same Achilles. And the Odyssean report (not anticipated in the *Iliad*) that what finally took Troy was not Achillean brawn but the ruse of the Trojan Horse is to adherents of Iliadic values somewhere between revisionism and defamation. Similarly, the latter parts of *War and Peace* no longer sound like quite the same author: Tolstoy opens the work in earnest pursuit of certain premises, only to end it by demonstrating their opposite. We can overlook Andrei's crankiness at the start since he is the only honest and thoughtful voice among the chorus of hypocrites that Anna Scherer has gathered in her salon. History looms large on the horizon; only Andrei has the courage to confront it. And what can be said against a man proving his manhood? The acrimony between those who adore Napoleon and those who fear him gives no hint that the ultimate heroes of the tale are those who at this point scarcely grasp the issue, types like the pregnant Princess Lise or Pierre, who will finally prove true manhood as doting father of Natasha's children. Beyond the convulsions of European history looms the yet larger specter of natural history, whose deities are all goddesses. Against this initially unsuspected touchstone of nature, the great hypocrite of the piece will be Andrei for constantly and variously deluding himself about his ability to see the Truth, when one must instead, like Pierre and Natasha, live it. Since war impends, on first reading one naturally sorts Anna's guests into tragic classifications: heroes, choral bystanders, victims. Lise and Pierre are natural victims. Once familiar with the peaceful idyll that lies beyond 1812, one can trust hindsight to spot the apparent fools as comic heroes (Pierre) and the celebrities as imposters. Andrei is such an *alazon*. But one must visit this landscape, like the Mount of Purgatory (*Inferno* I and *Purgatorio* I), twice to realize that it is not tragic. Paradise, not Golgotha, hides at the top. And the right people are going to find all of this woe therapeutic. Already the *Aeneid* uses such stratifications of outlook by beginning with a happy ending (of much wandering) which turns out to be the start of much woe. What was "Venus saves Trojans" (Book I) on first reading retrospectively becomes "Juno traps Romans." The epic leap *in medias res*, which *War and Peace* so faithfully makes, entails action so straightforward that it may begin at once and a perspective so complex that the only sufficient prologue is a preliminary reading of the whole work.

The individual parallels between Tolstoy and Homer continue in far greater detail than can be pursued here. Pierre's seven years with the temptress Helene replicate the seven years that Odysseus spent in captivity (initially willingly, then, like Pierre, less so) with Calypso. Years of wandering in fairyland have left Odysseus' wits a bit addled, and it takes the swineherd Eumaeus, whom he first visits in Ithaca, to put him in touch with the realities of his own land. For Pierre, confused by Freemasonry and similar distractions, the peasant Platon plays the same initiatory role. Odysseus customarily penetrates enemy territory disguised as a beggar — so once at Troy (Book IV), as in Ithaca; Pierre will finally be crafty enough to do much the same in Moscow. Neither Odysseus nor Pierre is much given to radical redefinition of social roles; they strive only to be given the chance to fulfill them in the normal way. In both of their protracted and dangerous homecomings the heroic quest is for the attainment of the ordinary.

The prizes are as similar as the heroes, most conspicuously in that both Penelope and Natasha are such paragons of resilient chastity. Both writers have found deft, if provocative, ways of letting these women experience life richly and in ways parallel to their future or returning husbands, but without losing their virtue in the process. Penelope and Natasha spend years being courted and learn much thereby without ever being won. Penelope faces her own Scylla and Charybdis between being too easy with her suitors (and losing everything) or rigidly resisting, thereby getting herself raped and Telemachus killed. Natasha must tack a similarly perilous course between disgrace, narrowly averted with Anatole Kuragin, and the sterile self-righteousness which leaves Sonia an old maid. The couples united or reunited at the end of the *Odyssey* and of *War and Peace* have used hardship and separation to grow more alike, while the unions which had prosperous and easy beginnings (Helen and Menelaus in the *Odyssey*; Helene and Pierre in Tolstoy) have collapsed from within. Tolstoy's Helene is in fact an unmistakable imitation of that Helen of Troy, and her entrance into Anna Scherer's soirée reenacts Helen's entrance onto the walls of Troy in the *Iliad* (Book III). Neither author attempts the details of a beauty which surpasses description; both rely instead on the crowd's reaction ("Surely there is no blame on Trojans and strong-greaved Achaians / if for long time they suffer hardship for a woman like this one" [III.156- 57].[19] "How lovely! said everyone who saw her" [p. 11]) along with the great beauties' gestures

---

[19] The translation is that of Richmond Lattimore, *The Iliad of Homer* (Chicago and London: University of Chicago Press, 1951).

of diffidence, which make them even more irresistible.[20] Both Helens have three husbands and pay for their scandal with childlessness (by barrenness and abortion, respectively).

Achilles and Andrei resemble each other in nothing so much as in their irreducible contradictoriness. As noted above, both have almost preternatural vision about the universe and their inner selves, but react erratically to the claims of society: that is, both can oscillate from petulant infant to selfless savior without any steady grasp of the manhood in between. Achilles begins Book I trying to save the Greek army at whatever cost to himself, and ends it tearfully begging his goddess mother to have it destroyed to salve his wounded pride. Andrei we see first as a man too big for small talk in Anna's parlor, but then not sufficiently mature to be decent to his pregnant wife. Both men alternate between periods of almost unbelievable heartlessness and of sublime moral perception. It is the same Achilles who can will his friends' death for his own childish reasons and then (as no other Greek could) accept Priam, not as the enemy king but as a grieving father like his own grieving father and as something like an extension of his own self (Book XXIV). Likewise, Andrei can abandon his own family and find Napoleon as an embodiment of greatness more important than the Russians who must die to establish that greatness, then after the battle of Borodino forgive the even more unlucky Anatole simply out of his love for all mankind — even though (or because?) he realizes that "now it is too late" (p. 908). Much can be read simply from the face, as we see in one of his animated moments with Pierre: "Every muscle of his thin face was now quivering with nervous excitement; his eyes, in which the fire of life had seemed extinguished, now flashed with brilliant light. It was evident that the more lifeless he seemed at ordinary times, the more impassioned he became in these moments of almost morbid irritation" (p. 28). Andrei's passions and sympathies, which can be overwhelming when they are not completely absent, direct themselves primarily in retrospect. Only his son's near death wrenches from Andrei the immense love he feels for this child whom he has earlier ignored. Life becomes beautiful for Andrei, as for Achilles, only in those moments (sometimes

---

[20] Cf. Georg Lukács' comparison of Homer's treatment of Helen to Tolstoy's Anna Karenina, Werke, Vol. VI: Probleme des Realismus III: Der historische Roman, ed. Peter Christian Ludz, Frank Benseler, György Márkus (Berlin: Luchterhand, 1965), p. 377.

misleading) when he feels that he is leaving it. Indeed, epiphany becomes Andrei's standard response to extreme pain, as when in the example just given he learns from the agony of Anatole that the meaning of life is in loving others and embracing the common mortality. Since his visions tend not to survive his recoveries, only the deathbed brings irreversible spiritual progress — and that a bleak turning inward that reverses earlier visions of Love. Similarly Achilles realizes his commitment to Patroclus only after he has thoughtlessly dispatched his companion to fight and die in his own armor. It is only after Achilles dooms Patroclus, Hector, and himself that he becomes the great and expansive humanitarian of Book XXIV. When we see him finally at ease with himself and with the enemy king, it is because both are in their last days. For both Achilles and Andrei, nothing in their troubled life becomes them so much as leaving it. Conversely, the *Odyssey*, the grandfather of all Baedekers, is memorable for all its introductions to new and exotic places; the poet tends to be much less interested in leavetaking and, indeed, ends the narrative simply by a bolt from the blue when the gods have seen enough. What we see of Pierre, for all the false turns along the way, is a protracted process of arrival: into society, into married life, into Freemasonry, into war, finally into true marriage and fatherhood.[21]

Apart from the steady habit of pursuing what is lost and resisting what impends, Achilles and Andrei are self-consistent only in living their lives in harmony with higher principles, while Odysseus and Pierre are mostly trying to get through the next hour. The higher principles, of course, tend to keep changing. In withdrawing from the siege, Achilles rejects the all-important esteem of his peers because he feels that he is "honoured already in Zeus' ordinance" (*Iliad* IX.608), that is, that he, unlike other men, has some claim to absolute status in the universe. Yet after Patroclus is killed, vengeance becomes the only absolute. When Priam arrives to reclaim Hector's body, even vengeance has given way to a transcendent sense of humanity which supersedes the difference of Trojan and Greek. Similarly, Andrei has no patience with mortals but worships the superhuman Napoleon; when even

---

[21] On Andrei, see especially John Hagan, "A Pattern of Character Development in *War and Peace*: Prince Andrej," *Slavic and East European Journal* 13 (1969): 164-90, which, however, argues that the work "culminates in the great spiritual quest of Andrej and Pierre, who emerge at the end and from their inner warfare to achieve the peace that passes all understanding."

he disappoints, the wounded Andrei fixes on the epiphany of the eternal sky. After his visit to Natasha, the blossoming of the oak tree symbolizes the absolute triumph of the life force, with which he willingly puts himself in harmony. Yet it is only the long process of dying that places him, like Achilles, substantially and finally in contact with any absolute principle. Only the proximity of death allows either hero any measure of serenity.

Both authors use the progressive disillusionment of the heroes to demonstrate at once the appeal and the hollowness of military glory. For the Greeks Achilles was the warrior par excellence, and yet it is from his lips that we hear that Menelaus' private grudge about the rape of Helen scarcely warrants the leveling of Troy; that aggression itself "swarms like smoke inside a man's heart / and becomes a thing sweeter to him than the dripping of honey" (XVIII.109-10). Similarly, Andrei can convey Tolstoy's larger point about the futility of militarism because he had once believed in it with almost religious fervor. The same Andrei who announced to Pierre at the outset, "I am going to war, the greatest war there ever was" (p. 28), learns by the end that "war is not courtesy but the most horrible thing in life; and we ought to understand that and not play at war" (p. 865). By contrast, Pierre and Odysseus can fight or not as circumstances demand because they have little coveted military glory for its own sake. To revert to Archilochus' terms, Andrei, like Achilles, is the fox who sees many things at once — too many; the nearsighted Pierre, like the hedgehog, sees only what is at hand. But that is what matters.

Finally, the heroes have quite different sorts of relationships with women and, by parallel, with the land itself. While Achilles' career is greatly affected by various women (Helen, then the slave girl taken from him by Agamemnon, then his mother), he plays very few scenes with them. Similarly Andrei's scenes with women are somehow peripheral to his experience and are often instances of noncommunication, as in his failure to appreciate Lise, Mary, and finally Natasha. By contrast, Odysseus has his best scenes mostly with women: Calypso and Circe, Helen, the princess Nausicaa, his old nurse, Athena, finally Penelope herself. Helene and Natasha similarly demarcate Pierre's spiritual odyssey. Nearly alone among epic heroes Pierre shows little susceptibility to male influence. He acquires and loses a real father, a spiritual brother (Andrei), a council of elders (the Freemasons), and admiring military comrades without much sign of permanent effect. His rebirth comes at the hands of the peasant Platon, whom he perceives, rather curiously, from his first words as an "old Russian peasant woman" and who embodies nonjudgmental mother love more purely than any other character in the work.[22] But then the earliest and greatest mystery about Pierre — glaring in a work so rich in the details of family life — is omission of any mention of his mother, a figure who retrospectively comes to seem the goal of his quest. The magic princess, Helene, certainly was not; Natasha is, but not in the aspect of the alluring maiden. Quite beyond her notable capacity to embody the spirit of motherhood and, indeed, of Russia itself, Natasha starts becoming more than a friend to Pierre when, as Andrei's widow, she lives in the same state of abandonment in which Pierre would always have known his mother.

With both sets of heroes, their relationship to the land parallels their dealings with the women who so often embody its spirit. Pierre and Andrei, often as their paths cross, seem to travel through different landscapes. For Andrei the path from the salon and the study to the battlefield is straight and unobstructed. He allows himself to be surrounded by only as much landscape as he can confer symbolic meaning on, as is characteristic of tragic heroes: For Oedipus there is only the wild Mount Cithaeron; for Lear, the stormy heath; for Macbeth, Birnam Wood; for Hamlet, the graveyard; for Achilles, only the dust with which he befouls his guilty self. Even the great flowering oak that symbolizes Andrei's awakening love for Natasha functions as a symbol in the text only because Andrei invites epiphany. As a well-read man of his century, he knows the redemptive powers of nature and, bored with his own emotional isolation, chooses to exercise this option. The object that he has picked as a symbol of regeneration is of the tritest: the Tree of Life or Tree of the World familiar already in the context of enchanted forests, golden boughs, and lairs of nymphs and dwarves to be found in everything from nursery tales to epics. Does a thoughtful adult identify himself with the barrenness of a great oak in mid-April without the anticipation that it will be verdant by June? The baleful, then the hopeful voices that Andrei projects onto the tree simply provide a supportive chorus for a scenario that he has mostly plotted out for himself. And what is there in the sky at Austerlitz but the meanings Andrei reads into it? The

---

[22] For a discussion of the attendant religious symbolism, see Robert Louis Jackson, "The Second Birth of Pierre Bezukhov," *Canadian-American Slavic Studies* 12 (1978), 535-42.

sky remains the same as always, only now Andrei's self-consciousness has need of it.

Similarly, there is no landscape at Ilium except as the poet or Achilles imports it in similes. And Achilles, like Andrei, is the single character who parallels the narrator's usual function of drawing parallels and imposing meanings. All of the other Greeks at Troy accept the scepter as a symbol of regal authority, but when Achilles hurls that symbol down in his petulant withdrawal from the camp (Book I), he imposes a new set of meanings on the scepter: He sees it rather as a lifeless branch that will never bear leaf again, as barren as the society over which Agamemnon presides. In speaking, Homer's characters rarely use that repertory of comparisons — charging lions, rushing rivers, cowering lambs — by which the poet makes the movement of battle precise and vivid. Only Achilles regularly shows that command of the language of simile, as for example to the cowering Hector: "As there are no trustworthy oaths between men and lions, nor wolves and lambs have spirit that can be brought to agreement but forever these hold feelings of hate for each other, so there can be no love between you and me, nor shall there be oaths between us" (*Iliad* XXII.262-66). Achilles and Andrei are conspicuous in their respective tales as the characters who speak and think most like the narrator, who are more often found perceiving their settings than being perceived within them. The landscape through which each travels is primarily in his own head: The dark chamber in which Andrei dies should be sufficiently confining, but it is less threatening to him than the dark chamber of which he dreams.

Where Andrei tends to *see* the landscape around him — and mostly in his own terms — Pierre, more passively and more responsively, hears and smells and touches as well. Andrei hears little in nature but the conflicting voices within him, as in the important meeting with Pierre on the raft at Bald Hills: "Prince Andrew felt as if the sound of the waves kept up a refrain to Pierre's words, whispering: 'It is true, believe it'" (p. 422). Pierre, by contrast, can sense mystical and quite unexpected messages even in smell and taste, as in the potato which Platon offers him. Pierre, too, can see symbolism in nature, as when the comet of 1812 symbolizes regeneration for him as the oak had for Andrei, just as the two men earlier voiced their despair in virtually the same words. Yet Pierre has not staged this epiphany, and there is nothing private or calculated in the comet's symbolism. Where the oak evokes Andrei's large and orderly repertory of epiphanic memories (the heavens at Austerlitz, the dead Lise's reproachful face, Pierre on the ferry, Natasha in the moonlight), the comet prompts Pierre instead to forget a painful past and, shedding a few tears, to conceive a hope which he will pursue. Pierre tends not to read meanings into nature closer at hand because he lives too close to it to see it in those terms. He is more a creature of earth, as his name already suggests (Pierre from the Greek *petros* 'rock'). He is compared to a bear at the outset, eats too much and drinks too much.

Similarly, Odysseus uses his eyes carefully in approaching new stops on his voyage, but only to ask the question, "Friend or foe?" Otherwise he is unself-conscious about his proximity to nature, even when he buries himself in leaves to survive the night cold or hides in a ram's fleece to escape the Cyclops. On land, he confronts godhead exclusively and quite variously in its feminine aspects: nymphs, witches, a flirtatious Athena. Likewise, the presiding deity of Pierre's ultimate felicity will be Mother Russia, especially as incarnated in Natasha — a spiritual presence inaccessible to those like Andrei who hear in nature no voices but their own. Through most of the work no note is made of Pierre's perceptions of nature. In the pivotal raft scene at Bald Hills, we hear only Andrei's perceptions, even though the setting is rich with symbolic overtones of boundaries and the crossing of them, the juncture of two worlds in this twilight, between light and darkness and perhaps even between life and death. Are we to be reminded of the raft of Charon in the classical underworld, where Odysseus and the dead Achilles meet a final time? Yet Pierre, as he rambles on about the Masonic Truth, grasps none of this. The earliest and most persuasive sign of his spiritual rebirth after the debacle at Borodino and his imprisonment is that we start seeing scenes through his eyes as he grows increasingly aware of his own perceptions. The progression recalls Dante: First, Pierre must be led through the infernal fires of a devastated Moscow and witness executions so horrible that they deprive him of his old consciousness: "He lost the power of thinking or understanding. He could only hear and see" (p. 1069). Gradually in the Virgin's Field a new and heightened perception begins to dawn, but not simply from within, not — as was always the case with Andrei — by an act of will but by the mysterious workings of Grace: "These bells reminded Pierre that it was Sunday and the feast of the Nativity of the Virgin" (p. 1066). The first promptings of this new and redemptive intuition are not conscious: "In place of the Russian order of life that had been destroyed, Pierre unconsciously felt that a quite different, firm, French order had been established in this ruined nest" (p. 1066). In place of Dante's emergence on Easter, Tolstoy has used the birth of the Virgin — or is she Mother Russia, whose minion, Platon Karataev, ministers to Pierre with a ritual based not on body and blood but on the smell and taste of the humble potato — a ritual as sensual and mystical as the eucharist, one (despite Platon's impending death) more purely bound up with growth and regeneration, and, above all, purely Russian.[23] The scene is an abandoned church, a manger-like structure, and Platon himself, who speaks largely proverbs and instructs through ritual, stands apart from the other characters of the work, almost in the realm of myth, an avatar of the Natural Man who precedes, initiates, or baptizes so many returning kings: the swineherd Eumaeus, who initiates Odysseus back into the life of Ithaca; the Aeneid's King Latinus; John the Baptist. Yet the childless and doomed Platon is also reminiscent of a Christ delegating a mission to a founder like Peter/Pierre; the French soldiers in misnaming Pierre "Kiril" from his patronymic remind us of a further step in the Apostolic succession to St. Cyril and hence to the Slavonic rebirth of Christian Witness, of which Tolstoy here gives a moving example. Moreover, Platon is and is not Plato, and his shed with the light of a surrounding reality breaking through at the cracks is and is not like Plato's Cave. In that analogy lurks much of Tolstoy's creative ambivalence to classical culture. As Platon is to Plato — more unprepossessing, closer to earth, altogether Slavonic — so is Pierre to Odysseus or any of the canonical heroes.

Now, no Christian writer can tie a turning point in his narrative to a protagonist's spiritual rebirth without stirring up possibilities of allegory almost too rich to control. And, indeed, the nexus of scriptural and mythological strands exceeds what we can account for here: Platon's dog recalls Odysseus' loyal Argus; Plato's Cave is itself an elaboration on the caves from which Odysseus is constantly emerging in his succession of rebirths and new beginnings; Pierre's peasant disguise for entering Moscow unmistakably recalls Odysseus' incursions first into Troy and then into his own palace dressed as a beggar, but in a sense it also echoes

---

[23] Cf. Jackson: "Platon emerges here as the source and symbol of renewal: as earth-mother, mother Russia, the people — the indestructible reality of the matrix. Pierre's 'resurrection' is accompanied, appropriately, by a sense of rebirth of the world, an experience of movement of the universe" (p. 541).

the carpenter's son who enters Jerusalem riding on an ass, just as Pierre's agonizing barefoot march is his *via dolorosa*. In a text as rigidly calculated as *War and Peace* to employ only allegories of its own making, this sudden revelation of mythological substrata may jar the reader only slightly less than would the waking of the dead. Then the allusions vanish almost as quickly as they appear; cumulatively there can be no sorting them out. Yet Tolstoy has provided a way out of this forest of symbols: the now strong integrating consciousness of Pierre — something we could not have relied upon earlier in the text. The unassimilable polysemousness of the text forces the reader to the humility which Pierre has lately perfected; we must rely on his response to this sudden and momentary efflorescence of meaning. And that response is to keep marching. As a piece of allegory, Pierre's rebirth is in small compass a *tour de force* comparable to the Dantesque and Miltonic triumphs in merging the accumulated riches of the classical and Christian traditions into a coherent parable about the growth of the single soul. Such allusiveness marks off the major turning in the text from the many small ones that have preceded it. The way out of this very complicated moment is indicated simply and clearly in the lesson on Loving Forgetfulness that Pierre has learned from Platon: "[Platon] loved his dog, his comrades, the French, and Pierre who was his neighbor, but Pierre felt that in spite of Karataev's affectionate tenderness for him (by which he unconsciously gave Pierre's spiritual life its due) he would not have grieved for a moment parting from him. And Pierre began to feel in the same way toward Karataev" (p. 1078). Pierre will attain to a consciousness as full as that of Andrei, and indeed will have the same epiphany of the sky: "And all that is me, all that is within me, and it is all I!" (p. 1130). Yet Pierre is laughing and immediately goes to sleep. The martyrdoms prepared in this section will proceed with a remarkable lack of allegory, with only meanings imposed by the participants. The meaning of Platon's death can adequately be read from Platon's own tale of the innocent merchant. In contrast to Andrei, who girded his sense of self with layers and layers of meaning until he was totally immobilized, Pierre has learned the power of forgetfulness: "the saving power [man] has of transferring his attention from one thing to another" (p. 1177). His realization of Platon's death recalls — "he knew not why" — a summer evening in Kiev, a Polish beauty, and dormant feelings toward Natasha which will grow to complete Platon's lessons.

Once the powers of earth have transfigured Pierre, the landscape itself vanishes from the text. Familiar locations recur a final time, stripped now of their enchantment. Once, for example, the children had all at one time or another ventured into a "fairyland" charged with good and bad possibilities for their growth. On a hunting trip Natasha had visited "Uncle," where by putting on a shawl and hearing a peasant air the Frenchified city girl gained the power to dance like the spirit of the Russian land itself. More balefully, in the nocturnal masquerade at the Melyukovs' country house, transvestitism suited the luckless Sonia all too well, and sorcery stirred up premonitions of Andrei's demise. Tolstoy did not exclude the possibility of chthonic powers that affect more than the imagination. For such scenes, pagan myth — be it classical or Slavonic — provides the clearest antecedents: journeys into the enchanted forest, descents into the underworld (Odysseus and Aeneas preparing the way for Christ and Dante), *Walpurgisnacht*. The old gods have always died slowly among the peasants.[24] Pierre's descent into Platon's cave makes the final and full revelation of this realm, and the old peasant's Delphic concatenation of Christian parables is richer and more mysterious than Christianity. That same mythic geography recurs for a last time in Petya's fatal initiation into battle, but now the text labels it as nothing but boyish dreams: "He was in a fairy kingdom where nothing resembled reality" (p. 1170). The worship of nature in *War and Peace*, then, follows a course very like that of the worship of war: Pierre's insights are pivotal in the deflation of both. At Borodino he is the first character to see war fully and completely as it is and no more; thereafter military glory lives on only as boyish dreams for such as Petya. Similarly, Pierre's almost visceral absorption of the powers of earth leaves it stripped of mythological meaning in the text. Such a transformation of the landscape is anomalous in novels, but nearly normative for Christian epic.[25] Dante-pilgrim moves from the pagan landscape of the Inferno into the Christian space of Paradise, which

---

[24] A similar merging of classical and Slavic elements in the landscape is to be found, perhaps as a legacy from Tolstoy, in Pasternak's *Doctor Zhivago*, for which, see Chapter 5 of this volume.

[25] The subject is much discussed of late, with surprisingly little reference to what is the beginning of wisdom on classical and later scenery, Ruskin's two essays on medieval landscape: "First the Fields" and "Secondly, the Rocks," Chs. xiv and xv in *Modern Painters*, III; in John Ruskin, *The Works of John Ruskin*, vol. 5, ed. E. T. Cook and Alexander Wedderburn (New York: Longmans, Greene and Co., 1904).

is also not space and which more purely figures the inner topography of the soul. If Milton's paradise is well lost, it is so because the outcasts may then advance to the "Paradise within." Tolstoy himself has taken the final and rather Calvinist step of leaving only so much landscape in the work's conclusion as has been converted to spiritual use by the redeemed and active soul: In his final vision of Edenic happiness, there is no surrounding garden. The work ends with a background as treeless and bare as that of Ilium. But then, as we have noted above, the book's final vision of felicity also entails quite a large reassertion of tragic earnestness thinly veiled as optimism.

War and Peace attains a synthesis of heroic modes when Pierre attains by grace what Andrei sought by force of will. For Pierre ends up not only with the domestic and affective side lacking in Andrei but also with that participation in Larger Principles which Andrei had wanted so desperately. He has that much desired oneness with nature, though more as gardener than Romantic. And he has the heroism possible in his age: indefatigable zeal for the ordinary. In much the same way, Odysseus merges at the end of his epic the skills of Achillean warrior (though on a reduced scale) and family man. Yet the fragility of Pierre as a synthesis of virtues becomes apparent in Epilogue One when the possibility of yet a fuller synthesis emerges in Nicholenka — born of Andrei; reared by that family among families, the Rostovs; intrigued by Pierre, though increasingly susceptible to the phantom image of his heroic father. Can one read Epilogue Two without wondering how Pierre could ever wade through these heady and important thoughts? The fragility of Odysseus as a combination of father and fighter similarly emerges from the unanimity of sequel writers in making his son his father's next adversary.

Tolstoy does not let his readers long forget that epics are what the great monsters of history carry around with them: Alexander carried his copy of the *Iliad* to India; Napoleon has his text of Ossian with him at Moscow. Some tyrants have written their own, as we are reminded when before their first conversation Pierre leafs through Andrei's copy of Caesar's *Commentaries*. When Napoleon first views Moscow, the perversity of his intentions emerges in nothing so much as his use of the extended comparison: for him, the city is a maiden waiting to be ravished. As we have already seen with Andrei, the calculated application of such elaborate comparisons — since Homer, the hallmark of epic style — tends to be a form of self-delusion, just as Platon's habit of spewing parables without much worrying about how they apply is a sign of spiritual health. The use of simile itself embodies just those qualities of suffocating traditionalism, glory-mongering, and artificiality which Tolstoy most resents, as we sense already when Anna Scherer is linked by a Homeric simile to the foreman of a spinning mill keeping "the conversational machine in steady, proper, and regular motion" (p. 10). Homer's similes of men charging like lions or rocks falling like snow epitomize vitality and energy usually beyond the reach of indecisive and often timorous mortals. Tolstoy turns the device quite oppositely to the mechanistic and life-denying activities he most detests, leading up to the climactic image (developed from *Aeneid* I.430-36) of Moscow as a queenless and doomed hive, an image paired with Napoleon's sick fantasy of the city as waiting maiden. Style itself, it is suggested, can glorify and justify the basest forms of human aggression.[26] The simile can figure the human in animal or mechanical terms (and justify carnage), as well as personify the inert and thereby turn empty abstractions (glory, honor, nationhood) into cruel deities. Similarly, to be susceptible of characterization by a fixed epithet — la belle Hélène, le charmant Hippolyte — no longer signifies heroic attainment, but rather viciousness. Just as these characters' faces are masks, the fixity of their epithets communicates the fixed depravity of their natures.

Like the landscape, the similes come to be used quite differently after Pierre's spiritual rebirth. The healthy clan of saved characters which we see at the end has, of course, no use for them, and the narrator uses extended metaphors about these characters only to figure the liberation from mechanistic perspectives, as when Pierre "threw away the telescope through which he had till now gazed over men's heads, and gladly regarded the ever-changing, eternally great, unfathomable, and infinite life around him" (p. 1227). Only the scientist — or the scientific historiographer — should be using this potent tool of analogy and in ways that point up the largest and inglorious patterns of collective life. Tolstoy uses the simile of ants returning to a ruined heap to explain how Moscow, purged and perfected, begins to be reborn (p. 1231). Such an affirmation of the instinctual life of the race contrasts diametrically with the generation of individual *gloire* and the

---

[26] On the similes, see especially James M. Curtis, "The Function of Imagery in *War and Peace*," *Slavic Review* 29 (1970): 460-80.

precise delineation of private psychology which epic similes had originally served. The process by which this literary device is parodied, rejected, then transformed and reapplied parallels the deflation and reconstitution of heroism accomplished by the shift from Andrei to Pierre. That the starting points for these reworkings of heroic values are so very traditional — returning to the first notes sounded in European literature — emphasizes all the more strongly how the final triumph of collective values, the slaying of the dragon of heroic solipsism, is a new departure for mankind. Thereby the Russian order consolidated in these events has all the stronger claim to being a new thing under the sun. But that dragon, of course, had been slain quite a number of times before. As the father of the European sensibility, Homer is a fitting guide for this second birth of Europe — as he had been for Virgil in proclaiming the new Roman dispensation, as Virgil had been for Dante in proclaiming the new Christian order, as all three had been for Milton in proclaiming a new Puritan order. All of these writers, like Tolstoy, proclaim their resistance to the epic style as they inherit it; that gesture of rejection (followed in every case by ceaseless cribbing from the same oppressive antecedents) is one of the surest markers of the genre.

We must also allow that Pierre ends up very much further from Odysseus than Andrei does from Achilles. The *Odyssey* does not imply that the meek shall inherit the earth in quite the way that Tolstoy means the parable; indeed, much the opposite is suggested. The deceptiveness of appearances in Homer counsels caution and guile more than humility. While Odysseus is profoundly unaffected by the disguises he wears, Natasha's strength lies in her ability to be transformed by wearing the peasant shawl at "Uncle's," just as Pierre's tattered disguise in prison allows the French-educated aristocrat to be reborn as Russian peasant. Though mythologically Pierre belongs with Odysseus among the ranks of unlikely saviors, that fatiguing operation of proceeding complexly under the guise of simplicity had hitherto called for an ironist: Socrates and Christ, no less than Odysseus. Now Andrei may at some moments (as in his retreat to being a country gentleman) flirt with the possibilities of such pastoral irony; Pierre, though steadily threatened and tempted by subtlety, emerges at the end unmarred by intellectual progress and no more guileful than when he began. Spared finally the Andreian thoughts that wander through eternity, he grows like a tree, imperceptibly and irreversibly. And where the ironists in the tradition repress, postpone, or outgrow their appetites, Pierre — self-indulgent in profoundly harmless ways — walks fatly through a thin man's role, lumbering where we have seen only artful dodgers and agile saints. Such heroes who triumph through passivity operate in the mode of paradox; Pierre is quite alone in being a staunch literalist.

Yet in all of the epics which show some form of bipolar heroism, the obsolescent (i.e., Achillean) mode is the closer to everything that precedes, while the more resilient (Odyssean) heroism that supplants it makes stronger claims of belonging to the writer's own time and place. The obsolescent mode tends, among other things, to recapitulate the concept of heroism as it has developed in cycle. Aeneas at Troy could have been a Homeric character; the later Aeneas could exist only in Italy. Dante-pilgrim with Virgil as guide could be one of Virgil's own characters; in Paradise he exists and perceives in ways never articulated in Latin. Milton's Satan is pointedly classical; his Christ wears the pagan trappings far more lightly.[27] All of these epics take up from and summarize the cycle that precedes, then advance us to quite different destinations. Tolstoy, then, is entirely typical in ending on a note that seems furthest from the tradition. He may have felt that in conferring something of the common touch on his surviving band of characters he was bringing the epic full circle. The historical role he assigns to Homer in "What is Art?" is alongside the Bible as the last "good, supreme art" still accessible to the masses.[28] In sloughing off, layer by layer, the tradition's accreted sophistications *War and Peace* may aim at an art "comprehensible to everybody."

What unites the major epics is not where they end, but that they almost cannot.[29] Comedy and tragedy have their respective principles of closure, as war and peace have their separate periodicities; but that epic synthesis which comes closest to the flow of history itself may, like the historical record, lack real and conclusive stopping points. Only the *Iliad* has the fully

[27] The traditional view that Milton's heavenly host is emphatically nonclassical has recently been challenged by Francis C. Blessington, Paradise Lost *and the Classical Epic* (Boston: Routledge and K. Paul, 1979), 19-49.

[28] Leo Tolstoy, *"What is Art?"* and *Essays on Art*, trans. Aylmer Maude (London: Oxford University Press, 1929), 178.

[29] *"In medias res*, then, is one way to describe the whole of an epic, not just its beginning. It is a narrative, a story, yet it begins in the middle and never concludes" (Joan Webber, *Milton and His Epic Tradition* (Seattle: University of Washington Press, 1979), p. 91).

satisfying conclusion that later epics would seek and fail to replicate. When Achilles and Priam, enemy chieftains, break bread together and then simply stare at each other as "an outright vision of gods" (XXIV.630-31) in the first moment of silence and first moment of full human recognition in the epic, the roles of warrior and family man become fully coincident for the first and only time in the *Iliad*: The men can accept each other as father and son because they will finally be implicated in each others' deaths; and those deaths, once foreseen with cold horror, begin to take on a rich and almost seductive meaning. Translated to a new level of significance, war and peace somehow reconcile themselves in the privileged sympathies of the doomed. However, the narrative irreconcilability of military and domestic values surfaces already at the end of the *Odyssey*, and so gravely that it provoked ancient scholars to surgery. Though the *Odyssey* has consistently maintained that it takes the same prowess (and maybe more wit) to wear a beggar's rags convincingly in the midst of one's enemies as to carry Hephaestus' glorious shield against Hector, the epic also wants to reassure us that Odysseus is equally good with his fists. Paradoxically, where we last saw Achilles at his most humane and tolerant playing a son-figure to Priam, Odysseus ends his epic as a warrior more ruthless than any seen at Troy. The scene of his slaughtering his wife's contemptible suitors in his own hall offers one particularly grisly reconciliation of devoted husband and serious warrior; likewise, he lovingly initiates his son into bloodthirstiness. Penelope thereafter accepts him only after he has lost (for the first time in the epic) a quite unexpected battle of wits, and as the grammarians Aristophanes and Aristarchus (3rd century B.C.) indicated by (apparently) ending the text here, we have at this point a full and satisfying conclusion to the Odyssean mode of the *Odyssey*.[30] Loose threads in the plot remain, hence Book XXIV (surely written last and perhaps much later and conceivably even by other hands) tries to pick them up, thereby ending all of the *Odyssey* (its late-emerging Iliadic themes as well), and indeed providing a conclusion to all preceding forty-eight books, partly by circling back to the beginning of

---

[30] The grounds for seeing everything after *Odyssey* XXIII.296 as later and inferior are forcefully summarized by Denys Page, *The Homeric Odyssey* (Oxford: Clarendon Press, 1955), 101-36. See, however, the counterarguments of Hartmut Erbse, *Beiträge zum Verständnis der Odysee* (Berlin and New York: De Gruyter, 1972), 166-244; John H. Finley, Jr., *Homer's* Odyssey (Cambridge, Mass., and London: Harvard University Press, 1978), pp. 200-08; and Dorothea Wender, *The Last Scenes of the* Odyssey (Leyden: E.J. Brill, 1978).

the *Iliad*, as well as repeating some of the format of that epic's final book. These several structural intentions lead to a disjointed and often lifeless text: The bickering of Achilles and Agamemnon started the *Iliad*; a detour into Hades shows them reconciled at the end of the *Odyssey*. But it is only a detour. A family man may be devoted to his wife; a real warrior must be far more concerned about his father, and so Odysseus must slip away from his reunion with Penelope to visit Laertes, who has withdrawn to the country. This final meditation on fathers and sons rehearses much of what we have seen with Achilles and Priam at the end of the *Iliad*; in both cases the son-figure rejuvenates the old man into his lost heroism. The local families, having lost older sons at Troy and younger sons in Odysseus' hall, take arms and allow Odysseus, with his heroic father and heroic son, a final glorious moment on the battlefield. But where will it all end? The gods are apparently as bored as the audience by this point, so Zeus sends a bolt from the blue to suspend a narrative that is proving itself incapable of concluding. Whatever hand was in fact responsible for this final disappointment, the compositional problems are evident: If Penelope is at the very end, then Laertes is not. If the epic at the last justifies itself as a worthy heroic sequel to the *Iliad*, it betrays the pacific Odyssean values. Having shown how twenty years of history, that is, twenty years of hardship and separation, can lead to one perfect moment between Odysseus and Penelope, the poet cannot finally abandon the momentum that that larger historical narrative has accumulated. It looks as if the narrative has such irrepressible life that it cannot be stilled; in the wake of literary triumph, the author cannot stop writing epilogues.

Should we be surprised, then, that Tolstoy, having replicated the vitality and scope of Homer's narrative so remarkably well, suffers the same inability to decide on the final moment? The first ending of *War and Peace*, like that of the *Odyssey*, presents the single perfect moment of a reunion that is all the richer for the years of postponement and trial. Natasha and Pierre, like Penelope and Odysseus, have had to suffer and grow to deserve this moment, and the author will not risk its perfection by lingering on it. The reader will sigh, turn out the light, go to sleep, and, awaking the next morning, remember that Natasha and Pierre are themselves so convincingly flesh and blood that they, too, will wake up the next day. To be sure, Andrei's life could be resolved in such a moment of romantic epiphany, but Natasha and Pierre are capable lovers because they inhabit the real world. Nor is Tolstoy's larger and absolutely vivid historical canvas so easily forgotten. Epilogue One satisfies our curiosity as far as 1820, thus continuing and concluding the less intimate mode of the narrative that has been family and historical chronicle. Again the shift from romance to heroism directs attention from men and women to fathers and sons. This epilogue, like the final books in both the *Iliad* and the *Odyssey*, focuses finally on the connection between heroic generations. The young Nicholas learns his heroism, rather impractically, from Plutarch here at the end of the tale just as it was Caesar's *Commentaries* that first came to hand in his father's library at the start of the book. It is doubly appropriate to use these classical texts here to effect the classical compositional device of *Ringkomposition*. Young Nicholas has been visited in sleep by a dream of his father; so Achilles by Patroclus, Aeneas by his wife and later by the shade of his father in Hades. Nicholas still represents the possibility of reconciliation of modes by being born of Andrei, but taken with nothing as much as with Uncle Pierre. Where his father apparently contemplated the idea of Caesar (as of Napoleon — both involving war with the French, one might note) as conqueror, Nicholas is taken rather by figures of heroic self-sacrifice, like Scaevola.[31] Yet in the midst of Pierre's and Natasha's, Mary's and Nicholas', bland happiness and their children, who are rather faceless compared to Nicholenka, Andrei's son seems to suggest the reassertion of Andrei's principles and thereby the possibility of continuing the oscillation of heroic modes. To the extent that Andrei dominated the start of *War and Peace*, this reassertion of his values structurally binds the end (like the end of the *Odyssey*) to the earliest phase of the narrative cycle.

By a final step toward generality, Epilogue Two tries to integrate the sprawling diversity of what precedes by the voice of the philosopher of history.[32] This voice, too, strongly recalls Andrei. To the extent that Andrei

---

[31] Therein lurks one of Tolstoy's childhood memories as he reported them to his biographer Birukov. His favorite "Aunt" Tatyana Alexandrovna Yergolskaya had herself as a girl imitated Scaevola's courageous act in burning himself. See Finch, 205.

[32] Cf. Ralph Matlaw's speculation that Tolstoy composed the second epilogue in 1886 from material originally located in the main body of the text "because he wanted the final impression to be didactic rather than novelistic, or to impose some final generalization in his massive work, a generalization that would raise the ending to a more universal meaning" (Ralph Matlaw, "Mechanical Structure and Inner Form: A Note on *War and Peace* and *Doctor Zhivago*," *Symposium* 17 (1962): 291; rpt. in Tolstoy, ed. Gibian, 1420).

expressed Tolstoy's own speculative and restless side (as Pierre does the physical and affective), his death leaves the author without a spokesman. It is as Andrei fades from the scene that the disquisitions on the meaning of history emerge into the text as a counterpoint to characters like Pierre who are living it moment by moment. Andrei's death, at the end of Book XII, is sandwiched between the final emergence of the two voices in the novel (Pierre's and the narrator's) which may be said to be heir to his own. For Andrei's final epiphany and death come in the midst of Pierre's spiritual rebirth presided over by Platon. The immanence of rebirth which Platon intuits in parable ("Lay me down like a stone, O God, and raise me up like a loaf," p. 1076) anticipates the terms of Andrei's characteristically intellectualized and specious reaction to his own dream of death: "Yes, it was death! I died — and woke up. Yes, death is an awakening!" (p. 1090). The darkened room of which Andrei dreams is an unmistakable reminder of Platon's shed in the preceding scene. Platon's great spiritual strength derives to some extent from his inability to articulate his values, values which Pierre appreciates and assimilates without analyzing.[33] The narrator is left to point the moral: "His words and actions flowed from him as evenly, inevitably, and spontaneously as fragrance exhales from a flower" (p. 1079). Or, in Biblical terms: "Consider the lilies of the field...they toil not, neither do they spin" (Matt. 6.28). Andrei remembers his epiphany at Austerlitz in precisely these terms "when he came to himself after being wounded and the flower of eternal, unfettered love had instantly unfolded itself in his soul" (p. 1087). Yet the metaphor here is self-elected and applied not to the self, as Tolstoy uses it of Platon, but to an abstraction of Love. Andrei's adduction of texts on his deathbed finally reveals the extent to which his self-images follow literary models: "The fowls of the air sow not, neither do they reap, yet your Father feedeth them" (p. 1086; cf. Matt. 6.26). This insight has nothing, of course, to do with Andrei's life and everything to do with "the little falcon," Platon. Impending death has liberated Andrei into the realm of pure theory without the hindrance of a continuing life that works otherwise. Only Natasha proves distracting: Love for her, too strong to be entirely lost, somehow does not mesh with universal, impersonal

---

[33] Tolstoy will repeat this situation at the end of *Anna Karenina* (Part VIII, Chs. xi and xii) when, through the tutelage of a peasant named Platon, Levin comes to identify reason as a stumbling block to truth.

Love. The details do not fit. The rhythmic clicking of her knitting needles is comforting just as Platon's regular snoring is for Pierre. But where Pierre will let that humble sound embody a sense of order for the moment, Andrei is soothed but unenlightened by the clicking and staunchly looks within for his vision of an Ordering Principle. But at least the theory has finally consolidated itself for Andrei. His final service to the reader in supplying the explanatory texts for a reality being lived by the prisoners in the preceding chapter makes him finally and purely the Word of which Platon is the Flesh, the prophet of a truth increasingly to be incarnated in Pierre.

Now, for Pierre the loss of Andrei as spiritual advisor is a great liberation. The philosophizing voice does not vanish from the text, however, but is instead institutionalized, starting with the next chapter, where the Historian makes his first full affirmation of the Andreian vision of true causes perceptible only with the abandonment of self: "The discovery of these laws (sc. directing events) is only possible when we have quite abandoned the attempt to find the cause in the will of just one man, just as the discovery of the laws of the motion of the planets was possible only when man abandoned the conception of the fixity of the earth" (p. 1096). As the earth is no longer the center of the universe, neither should the individual be. The reader may recoil at the analogies drawn between mechanics and morals, but they could not be more Andreian, for he, too, similarly deduced spiritual destiny from atomic theory: "To die means that I, a particle of love, shall return to the general and eternal source" (p. 1089). In transforming Andrei finally into pure theory, Tolstoy discredits him as a character, perhaps, and distances him from our sympathy, but thereby brings him all the closer to himself as author. Andrei's heroic immolation in renouncing life to become pure text unmistakably replicates on another level the author's own creative process and openly acknowledges the contradictoriness of writing books to affirm the virtues of living life without them. Andrei's final epiphany, surely not lost on the hand that wrote it, is that the ultimate virtue of insight is to establish its own futility: "Is it possible that the truth of life has been revealed to me only to show me that I have spent my life in falsity?" (p. 1089). Tolstoy knows perfectly well that people who face the end saying things like this have almost always been saying them all along: Andrei's vision of futility was complete already at Austerlitz. One wonders, then, if the young Tolstoy who so acutely diagnosed the syndrome did not anticipate that he would spend his latter decades as one of this desolate tribe. It is only at the start of Book

XIII, immediately after Andrei's death and Pierre's rebirth, that Tolstoy's theoretical panoply — deterministic historiography, Newtonian mechanics, desacralized Christian ethics — is fully revealed: the astronomical analogy here first adduced will also end Epilogue Two. And just as the *Odyssey*, after working us away from the Achillean values for many books leaves us by an odd turn uncomfortably stranded at the end in Iliadic territory, out on a battlefield, so in *War and Peace* the progress from Andrei to Pierre turns in this second epilogue to a final reassertion of the Andreian side of Tolstoy himself, who, like Andrei, was to be cured of philosophizing only by death. With every successive ending, the Andreian mode creeps back more and more into the text to the point that many readers have the uneasy sense that Tolstoy himself has caught the diseases of which he has cured Russia as reborn in 1812. In any case, these three successive endings in *War and Peace* allow the reader the choice of seeing the work end as novel, as chronicle, or as tract, but prevent him from reading the work as any one of these forms to the exclusion of the others. If the reader, having entrusted his sympathies to the narrative, feels betrayed, distanced, and compelled to decisions when he might prefer merely to carry away a feeling, his reaction may come close to that of the spectator of Brecht's epic theater, who "steht gegenüber, studiert."[34] Indeed, ruptured closure may be the only narrative means for Tolstoy, as for Brecht, to maintain "der Mensch als Prozess," not "als Fixum." In any case, the door is also left open for *Anna Karenina*, even as the fumbled ending of the *Odyssey* accommodated further tales, both the lost Telegony and Kazantzakis' modern sequel. A proper epic must allow the cycle to continue.

Tolstoy's didacticism per se does not disqualify the work as epic, but rather certifies it as that "tribal encyclopedia"[35] which the Greeks held Homer to be, the canon of traditional culture, just as the Bible and the *Aeneid* (allegorized into a Christian text) were for later Europeans. The epic has never rivaled the novel's capacity to observe precisely *how* lives get lived because of its larger burden of explaining ultimately why. Where novelistic action transpires against a background of implied causality,

---

[34] Bertolt Brecht, "Anmerkungen" to "Aufstieg und Fall der Stadt Mahagonny," in *Stücke*, vol. 3 (Berlin: Suhrkamp Verlag, 1955), 267.

[35] See especially Eric A. Havelock, "The Homeric Encyclopedia," in *Preface to Plato* (New York: Grosset & Dunlap, 1967), 61-86.

epics proudly reveal the workings of their divine "Machinery" (Pope): Olympus, a still meddlesome Creator, or (in lighter moments) Sylphs, Gnomes, and Salamanders. Tolstoy at the beginning of *War and Peace* reverts to the simplest format of dramatizing such causality: action on two tiers.[36] Tolstoy's noblemen, like Homer's kings, look up to a plane of beings very like themselves (the all-too human gods; soi-disant Olympians like Napoleon and the Czar), presumed to be in charge. Both narratives open with gatherings (assembly and soirée) in which the protagonists begin to deal with the aggressions of their betters (Apollo and Napoleon); both assemblies rely on the information of mediators to these higher councils (the priest Calchas; Anna Scherer, maid of honor of the Empress) and both quell internal disputes by the sheer verbiage of peacemakers more wordy than wise (Nestor, Prince Hippolyte). Though the Olympians begin the *Iliad* grandly in charge, the magnificent self-destructiveness of mortals makes divine malice increasingly redundant. By the end the gods have devolved to squabbling among themselves and taking pratfalls, while men advance to the tragic stature denied to Olympus' eternal children. Tolstoy is even more intent on debunking the infallibility of titans like Napoleon, as well as his impact, and by the end has taken the further step of removing the upper tier from causation, from the esteem of the heroes, and indeed entirely from the narrative, to be replaced by his clockwork universe. But the final reversion to cosmology in the historiographical disquisitions is itself an aspect of epos as old as Homer (e.g., the Hesiodic school), often nearly as expansive (Aratus, Lucretius), and lately as prone to lecturing as Tolstoy here shows himself: Beatrice, Bernard, Michael.

In the larger epic tradition, nothing establishes Tolstoy's credentials more persuasively than this failure to end as vigorously as he has usually narrated. With suspicious frequency the epic writers who most successfully distill the meaning of human history into a riveting particularity show the greatest tendency to trail off finally into a generality that leaves their readers behind. All but the most devoted English readers of the *Divine Comedy* tend to know that the end of *Paradiso* is sublime largely because Mr. Eliot says it is. Sensibilities transformed by Milton's garden and his hell have

---

[36] On the development of this narrative format between Homer and Milton, see Thomas Greene, *The Descent from Heaven* (New Haven and London: Yale University Press, 1963).

trouble staying awake through the final two books of historical catalogue. Yet *Paradise Lost* at its best has the virtues of drama, and it was to this mode that Milton, perhaps himself unconvinced by the narrative inconclusiveness surrounding his epic's doctrinal closure, reverted in *Paradise Regained*.

In many of these failed conclusions, one notes the indestructability of the Achillean-Satanic hero. These firebrands, aloof and self-destructive, all exist to be deflated, made obsolete, and replaced. Yet after we move on to the new heroism — from Achilles to Odysseus, from the Trojan Aeneas to the Roman, from Dante necromantic student of Virgil to Dante the lover of Beatrice, from pagan Satan to Puritan Christ, from Andrei to Pierre — the old heroism tends never to be quite as dead or as boring as the author's piety and pacificism would have it be. Tolstoy's own final reversion to his own more Andreian side must remind us of the pagans, Homer and Virgil, who lapsed in that more vivid direction at the end of the *Odyssey* and the *Aeneid*, as well as Dante and Milton, who seem to have averted such lapses into Satanic territory at the cost of ending on a high, hollow note. However the axis is drawn — war and peace, damnation and salvation, solipsism and community — the larger drift of the texts toward edification and redemption never quite manages to carry most readers with it. Tolstoy is only the latest to discover that having first described an earlier more fallen, more colorful world — a world (like Virgil's Troy and Carthage, Dante's Inferno, Milton's lively Hell and lapsing Paradise) still open to the incursions of older and rawer forms of heroism, the author cannot at will shepherd the reader into the happier and duller vision of his conclusion.

Tolstoy is distinctive perhaps only in that in ending *War and Peace* he numbs and disappoints the reader twice and quite contradictorily. Though concluding the same text, the first and second epilogues are no more intrinsically unified by that common function than are Helene and Natasha by being married to the same man. The happy participants in the "real life" of Epilogue One stand in no need of the edification of Epilogue Two. There the historian is called to the objectivity of astronomers, who have learned to discount the sensation of fixity that their planet gives them (p. 1351); but, as we have seen, for Pierre life becomes possible when he throws away his telescope. Andrei, who in having both ideas and offspring had represented the possibility of joining the theoretical and participatory modes, has disappeared from the text, and the deep chasm between the two epilogues forebodes the latter half of Tolstoy's own life, to be spent in an awkward attempt to live Epilogue One while restricting his writing to the didacticism of Epilogue Two (*The Kingdom of God is Within You*, *My Religion*, *The Gospels*). In retrospect it comes to seem that the narrative forms in which Tolstoy in his later and more pious phases indulged himself only covertly and abashedly (as with *Hadji Murat*) had served him well by that very treacherousness, turning single tales double, which gave both *War and Peace* and *Anna Karenina* a life of their own as they were being written. Tolstoy's later disciplined fixation on the single hero, at once Christ and Everyman, kept unexpected guests like Pierre and Levin from arriving and stealing the show. Yet at that point literary form ceased to serve the vigorous contradictoriness of Tolstoy's own sensibility, and he ceased to be heir to the mysterious capacity of the epic canvas to be not only the largest but, at its best, the liveliest of literary forms and the hardest to bring to an end. It was no more possible in Tolstoy's day than it had been in Homer's to reduce life seen on the largest manageable scale to either a tragic or a comic perspective, to let either private meaning or historical achievements overshadow all else. It is the form par excellence for minds too big to be made up — at once the most presumptuous of literary acts and the humblest. For epic is not a genre in the way that tragedy or romance are genres — traditions of separate and similar works — but has been since well before the *Iliad* a cycle of tales taking up one from another, of old forms of heroism flourishing a last time as they are being supplanted by something less imposing and more resilient: Odysseus in place of Achilles, Beatrice instead of Virgil, Christ instead of Satan, Pierre in place of Andrei, then Levin in place of either. The price of entering *la bella scuola* of epic writers is to submit to the inherited terms of the cycle and to accept that it will be continued by someone other than oneself. The experience of having outlived one's service in this company is apparently not a happy one. One thinks of Milton in his last years and of Tolstoy reflecting on *Anna Karenina* (and doubtless on *War and Peace* no less): "I assure you that this abomination does not exist for me and that I am only vexed that there should be people who have need of it."[37] Those people would turn out to include Sholokhov and Pasternak, who would continue the cycle which Tolstoy had imported to the Russian landscape.

---

[37] Letter of May 1, 1881, to V. V. Strakhov, quoted in Gusev, p. 535.

5. *Doctor Zhivago*
and the Tradition of National Epic

In 1927 Boris Pasternak wrote, "I consider that the epic is what our time inspires, and accordingly in the book *Nineteen Five*, I move across from lyrical thinking to epic, though this is very difficult. Subsequently I mean to work at prose."[1] In the two decades since the sensational publication of *Doctor Zhivago* in the West, readers and critics have been most uncertain about how Pasternak's masterpiece is to be read as a work of prose: how much did he finally abandon "lyrical thinking"? Clearly the work is heir to the nineteenth-century Russian novel, in particular to the religious and philosophical preoccupations of Tolstoy and Dostoevsky. The ineffectual Yuri Zhivago perpetuates the type of superfluous man so familiar from *Eugene Onegin*, *A Hero of Our Time*, *Rudin*, and *Oblomov*. But the language of *Doctor Zhivago*, its diction and imagery, clearly come from the pen of a poet, a man who had heretofore published mostly verse. Perhaps, as one critic suggests, we have a "poem in prose,"[2] a phenomenon familiar enough in Russia, where novels have a long tradition of trying to become something else. Pushkin wrote *Eugene Onegin* in iambic tetrameter and subtitled it a "novel in verse"; Gogol wrote *Dead Souls* in prose and called it a poem. Lermontov's *A Hero of Our Time* is actually a cycle of five stories with a common hero, while Turgenev distinguished his short novels from his long short stories only on the basis of theme.[3] And in telling the great tale of the Russian nation, Tolstoy's major rivalry is often not with the novelists at all, but with Homer. The faithless Helene Kuragin is not just an emigree from a French novel, but clearly and distinctly the avatar of her namesake, Helen of Troy.[4]

---

[1] Boris Pasternak, *Sochinenija* (Ann Arbor, Mich.: University of Michigan Press, 1961), III, 215-16; the translation is our own.

[2] Alexander Gerschenkron, "Notes on *Doctor Zhivago*," *Modern Philology* 58 (1961), 196.

[3] Turgenev originally called only *Virgin Soil* (1876) a novel. In his letters he refers to the six works that he ultimately categorized as novels (*Rudin, On the Eve, A Nest of Gentlefolk, Fathers and Sons, Smoke, Virgin Soil*) as "long tales."

[4] One recalls Tolstoy's remark to Maxim Gorky that "without false modesty, *War*

Tolstoy is very much on Pasternak's mind in *Doctor Zhivago*, especially, as Poggioli notes, in the book's epilogue.[5] It has been charged that the novel lacks Tolstoy's "epic sweep";[6] yet the book covers more years than *War and Peace*, a larger and incomparably more horrible war, and a more significant turning point in the life of the nation. Already in 1927, as we have seen, prose and epic seemed to be a common destination for Pasternak. What then of the possibility that he means *Doctor Zhivago* to be read not just with *War and Peace* but, like Tolstoy's own heroic canvas, beside the epics of other nations as well?

Writers of epic, we recall, have clear and efficient ways of attaching their works to the tradition as it stretches forward from Homer. Virgil's *Aeneid*, as every schoolboy once knew, begins with a proper obeisance to both Homeric epics: *arma virumque cano*: "Arms (*Iliad*) and the man (*Odyssey*) I sing." So it is that from the opening of Dante's *Divine Comedy* comes Zhivago's sense at the crisis of his middle years of standing in "the dark forest of his life" (p. 444).[7] Much earlier in Moscow, during his nearly fatal bout with typhus, Yuri had revealed his ambition to depict in poetry the three days of Christ in Hell. His unconsciousness had allowed him to participate in that passage through death, even as Dante had envisioned himself doing in the *Inferno*. Pasternak's allusion is not just symbolist posturing, for it reinforces our sense of the scope of the symbolic reference: Zhivago's spiritual pilgrimage, his own imitation of Christ as it develops throughout the whole of the work, reflects as broadly on all mankind as

---

and Peace is like the *Iliad*." Maxim Gorky, *Reminiscences of Tolstoy, Chekhov and Andreev*, trans. Katherine Mansfield, S.S. Kotelianky and Leonard Wolf (London: Hogarth Press, 1948), p. 57. For a brief discussion of Tolstoy's relationship to Homer, see Chauncey E. Finch, "Tolstoy as a Student of the Classics," *The Classical Journal*, 47 (1952): 205-10; R. F. Christian, *Tolstoy's* War and Peace: *A Study* (Oxford, Clarendon Press, 1962); and George Steiner, *Tolstoy or Dostoevsky* (London: Faber and Faber, 1960).

[5] Renato Poggioli, *The Poets of Russia* (Cambridge, Mass.: Harvard University Press, 1960), p. 332. Poggioli extended his discussion of the novel in "Boris Pasternak," *Partisan Review* 25 (1958): 541-54.

[6] Vladimir Markov, "Notes on Pasternak's *Doctor Zhivago*," *Russian Review* 18 (1959): 18.

[7] Translations and page references to *Doctor Zhivago* are from the Pantheon edition (New York, 1958), prose translated by Max Hayward and Manya Harari, poems by Bernard Guerney.

Dante's had. Christian typologies will become inescapable by the end of the work, when Yuri and Lara come to figure Adam and Eve in their troubled idyll in Varykino, as well as Christ and Magdalene in the concluding cycle of Yuri's poems.[8] But early in the story Pasternak, by evoking the model of the *Divine Comedy*, gives the reader terms with which to interpret the level of spiritual allegory in the work.

A yet older legacy from the tradition of epic is present in the revenge theme through which such sagas are regularly resolved. Achilles' companion Patroclus, a gentle soul, after his one day of glory on the battlefield, dies at the hands of Hector in what may be for the reader the single most painful scene in the epic. What follows is Achilles' vengeance. Virgil heightens the pathos of this theme by making the victim a mere boy, Pallas, who likewise has his single day of battle and dies. For this his murderer, Turnus, will be killed by Aeneas when he might better have been spared. From Pallas we find the boy-warrior Petya Rostov in *War and Peace*, whose relationship with Pierre Bezukhov is very much like that of Pallas and Aeneas. Again the boy dies pathetically in his first taste of battle. Finally, Pasternak creates his own version of this figure as Zhivago's and Lara's lost daughter tells the concluding tale of savagery in the book, the strangling of a crippled boy, again called Petya, the last and in some ways the most pathetic victim of the tale. This is a curious moment in the work, when the writer has almost exhausted his tale, and we are at the furthest margins of Zhivago's biography, in a backwater of history. But suddenly tradition shows through, so that *Doctor Zhivago* ends its action precisely as does the Aeneid and no less disconcertingly, with the revenge for the boy and a particularly grisly murder. Where Aeneas had slaughtered the unarmed Turnus, Petya's murderer is lashed to the rails and run over by a train. Thereby the deepening chaos of history comes to stand in piquant counterpoint to the constancy and continuity of the literary tradition. In epic, more than in any other genre, the chains of transmission are strong and unbroken. Not a few of them lead to *Doctor Zhivago*.[9]

---

[8] Typological interpretation is demonstrated later on by Sima Tuntseva in explaining the correspondence of the miraculous crossing of the Red Sea to the Virgin Birth (p. 412).

[9] For comparable themes recurrent in the epic tradition, see for example Thomas Greene, *The Descent from Heaven: A Study in Epic Continuity* (New Haven and London: Yale

The single book of which we are most often reminded in the narrative and especially in the cycle of poems that ends the work is, of course, the Bible, in particular Genesis and the Gospels. Pasternak inherits from Dante and other Christian poets the double time sense, the steady cross-referencing of the current moment to the life of Christ. The same device had been used in Russia for political commentary by Mikhail Bulgakov in his brilliant satirical novel, *The Master and Margarita* (1940), which periodically shifts the action from Russia to Jerusalem under Roman hegemony. The interweaving of the main plot line with the story of Christ's persecution by Pontius Pilate suggests an analogy to Stalinist destruction of individual dignity which could never be openly articulated. Pasternak, no less concerned with making a response to the political order, similarly evokes the age of Christ with a strong reminder that it is equally the age of Caesar. Indeed the first political pronouncement in the book, from Yuri's adored uncle, Nikolai Nikolaievich, centers on Rome: "There was no history in [the spiritual] sense among the ancients. They had blood and beastliness and cruelty and pockmarked Caligulas who do not suspect how untalented every enslaver is. They had the boastful dead eternity of bronze monuments and marble columns. It was not until after the coming of Christ that time and man could breathe freely. It was not until after Him that men began to live toward the future" (p. 10). An informed reader, as Vladimir Markov has observed,[10] would not miss the image of Stalin, nowhere mentioned in the work, lurking behind the pockmarked tyrant Caligula. The optimism of this statement, of course, will be betrayed by the narrative to follow, as Pasternak hints with increasing clarity that "this holy city" of Moscow (p. 519) has truly and regrettably fulfilled her centuries-old boast to be the third Rome. She is not Rome in the religious sense of a final and flourishing bastion of pure, uncorrupted Orthodox Christianity, as the sixteenth-century prophecy had suggested. Rather, she is Rome, the vast imperial state founded on absolute centralized authority and internal ideological conformity. By the time Pasternak wrote, Russia herself had conquered nations, and Pasternak does not overlook the lesson that empire

University Press, 1963), and A. Bartlett Giamatti, *The Earthly Paradise and the Renaissance Epic* (Princeton N.J.: Princeton University Press, 1966). See also C. M. Bowra, *From Virgil to Milton* (London: Macmillan and Co., 1945).

[10] Markov, p. 22.

had left Rome a "flea market of borrowed gods and conquered peoples" (p. 43). Similarly, Lara observes that it was an access of "the ancient Roman virtue" (p. 299) that transformed her gentle Antipov, the teacher of classics and mathematics, into the demonic Strelnikov. *Doctor Zhivago* ends with Misha Gordon's direct confirmation that the sins of the new imperialist Soviet order renew those of ancient Rome: "It has often happened in history that a lofty ideal has degenerated into crude materialism. Thus Greece gave way to Rome, and the Russian Enlightenment has become the Russian Revolution" (p. 518).

Pasternak, then, fixes his gaze steadily on Rome, both in religious and political contexts. Yuri even finds his inspiration, Lara — and with her the ability to set down the poetry so long latent in him — across from the House of the Sculptures, a monument of an earlier age decorated with the classical Muses. The question presents itself whether Pasternak in chronicling the revolution could have overlooked the poet of the new Augustan order — Virgil, who was long credited with foreknowledge of the coming of Christ as well.[11] Of poets, Virgil alone had the status among Christians of a prophet, the man whose poetic vision escaped the confines of paganism both in the Fourth or Messianic Eclogue and in an epic that can be read as an allegory of the soul's progress. In the *Inferno* Dante had canonized Virgil as the great representative of the religious, political, and literary legacy of Rome. At least until the time of Milton, the burden of the epic poet was simply to write the *Aeneid* of his own age and nation. It was Virgil who set the pattern for focusing the history of a people through the myth of a single life, precisely as Pasternak does. Virgil stands therefore at the head of a two-fold tradition, the national *and* Christian epic, a double legacy to be felt throughout *Doctor Zhivago*. He is also a man whose historical moment and career strikingly parallel Pasternak's own. Both began as poets of small and perfect poems of a pastoral cast; the love of nature is everywhere to be seen in their masterpieces as well. Both saw their worlds turned upside down by civil war and by the founding of a new and in some ways inhuman order. Yet both managed to survive in that order where others did not. And as the two writers approached their monumental final statements, both turned away from "modern" movements, the *poetae novi* and the symbolists

---

[11] See, for instance, Domenico Comparetti, *Vergil in the Middle Ages*, trans. E. F. M. Benecke (New York: Macmillan and Co., 1896).

respectively, reaching further and further back in time for their models — Virgil to Homer, Pasternak to the epics and the Bible.

Does *Doctor Zhivago*, then, represent Pasternak's attempt to distill the experience of Russia in the way that Virgil had memorialized Rome in the *Aeneid*? As we have seen, the endings of the two works are very similar. Both begin with their heroes desolate in the midst of a storm and return to that image to mark the crises of the stories. Their central and most memorable images are also remarkably similar, for Pasternak associates his work with the *Aeneid* by taking from its centerpiece, that is, from Aeneas' descent into the Underworld in Book VI, the pattern and imagery of Zhivago's own spiritual death and rebirth in Chapter xii, "The Rowan Tree" (in the original, "Rowanberries in Sugar"). This chapter marks Zhivago's liberation literally from Liberius and the partisan Forest Brotherhood, and more broadly from a current in history that conspires to silence and destroy him. Henry Gifford's formulation that "Liberius, in his confidence that the future can be easily moulded to design, represents the dead opposite of talent"[12] is especially appropriate, for Zhivago's escape from these hostile forces signals the imminent birth of his creative energy, the inevitable fulfillment of his calling as a poet. It is precisely at this point in the work that the hero will be able to return to Lara, and through her finally to write down the poetry which has long been germinating inside him. It is in this brief interlude and supreme moment of personal freedom that Zhivago, we feel, can become himself for once, can finally, recalling Lara's similar purpose in life, "grasp the meaning of [earth's] wild enchantment and call each thing by its right name" (p. 75).

Zhivago consecrates his moment of escape by a pledge to the rowan tree: "The footpath brought the doctor to the foot of the tree, whose name he had just spoken. It was half in snow, half in frozen leaves and berries, and it held out two white branches toward him. He remembered Lara's strong white arms and seized the branches toward him. As if in answer, the tree shook snow all over him. He muttered without realizing what he was saying, and completely beside himself: 'I'll find you, my beauty, my love, my own flesh and blood'" (p. 375). Many of the work's dominant images converge here. The sacramental quality of the scene is realized primarily in Christian

---

[12] Henry Gifford, *Pasternak: A Critical Study* (Cambridge: Cambridge University Press, 1977), p. 192.

terms, as is customary for Pasternak. Zhivago passes the sentry by voicing his intent to eat the berries, an image of the Eucharist drawn out by their blood-red color against the white snow, as the chapter title emphasizes. Zhivago symbolizes his emotion in an image of transubstantiation, speaking of Lara as his "flesh and blood," as Christ had with the bread and wine. The outstretched arms of the tree are the image of the cross, so familiar in this work. We are further reminded of Christ's sacrifice when, at Strelnikov's suicide in the snow, the drops of blood are compared to rowanberries. It had initially been Zhivago who was contemplating suicide; Strelnikov in dying comes to bear this burden for him. The falling snow may also represent baptism.

But, as everywhere in Pasternak's pantheistic landscape, there also lurks an element of pagan mythology in Zhivago's private ceremony, about which the reader may inform himself in Sir James Frazer's *The Golden Bough*, indeed in its title chapter.[13] For the rowan tree, bearing its bright fruit in the dead of winter and thus symbolizing regeneration, is, as Pasternak emphasizes (pp. 352-53), a parallel to the mistletoe, to which Virgil links his image of the golden bough, perhaps the most famous in the epic. By this bough, which enables Aeneas to penetrate into the underworld, Virgil's hero gains a unique measure of freedom, in many ways not unlike that of Yuri Zhivago. In a life entirely directed from above, dictated by Roman destiny, Aeneas' trip into the underworld is the moment when volition and duty coincide most closely. The questions he asks of the dead are the last signs of personal curiosity we see in him. Indeed, the oracle cautions against the venture. We have, then, a rare example of Aeneas' pursuit of private desires against official advice. For Yuri, too, the rowan tree initiates a period of release, a momentary intermission — to recall the image of his poem "Hamlet" — between the acts of the drama which is history.[14] Not

---

[13] Sir James Frazer, *Balder the Beautiful* in *The Golden Bough*, vol. 11 (London: Macmillan and Co., 1914), p. 281 f.

[14] For Pasternak's most explicit statement regarding Yuri's direction from above, see Chapter xiv, "Return to Varykino," Part 8: "At such moments Yuri Andreievich felt that the main part of the work was being done not by him but by a superior power which was above him and directed him, namely the movement of universal thought and poetry in its present historical stage and the one to come. And he felt himself to be only the occasion, the fulcrum needed to make this movement possible" (p. 437). Of course, as in Aeneas's case, Yuri's "divine guidance" in no way removes him from his age, but rather places him in the very center of its major historical and philosophical issues.

coincidentally, just as it is a sibyl who directs Aeneas to the golden bough, so in Pasternak it is the witch Kubarikha who prophesies the rowan tree. Both the sibyl and the witch have baleful prophecies of a more general sort, all of which will be fulfilled. Most strikingly, Kubarikha not only claims the power to cast a spell even on such as Strelnikov, but says, "I will stick a knife into such a pillar of snow, right up to the hilt, and when I take it out of the snow, it will be red with blood" — a clear foreshadowing of the blood on the snow that marks his death, the "rowanberries in sugar."[15] And as the rowan tree is bound up in Zhivago's mind with the memory of Lara and the image of home, so Aeneas is led to the golden bough by the doves of his mother, Venus.[16]

In broader structural terms, Zhivago's meeting with the rowan tree is as much a watershed in the book as is Aeneas' discovery of the golden

[15] That Pasternak did in fact consult Frazer is suggested by the constellation of rowan trees, cattle, hares, and witches within a single page of *Doctor Zhivago* (p. 363) and a single page of *The Golden Bough* (Frazer, vol. 2, 53). Frazer notes a Scottish custom of using rowan trees to protect cattle against witches; cattle in *Zhivago* are the specialty of the witch Kubarikha, who wears "a pea-green Royal Scots Fusiliers overcoat" (p. 352). Frazer mentions in passing the comparable Irish custom of killing hares among the cattle on May Day in the belief that they are old women trying to steal the butter; it is a hare who speaks to the rowan tree in Kubarikha's mysterious chant, possibly "an old Russian song," possibly improvisation. There is a suggestion that the song is a spell binding Zhivago to the camp, for the hare sings as a "poor soldier, kept in foreign parts" longing for "my grieving love, my bride" exactly as is Zhivago. The last lines — "I'll break from durance bitter, / I'll go to my red berry, to my lovely bride" — directly presage Zhivago's escape, at which point he too will identify the rowan tree with his love. If, then, Zhivago's confinement has resulted from Kubarikha's malign influence, the rowan tree which brings his escape is simply revealing its fabled powers as a protection against witchcraft.

[16] On the symbolism of the golden bough, see especially R. A. Brooks, "*Discolor Aura*: Reflections on the Golden Bough," *American Journal of Philology*, 74 (1953): 260-80. On the golden bough as a symbol of the timeless potency of art, compare W. B. Yeats's lines in "Byzantium":

> Miracle, bird or golden handiwork,
> More miracle than bird or handiwork,
> Planted on the star-lit golden bough,
> Can like the cocks of Hades crow,
> Or, by the moon embittered, scorn aloud
> In glory of changeless metal
> Common bird or petal
> And all complexities of mire or blood.
> (lines 17-24)

Quoted from W.B. Yeats, *The Variorum Edition of the Poems of W. B. Yeats*, ed. Peter Allt and Russell K. Alspach (New York: Macmillan, 1957), pp. 497-98.

bough and his subsequent trip to the underworld. To this point, Aeneas has faltered in his progress largely because of a gaze cast steadily backward. As he confesses to the angry Dido in Book IV, his fondest hopes still direct themselves to what might have been. And looking always to his father, to the past, to Troy, he has proved very uncertain as a leader. But his final pilgrimage to the dead Anchises proves a radical turning point, for his father directs him to a vision of the Roman future, a great historical pageant. And from that point, Aeneas' gaze is steadfastly forward, even if Virgil cannot quite ignore the dangers of this blinkered vision.

It is not from the past that Zhivago escapes through the enchanted grove, as had Aeneas, but from the burden of the future. He has tried, with diminishing success, to integrate himself into history, to go forward with it. But the more he accepts his mission as poet, the more he realizes that the times are against him: "He reflected again that he conceived of history, of what is called the course of history, not in the accepted way but by analogy with the vegetable kingdom" (p. 453) — a heresy in the Marxist worship of progress. Yuri had at first looked joyfully and confidently to the rebirth of Russia, whether it was to result from the revolution which "had been understood by the students, followers of Blok, in 1905" (p. 160) or from the abdication of the Czar in February 1917. But with the Bolsheviks' seizure of power, his historical perspective changes radically, and he finds liberation only from within the past. It is only after fleeing the Forest Brotherhood that Zhivago escapes Nikolai Nikolaievich's naïve hope to "live toward the future"; only now does he begin to live toward the past. He finds Lara and with her a view of the old neoclassical House of the Sculptures. Its bottom story is defaced by party circulars which day by day strip men of their freedom and divest language of its meaning; but above it there still remains a vision of the last century — an age perhaps decadent, like the rich merchant who built this theater as a monument to the Muses, but nonetheless brilliant, indeed unrivaled, in literature.

For Zhivago to create, to call things by their right names, he must literally depart from history, leaving Yuriatin for the Mikulitsyns' inaccessible house. For Pasternak, no less than for Virgil, to move through space is to move through time as well. Yuri's train ride to the Urals with Tonia takes him back in time, layer by layer uncovering rich new literary resources. In Moscow one reads Blok and the symbolists. But in Yuriatin one has time for other times and other nations: Tolstoy, Pushkin, Stendhal, Dickens, Kleist.

Finally, alone and snowbound, one can write oneself. Clearly the East offered from the first the promise of a liberation from time and history, just as Nikolai Nikolaievich had had to flee to the neutral territory of Switzerland to compose his reflections on Russian society. The names in the East — Bacchus, Lupus, Faustus, Liberius, Samdeviatov (from San Donato) — are but one indication of the escape from the immediate confines of the Russian destiny: "History had not caught up with this remote provincial life" (pp. 264-65). Just off the train, Yuri and Lara meet the carriage driver Bacchus — not the Bacchus whom Tonia's mother had once described, the mythic figure who had forged himself a new stomach of iron, but another man entirely. Yet the continuity of the name, not just from man to man, but down from Rome, suggests that Yuri is now in touch with a mythic realm beyond time and nationality. For of course the myths of all nations, whether of Bacchus or of the rowan tree, are essentially the same. Zhivago finally recognizes with Lara the drift of his transformation: "You and I are like Adam and Eve, the first two people on earth . . . the last remembrance of all that immeasurable greatness which has been created in the world in all the thousands of years between them and us" (p. 403). Indeed, Zhivago penetrates even further back in time, for he dismisses even Lara from his snowy Eden and conceives her in her absence as the primal, all-creating sea, the beginning of creation (p. 452). Then comes the poetry and Yuri quite literally finds his moment of creation. Pasternak's hero, like Virgil's, can come to terms with his mission only by a major reorientation of his sense of time, a change so radical that it requires a symbolic death and rebirth like that which follows from the sacraments of the rowan tree and golden bough.

As heroes, Aeneas and Zhivago disappoint readers in much the same way. Temperamentally alike, both confront a tumultuous age with a strange passivity and resist the burden of decision which descends to them. Through much of the epic, Aeneas seems almost to be expecting Hector to appear and take charge; Zhivago on the whole is most comfortable following someone else. In the *Aeneid*, the stage direction for the hero's entrance would have to be, "Enter Aeneas, fainting." Tossed at sea, he wishes only that he had died somewhat earlier. As is often noted, each small triumph of his leadership brings Aeneas closer to being the spiritless, official man. He himself, in killing the defenseless Turnus at the end of Book XII, becomes the final victim of the very barbarity, the *furor* that his life had chiefly served to combat. For all his great services to the Roman race, Aeneas' personal journey goes from helplessness to helplessness. Yuri, the poet, begins and ends in inarticulateness. Over his mother's grave he has neither the expressiveness of human speech nor that of animal cries; he simply sobs. He dies, mute and unrecognized, from the suffocation of a deteriorating streetcar. Both he and Aeneas are involved in the creation of a new historical order which they may assist, but cannot finally shape. Their moments of fulfillment are extraordinary in their passivity: Aeneas comes to see the site of the future Rome as his ship is guided up against the current by Father Tiber; Zhivago's poetry comes as naturally and inevitably as water flowing downward (p. 437). Both are consistently denied the dignity of self-immolation; both survive to lose more than they might have imagined possible.

The private affections of both men are, in the last analysis, not private at all, but symbolic of the larger rhythms of the national experience. In this, *Doctor Zhivago* ventures very far indeed from the customary concerns of the novel and comes to parallel the symbolic structure of the *Aeneid* almost step by step. Both Zhivago and Aeneas have in effect three wives who are symbolic — in much the same way — of the cultural shifts that the heroes experience. For each, the first wife represents a national identity which must be abandoned. Creusa is too much the Trojan to be transplanted to Italy. Virgil will credit males with the capacity to change; bit by bit the women are left behind. So Tonia, the aristocrat, must be forgotten in the new Russia; although Yuri could surely join his wife and family in Paris with the help of his wonder-working brother Evgraf, there can be no doubt about the emotional impossibility of return. Both wives prove surprisingly obliging in giving their men their freedom. Creusa returns in a vision to release Aeneas; Tonia writes a letter — gallant in its way, if not without recriminations.

For both heroes a brief love found midway, with an equal, proves most moving: in the *Aeneid* it is the hero's love for Dido; in *Doctor Zhivago*, Yuri's passion for Lara. It is in their own manly sphere of activities, at the Carthaginian court and in the hospital at Meliuzeievo, that the two men come to know these women. Both pairs are united from the first by common sufferings: Dido, like Aeneas, is widowed; Zhivago's life, no less than Lara's, has been devastated by Komarovsky. In each book, both lovers have already been married. Both pairs form a pseudo-family, with Dido as mother to

Aeneas' son just as Zhivago becomes father to Lara's daughter. Lara has a child by the departed Zhivago — precisely what Dido had desired from the fleeing Aeneas. Neither hero ever quite wins his beloved from her former husband. Dido's disappearance into the forest of shadows, during Aeneas' underworld visit in Book VI, "where Sychaeus, her husband of earlier days, answers her grief and gives her love for love" (line 473),[17] finds an important parallel in Lara's admission to Yuri that, if possible, she would crawl on her knees to Pasha Antipov, for "I could never hold out against the call of the past, of loyalty" (p. 403).[18]

In both works the hero's duplicitous abandonment of his love has become a major point of controversy. How could Aeneas or Zhivago be so cruel? Why must they cheat themselves of their most profound loves? On this point, the two works elucidate each other profoundly. Both Dido and Lara are symbols, though spurious ones, of the hero's mission. If Aeneas' overriding concern is the founding of a nation, Dido offers him that opportunity in her new city. Yet Carthage is not Rome, and so he must leave. Lara is for Zhivago a symbol of Russia itself, to which he feels bonds of duty and affection no less than those of Aeneas for Rome. Yet finally to follow Lara and Komarovsky in their flight to the East would entail abandoning the real Russia. Zhivago must choose instead to return to Moscow, the clear symbol of the nation and the new order. He does so with the most intense conflicts, as we can see in the *apologia* which he rehearses to Lara in the poem "Explanation":

> And yet, no matter how the night
> May chain me with its ring of longing,
> The pull of separation is still stronger
> And I have a beckoning for the clean break.
> (p. 530)

Aeneas had fought the same battle to the same effect:

> But long as he might to ease her grief,
> To speak and calm her cares, Faithful Aeneas, full of sighs,

---

[17] Translations from the *Aeneid* are our own; the edition is R. A. B. Mynors' *P. Vergilii Maronis Opera* (Oxford: Claredonianus, 1969).

[18] The imagistic linkage of storm and deception which Zhivago uses to figure seduction in "Hopbines" may itself derive from the ominous backdrop to the spurious nuptials of Aeneas and Dido as they are trapped in a cave by a thunderstorm (IV.160 ff.).

And shaken at heart by the strength of his love,
Still obeys the gods and returns to his ships.
(IV. 393-96)

Immediately before Lara's departure, the new moon shining like "an omen of separation and an image of solitude" (p. 444) recalls the simile used to introduce Aeneas' final rejection by Dido, whose wraith glimmers through the shadows of Hades like the new moon through the clouds (VI.453-54). Emotionally, Zhivago will no more awaken from that night than will Aeneas. Neither will ever love again.

Finally, after abandoning their passionate lovers, both heroes marry women who symbolize the new order, Aeneas with the Italian Lavinia and Zhivago with the proletarian Marina, each as faceless as the other. They represent the submersion of the hero's character into the security — or is it the stultification? — of the new political realities. The peculiarly Roman quality of Zhivago's final entrapment and silence is suggested in the Latin names of Marina and their daughters Capitolina and Claudia.

But the most telling characteristic of both Aeneas and Zhivago is that neither can hold his place finally as hero of the work. Once Aeneas has deciphered and accepted the instructions of the gods and Zhivago has set down his poetry, the character of each becomes inconsequential. They simply fade. When Achilles in the *Iliad* initiates his final triumph by raising the magnificently embossed shield, its figurative compression of all of human experience symbolizes his own godlike perspective, the scope of his own more-than-human personality. Aeneas carries on his shield images of the Roman future, a scene contingent on his valor, but one with no room for him. Where Achilles alone could bear to gaze on the brilliance of his shield, Aeneas looks on Vulcan's work gratefully, but without understanding what he sees. The founding of Rome, like the Russian Revolution, brought the bearers of the fine old virtues to conspire at their own obsolescence. Like Zhivago, who never comes to know the impact of his own writings and is forgetful of his own prophecies by the time they are fulfilled, Aeneas can win Italy but never really inhabit it. Both are types of Moses who, in the end, cannot enter the Promised Land. Indeed after the disabling of Turnus, the *Aeneid* takes its protagonist one short and painful step beyond his usefulness, into the rage that will undo much of what he has done.

To the Romans, Rome was an identity palpable enough to be worshiped as the goddess Roma. She is the true hero of the *Aeneid*, despite the shortcomings of her servants like Aeneas. Similarly, at the end of *Doctor Zhivago*, "Moscow now struck [Dudorov and Gordon] not as the stage of the events connected with [Zhivago] but as the main protagonist of a long story" (p. 519). The future clearly belongs to a new order, in both cases marked by cultural heterogeneity.[19] Aeneas' heir will be his half-Italian son Silvius, as Zhivago will bequeath his work and even his daughter to his half-brother Evgraf, "with the Kirghiz eyes." Just as Rome is not simply Latin, but Trojan and Greek as well, so Russia's destiny is founded upon a mixture: it is Eurasian. And it is in the nature of such historical shifts that no single hero can see them through all the way to the end. Zhivago and Aeneas do, however, show the capacity necessary if we are to have an observer of such ages: endurance. The weak, like Tonia and Creusa, are soon lost. And the old-style heroes who make a strenuous commitment to the moment — Hector, Turnus, Strelnikov — are the first to go. Finally only the city endures. Zhivago's own articles and poems had turned to this theme before ceasing altogether (p. 488).

Where the city displaces the individual as the focus of attention, we may well wonder what role remains for the artist in these brave new worlds. Zhivago clearly and Aeneas more subtly have from the first figured the experience and outlook of their creators; both heroes are equally impeded by an excess of sensitivity. As they gradually lose our sympathy in succumbing to the new order, they pose the question of Pasternak's and Virgil's own relationship to society. Virgil's underworld, like Dante's, is filled with poets — but there are none in Aeneas' vision of the Roman future in Book VI. Aeneas takes none on his ship, finds none in Italy. The Italians are more vigorous than the Carthaginians because their art is for the most part rude and sacramental. They do not beguile their evenings with poetry. Father Anchises' famous charge to his son in the underworld may be read for its omissions (VI. 847 ff.): Other nations will produce better sculptors, orators, and astronomers. "But you, Roman, remember to rule the nations with your power — these will be your arts — to enforce the law of peace, to spare the conquered and tame the proud." And poets? At best they do not

---

[19] In this respect both works stand in sharp contrast to their immediate predecessors: one to the Homeric suspicions about the Oriental tinge to Trojan society and the other to Tolstoy's abhorrence of Francophilia and the French. On the theme of cultural heterogeneity in Pasternak's work, see R. E. Steussy, "The Myth Behind *Doctor Zhivago*," *Russian Review* 19 (1959): 184-89.

figure very largely in this destiny. One has the sense of the poet becoming the superfluous man, as Pasternak later describes him.

In these discouraging circumstances, writers can be put into conflict even with their revered predecessors, whose very brilliance can stand as a reproach to the spokesmen of such later and less-favored ages. By functioning within a great tradition, Virgil and Pasternak risk devastatingly unfavorable comparisons — with Homer and Tolstoy respectively. There must therefore also be a breaking away, an assertion of freedom in the very act of imitation — but the epic tradition richly provides the means for this too.

We may take again as examples the golden bough and the rowan tree. Book VI of the *Aeneid*, the descent to the underworld, is perhaps the most closely and consistently Homeric book of the epic, deriving step-by-step from Odysseus' descent in Book XI of the *Odyssey*. Yet its introductory and dominant symbol, the golden bough, had not before figured in poetry[20] — a rare move for Virgil. Odysseus had gained his vision of the underworld simply by slaughtering sheep for blood to vivify the strengthless dead. But in place of this raw physicality, Virgil offers a delicate image of artificiality against the backdrop of nature, of golden foil glimmering in the darkness of the forest. Homer had been the founder, the great original. And that Virgil cannot claim to be. As Anchises will shortly remind us, to be such is not Roman. Yet who can deny the fascination of this uncanny bough, so like art itself, glimmering gold against the dim forest — life out of death and suggesting a capacity in nature to generate something that goes beyond itself, perfect in its mimesis of organic form, but enduring. Aeneas may be going down to an underworld already created and discovered by Homer, but he goes with a symbol of this new art, elegant rather than vigorous, newly born from the old tradition. In the ages since Homer, the one great literary sin, the worst folly, had been to try to rival Homer at his own game. Virgil clearly never came to terms with the presumptuousness, the scale of his own project: "I must have been mad to try," he is reported to have said (Macrobius, *Sat.* I.xxiv.11).[21] On his deathbed, he ordered the work to be burned. Yet, through all the vagaries of critical fashion, one point

---

[20] This is the conclusion of Eduard Norden in his masterful review of the evidence in *P. Vergilius Moro Aeneis Buch VI* (Leipzig: B.G. Teubner, 1903), pp. 161-80.

[21] In a letter to Augustus: "Sed tanta inchoata res est, ut paene vitio mentis tantum opus ingressus mihi videar."

on which Virgil's reputation remains unassailable is his unrivaled capacity to incorporate in his poetry his predecessor's most imposing monuments as a mirror for his own genius.[22] Even in falling short of the Homeric achievement, Virgil left to all ages the still inescapable legacy of reading the Homeric poems through the filter of the *Aeneid*. He does not surpass his model but overshadows it.

Pasternak's rowan tree entails a similar declaration of indebtedness and freedom in regard to the imposing presence of Tolstoy. Zhivago sees the rowan tree twice, and only the second time recognizes its meaning for him as a symbol of Lara. Tolstoy's Prince Andrey Bolkonsky had passed an oak tree and saw in its bare limbs a symbol of his own lifelessness. But after meeting Natasha Rostova, he sees in that same oak, now in bloom, personal regeneration. The rowan tree, then, calls to mind what may be the most memorable image of *War and Peace*. There is piety in this, as often in *Doctor Zhivago*, toward the great master whom Pasternak met in his father's house. But there is rebellion as well — against Tolstoy's positivistic view of history, his dreams of family happiness, and most of all against the legacy of *War and Peace* as an art form. The difference between Tolstoy's oak and Pasternak's rowan as symbols reveals at once how very different the works are. Tolstoy could not, in the end, accept Andrey's vision of individual transformation. Andrey is shown finally as deluding himself, for the love of Natasha will not work out; Andrey will remain as aloof and lonely as ever. But for Pasternak, the transformation experienced by Zhivago is real and profound; there is poetry where there was none before. The ephemerality of the love to come makes it all the nobler. Tolstoy's symbol has only the meanings Andrey reads into it and these finally fade; *War and Peace* is not bound together by such images. But Pasternak's figure, as we have seen, is a perfect example of the many-tiered symbolism of the work — at once personal, historical, aesthetic, and religious. Tolstoy took his image, as usual, from the Russian land; Pasternak's is more complexly literary, going back not only to Tolstoy but also to Virgil and the Gospels.

At many other points Pasternak brings *War and Peace* no less clearly to mind, even in small touches like the bullet deflected by a holy token,

---

[22] As a rough index to the debt we may consider Georg Knauer's register of Virgil's Homeric borrowings in *Die Aeneas und Homer* (Gottingen: Vandenhoeck and Ruprecht, 1964), which runs to some 550 pages.

the viewing of the Czar, the ruinous gambling of the heroine's brother. The intellectuality and isolation of Tolstoy's Prince Andrey make him a clear ancestor of Yuri Andreievich. Thereby, of course, Pasternak pays his respects to Tolstoy, and necessarily, for the second great chronicle of the Russian nation must acknowledge the first, just as the Latin master of classical epic everywhere treats his Greek predecessor with clear, if subversive, reverence. But in breaking free, in using the same sort of images so very differently, Pasternak also responds to the shadow that the extraordinary legacy of the nineteenth century had cast over his own generation. As Misha Gordon reflects in the passage quoted above, we are the arid successors of a brilliant age. Pasternak feels the burden not only of creating worthy art, but of proving that art itself can still exist, that the House of Sculptures is not entirely papered over. And as Gordon indicates, this was precisely the position of the Romans as well: no literature had felt the burden of self-justification more severely. Pasternak reveals no easy confidence about his mission. Yes, this, too, like the first century, is an age of miracles: a deaf-mute speaks, perhaps with an element of clairvoyance. But what Pogorevshikh, this "imperturbable oracle" (p. 163), says, like the language of most oracles and most revolutionaries, is a babble that destroys meaning. The imagery of the Book of Revelation pervades *Doctor Zhivago*,[23] and Pasternak's own self-appointed rôle shows obvious similarities to that of St. John, apocalyptic prophet and cryptic foe of Roman oppression. But Pasternak no less freely allows that Zhivago, and hence perhaps he himself, may be much more a Cassandra (p. 197), a prophet fated never to be believed and therefore burying the truth in the very act of perceiving it. Pasternak's every formulation of the problem reminds us that it is not a new one.

To return to our central question: to what extent does Pasternak mean for us, in reading *Doctor Zhivago*, to recall that comparable statements in other ages have been epics? At the very least he has made the links between

---

[23] The first of Zhivago's meditations on the nature of art, after the funeral of Anna Ivanovna, announces this spiritual allegiance: "In answer to the desolation brought by death to the people slowly pacing after him, he was drawn, as irresistibly as water funneling downward, to dream, to think, to work out new forms, to create beauty. More vividly than ever before he realized that art has two constant, two unending concerns: it always meditates on death and thus always creates life. All great, genuine art resembles and continues the Revelation of St. John" (pp. 89-90).

Soviet Russia and Augustan Rome unmistakable: the decay of the old order; the hideous civil war; the coming of a perhaps necessary, but terrifying new authoritarianism. Clearly the similarity of historical circumstances would by itself dictate rhythms in the tale similar to the *Aeneid*, such as the drift toward cultural and racial heterogeneity, the impossibility of shaping the tale of such a movement around a strong, self-willed hero who runs eagerly to this future. Doubt, hesitation, and remorse are as appropriate to Aeneas as to Zhivago, given the horrors of the age. Yet the larger structure of *Doctor Zhivago* and images like that of the rowan tree suggest that far more than historical coincidence is involved, that Pasternak is using and acknowledging the *Aeneid* as the prototype of the national epic, and associating his work with that poem in a way that parallels and enhances its connection with the Gospels.

It is by no means too late in the world's history for Roman Virgil to be exercising such an influence. Consider, for example, Jorge Luis Borges' recent observation that "for me, he *stands* for poetry... If we take a line from Virgil we might as well say that we took a line from the moon or the sky or the trees."[24] And, of course, for prophets of the national experience, the stance of revenant Virgil proclaiming a new Rome has long been such a commonplace that we might be more surprised if it did not at some point penetrate to Russia. Yet it is in light of the strong continuities of epic that Pasternak's originality becomes most striking. His observation, made so soon after the revolution, that "epic is what our time inspires," seems in retrospect less the heroic posturing of Virgil's earlier heirs than an indictment of the perverse "heroism," the inhuman collectivism — the Romanness — of the new Russian order that was for so long to silence one of its finest lyric voices. *Doctor Zhivago* in fact ends with a powerful betrayal of the traditional respect for monumental form, that is, for the epic, as the pinnacle and consummation of literary activity. For here the great canvas stands not simply as an end in itself, but serves finally to create imaginative space and a fictional shield so that Pasternak may issue his final cycle of lyric poems. The prose saga of triumphant collectivism may also be seen as no more than a prelude to the final assertion, in the poems, of an

---

[24] Jorge Luis Borges, *Borges on Writing*, ed. Norman T. di Giovanni, Daniel Halpern, and Frank MacShane (New York: Dutton, 1973), p. 81.

individual voice which the larger movements of history had overwhelmed, but of which some fragments miraculously survive.

Yet the very unease of Pasternak's complicity in the great tradition of celebrations of nationhood puts him, ironically, in the closest proximity to its master. For Virgil, far more than his imitators, can never forget the human cost, the chilling impersonality of the brilliant national destiny.[25] When Aeneas, at the very center of the epic, emerges from his underworld vision of the Roman future, it is through the Gate of Ivory, the gate of false dreams. If the falseness of these heroic dreams, like the sad barbarity of Aeneas' final moments, is too ambiguous an image to stand as a clear disclaimer of the poet's epic calling, a final retreat from heroic assertion, we may at least say that each half of the Aeneid, like Doctor Zhivago with its concluding lyrics, ends more with a question than a benediction. It was Virgil who set the pattern, to be seen again in Yuri Zhivago, of a hero whose life in history becomes a descent into silence. The tragedy of the stilling of the individual voice cannot, of course, belong to Russia alone or to Rome: Pasternak clearly means Zhivago to be of more than local or momentary interest. And one of the ways that he brings the experience of Russia to speak for more than Russia is to phrase it, at certain crucial moments, in the language used of other places and other times, of Rome and Florence, no less than of Jerusalem.

---

[25] On "the continual opposition of a personal voice which comes to us as if it were Virgil's own to the public voice of Roman success," see especially Adam Parry, "The Two Voices of Virgil's *Aeneid*," *Arion* 2 (Winter 1963): 66-80.

6. Stalin and the Death of Epic: Mikhail Bakhtin, Nadezhda Mandelstam, Boris Pasternak

Does epic belong to princes? Imperialists have often assumed that it does: Alexander of Macedonia, after pausing at Troy to envy Achilles for having found a Homer, swept on to India with an *Iliad* in a jewelled casket. Caesar Augustus extracted the *Aeneid* from an apparently reluctant poet of shorter forms. Napoleon took a copy of Ossian on his march to Moscow. And Mussolini's favorite play was Shakespeare's *Julius Caesar*, which, speaking better than he knew, he proclaimed to be a textbook for statesmen. Ezra Pound seconded the impulse, while trying to educate the taste.

Among general readers, few might dispute the association. The unfading image of Hitler at Bayreuth indicts the influence of all heroic art. Even with the battlefield replaced by the dynamo and the collective farm, what is bad about Stalin's socialist realism, like his architecture, is heroically bad. Poets of the first rank are not easily tarred by this brush. When epic poetry has gratified the naked bellicosity of the Alexanders and Napoleons, it has usually done so late and mistakenly, for Homer's most esteemed heirs have more often satirized than gratified regal claims to grandeur. Alexander presumably overlooked how Homer actually portrays the leaders of expeditions through the ineffectual, blustering, and ingloriously doomed Agamemnon. However much Virgil fostered Augustus' vanity in seeing himself as the new Aeneas, the poet also sees Turnus' self-presentation as the new Achilles as a mask for weakness. Dante lets the old heroism sink into the pit on the weight of its own presumptions, as we see in the unbending, unlearning Farinata; in a Ulysses eternally trapped in the tales of Ulysses; and in the great joke, Satan, throned in unyielding ice of his own creation.

Dante's case reminds us that the great national visions tend not to come from the political center of things, but depend instead on the distance and nostalgia of exile or expatriation (from Dante to Joyce to Walcott), lost partisan causes (Virgil and Milton), or, at the very least, getting out of town: Nikolai Gogol fled to Rome in 1836 to write Russia's great national book, which turned out to be *Dead Souls*. That lesson was not lost on the outcast intelligentsia of the Stalinist era. In his "Conversations about Dante," Osip Mandelstam, who always carried a compact *Divine Comedy* in case he should suddenly end up in prison, did not name the unmentionable Stalin in connection with Farinata and Ulysses but assumed the reference as damningly self-evident: "It is unthinkable to read the cantos of Dante without aiming them in the direction of the present day. They are made for that. They are missiles for capturing the future."[1] Alexander Solzhenitsyn adapted Dante's image of self-cancelling heroics on the first page of *The First Circle*, where we first see the Soviet inferno through an eery light that cuts through the Moscow night: "...from ten o'clock on, thousands of windows in sixty-five Moscow ministries would light up again. There was only one person behind a dozen fortress walls, who could not sleep at night, and he had taught all official Moscow to keep vigil with him until three or four in the morning."[2] In this infernal Moscow, the lucky ones are the imprisoned intellectuals out in the audio research center on the edge of the city, who, like Dante's worthy pagans in the first circle, occupy the comparatively pleasant rim of the pit. But at the center behind the dozen walls is the unmoved Mover, exiled from nature (for night brings no sleep), imprisoning others so as to lock himself the more firmly in the ice. Solzhenitsyn freely concedes all of the Great Insomniac's claims to be at the center of things, the dead center.

Heroic antiquity is one of the preferred ways of satirizing Stalin: Mandelstam styles him "the Assyrian." Pasternak allegorically uses the pockmarked Caligula for the pockmarked Stalin.[3] Mikhail Bulgakov in *The Master and Margarita* interlards a tale of political cowardice in contemporary Moscow with the case of the Roman bureaucrat Pontius

---

[1] Osip Mandelstam, *Osip Mandelstam: Selected Essays*, trans. Sidney Monas (Austin and London: University of Texas Press, 1977), 24.

[2] Aleksandr I. Solzhenitsyn, *The First Circle*, trans. Thomas P. Whitney (New York: Harper and Row, 1968), 1.

[3] Masing-Delic argues that Pasternak uses Rome allegorically to trace the origins both of capitalism and socialism in their common use of wealth and spectacle, "bread and circuses," to suppress individuality. I. Masing-Delic, "Capitalist Bread and Socialist Spectacle: The Janus Face of 'Rome' in Pasternak's *Doctor Zhivago*," in *Boris Pasternak and his Times: Selected Papers from the Second International Symposium on Pasternak*, ed. Lazar Fleishman (Berkeley, Calif.: Brekeley Slavic Specialties, 1989).

Pilate. The analogy to Rome is easily made for Moscow. The sixteenth-century monk Philotheus called Moscow the third Rome, that is, a third and final capital of Christendom after Rome itself and Byzantium. With bitter irony Pasternak's sweeping historical narrative in *Doctor Zhivago* suggests that indeed Moscow has become a Rome, not the final capital of Christendom, but the Rome of Augustus and the Mediterranean empire. Rome is described as "a flea market of borrowed gods and conquered peoples" (Pasternak 1958, 43).[4] As Zhivago's friend Misha Gordon reflects in the epilogue, "It has often happened in history that a lofty ideal has degenerated into crude materialism. Thus Greece gave way to Rome, and the Russian Enlightenment has become the Russian Revolution."[5] The disappointed hopes of the revolution inspired Osip Mandelstam to speculate about a "Fourth Rome."[6]

On this evidence, Boris Pasternak and Osip Mandelstam should figure among those who scorn heroic art, even that of antiquity, because of the atrocities of this century and who therefore turn away from Wagner and even Virgil as one would from German or Roman imperialism. Yet we shall argue that the oppressions of Stalinism deepened the classicism of both poets. Stalin once did, to be sure, serve as Muse for Mandelstam, when in the winter of 1936-37 he conceived the hope that a conciliatory gesture might save him or his wife. As Nadezhda Mandelstam recalls:

> His attempt to do violence to himself was meeting stubborn resistance, and the artificially conceived poem about Stalin simply became a matrix for the utterly different material seething inside him — real poetry which was antagonistic to the "Ode" and canceled it out... A mention of Aeschylus and Prometheus in the "Ode" led on in the "free poems" to the theme of tragedy and martyrdom....[7]

In the fatal gap between a dictator waiting for Aeschylean encomium and a poet who turns to Promethean refusal, we can see the double life of heroic

---

[4] Boris Pasternak, *Doctor Zhivago*, prose trans. Max Hayward and Manya Harari, poems trans. Bernard Guerney (New York: Pantheon, 1958; repr. New York: Ballantine, 1981), 43. Page numbers for *Doctor Zhivago* are to the 1981 edition.

[5] Ibid, 518.

[6] Nadezhda Mandelstam, *Hope Against Hope*, trans. Max Hayward (New York: Atheneum, 1970), 178. Mrs. Mandelstam's title is *Vospominaniya*, "Memoirs."

[7] Ibid, 200.

literature in our century. Although epic traditionally presents itself as the singing of praise, it may have survived into the modern era more as an act of resistance.

After his death, Stalin's negative inspiration showed itself in the publication of three important bodies of work that in quite various ways try to undo the reign of the lie by what we may call monumental "histories of voice": Boris Pasternak's *Doctor Zhivago*, the memoirs of Nadezhda Mandelstam, and the cultural theories of Mikhail Bakhtin.[8] All three writers were born in the 1890s, shared the hopes of the 1917 revolution and the disillusionment of the 1920s, suffered silencing during the Stalinist era, and, in the case of Bakhtin and the Mandelstams, internal exile. From their various beginnings — as philologist, lyric poet, wife of a lyric poet — they were driven by oppression to prophecy on a grander scale than they might have imagined at the start of their careers. In their various ways, the three contend that the most fragile and evanescent of tones, be it lyrical or ironic, can survive and prevail in history and prove mightier than the organs of state terrorism. Some of the few who ever returned from the camps, as Mrs. Mandelstam notes, brought back snatches of her husband's verse.

Pasternak's semi-autobiographical *Doctor Zhivago* and the memoirs of Nadezhda Mandelstam tell similar tales of the silencing of a poet by the inhuman forces of the age. Both prose narratives aim to preserve and explain cycles of lyric poetry: the "Poems of Yurii Zhivago" printed at the end of the volume — implicitly the remains of Pasternak the lyric poet — and the poems of Osip Mandelstam, still unpublished in Russia when his wife wrote in the 1960s.[9] Both accounts invert materialist perspectives by making even the greatest historical events mere background to the lives of poets (the October Revolution happens between chapters in *Doctor Zhivago*), and those biographies in turn a footnote to the poems. The widows in these books tell similar tales. Lamenting over Yurii's corpse, Lara sums up his — and the novel's — view of history: "The riddle of life, the riddle of death, the enchantment of genius, the enchantment of unadorned

---

[8] We shall concentrate on "Epic and Novel" (1941) and "From the Prehistory of Novelistic Discourse" (1940) in Bakhtin (1981).

[9] The last collection of Mandelstam's verse to be published in the USSR was in 1928 under the title *Stikhotvoreniya*. Only after a forty-five year hiatus, in 1973, would a volume of his poetry appear in the USSR.

beauty — yes, yes, these things were ours. But the small problems of practical life — things like the reshaping of the planet — these things, no thank you, they are not for us."[10] Concerning the speculation of her husband's American editor that Mandelstam went to Armenia to avoid the Five Year Plans, Mrs. Mandelstam similarly expostulates: "Why should he have been put out by the planned organization of the economy? As if that mattered! What mattered was that, as M[andelstam] saw them, by virtue of their links between the Black Sea and the Mediterranean, the Crimea, Georgia and Armenia were part of world culture."[11]

Both Boris Pasternak and Nadezhda Mandelstam serve the fundamental need to provide witness once the terror has subsided. As a preface to her own memorial, *Requiem*, their friend and fellow sufferer Anna Akhmatova replaces the traditional visit of the Muse or scene of poetic vocation with a vignette from the prison queues of Leningrad. When someone recognized her, a woman with blue lips "came out of the numbness which affected us all and whispered in my ear — (we all spoke in whispers there): 'Can you describe this?' I said, 'I can!' Then something resembling a smile slipped over what had once been her face."[12] Having survived and maintained her own lyric voice, she could speak for the fallen succinctly in the mode of elegy. Nadezhda Mandelstam noticed the same vocation to witness in Pasternak already in the 1930s: "…every time we met him he told us he was writing a prose work 'about us all.'"[13] Unlike Akhmatova's, Pasternak's memorial after decades in the writing attained monumental scope, though the work seems uneasy about its own scale. As Zhivago's career follows Pasternak's own progression from poetry to prose (that is, the writing of this very novel), the narrative confesses its involvement in the Tolstoyan paradox — fighting fire with fire — of countering the old, deluded heroics through a sweeping vision that may in time prove just as clumsy and oppressive. Zhivago ends the creative and poetic part of his solitude at Varykino and begins the final, futile phase of his career as a voluminous writer of prose by a vision of how the Tolstoyan "great men" and Napoleons of history have

---

[10] Pasternak, 418.

[11] Nadezhda Mandelstam, 251.

[12] Anna Akhmatova, *Poems of Anna Akhmatova*, trans. Stanley Kunitz and Max Hayward (Boston: Little Brown and Company, 1973), 91.

[13] Nadezhda Mandelstam, 299.

been replaced by fanatical revolutionaries.[14] Pasternak's melancholy about how an inhuman age has reduced him to speaking in monumental terms does not make him the less like Virgil.

Nadezhda Mandelstam writes on the same scale but with less self-consciousness about the form. Despite the real uncertainty of her position, especially while her husband's poems remain unpublished in Russia, her tones are more triumphant than Pasternak's, as well as sometimes starker. She confesses herself an optimist, like her husband. What she narrates, from the 1934 arrest up to the second arrest in 1937, is a struggle that inspired Richard Pevear to make the comparison to Homeric battle.[15] The narrative begins with a famous leap *in medias res*: "After slapping Alexei Tolstoi in the face, M[andelstam] immediately returned to Moscow."[16] What matters in her world, as in Homer's, is that the tale, the kleos, endure: "If nothing else is left, one must scream. Silence is the real crime against humanity."[17] Yet she is already willing to declare victory, since the Stalinist battle was waged not just against perishable human resistance but against the Mind itself. Her husband's experience, like that of the fictional Zhivago, speaks for his generation, for Russia, and ultimately for the experience of man in history:

> Russia once saved the Christian culture of Europe from the Tatars, and in the past fifty years, by taking the brunt on herself, she has saved Europe again — this time from rationalism and all the will to evil that goes with it. The sacrifice in human life was enormous. How can I believe it was all in vain?[18]

Russia's sacrificial role in history, as it inevitably recalls that of Israel, figures in the Judeo-Christian tradition of apocalypse, of which these memoirs are a chapter: "M[andelstam] taught me to believe that history is a practical testing-ground for the ways of good and evil."[19]

---

[14] Pasternak, 378.

[15] Richard Pevear, "On the Memiors of Nadezhda Mandelstam," Hudson Review 24, no. 3 (1971): 427-28.

[16] Nadezhda Mandelstam, 3.

[17] Ibid, 43.

[18] Ibid, 329.

[19] Ibid, 328.

Though Bakhtin does not center his larger history of culture on the case of a single writer, his theoretical overview shares many of the same assumptions as the other two and provides terms to interpret them. He, too, charts through history the triumphant emergence of the voices of resistance, which he identifies not in terms of lyric but of irony, humor, and polyphony — the constellation of qualities that constitutes the "novelistic." This honest, joking, subversive tendency has long been at war with the deadening hand of authority, centralization, and tradition, which in now influential essays from the 1940s Bakhtin labels the "epic." Like the other two, he sees cultural creativity as centrifugal, to be found not in the centers of power and cultural authority but on the margins, especially where languages and cultures intermingle: not the court, but the marketplace; not Athens, but the Hellenistic cities; not Rome, but Lucian's polyglot Samosata in Syria.

Confirmations of this centrifugal tendency can be noted in the careers of Yurii Zhivago and Osip Mandelstam. It is Zhivago's trip to the Urals, to Varykino, that calls forth the poems in the concluding poem cycle, just as in fact Osip Mandelstam's visit to Armenia ended five years of writer's block. In his wife's view his status as a perpetual wanderer was fundamental to his creativity, while his "antipode" Pasternak paid a steep artistic price for the privilege of staying in Moscow. Moscow in both works ends up seeming hostage to a hollow and tyrannical "now," and it is on the margins that one enters into another, more natural and human reality that also gives access to antiquity. In the Urals Zhivago runs into figures named Bacchus, Lupus, Faustus, Liberius; Mandelstam's Armenia is in contact with Italy and antiquity. Of Sevan Island Mandelstam observes, only half-humorously: "The entire island is Homerically strewn with yellowed bones — remnants of the local people's pious picnics."[20]

While Bakhtin's resistance to state authority and its attempts to monopolize meaning is similar to that of the other two, though far more deeply encoded, his reaction to literary authority seems, at least on the surface, almost to be the opposite. Though trained as a classical philologist, Bakhtin resists classicism, traditionalism, and canon-building. Pasternak and the Mandelstams welcome classic writers as collaborators in their escape from the terrors of the current age. Even exile itself has its

[20] Mandelstam, 174.

own venerable traditions. Where the exiled Pushkin invoked Ovid, Osip Mandelstam invokes Pushkin, as well as Dante, to figure his own wandering. Zhivago's second visit to Varykino brings him to "the dark forest of his life,"[21] where wolves worthy of *Inferno* 1 appear on the horizon. Yet in Bakhtin's formulation, such invocations of literary authority must stand as part of the deadening "epic" mentality. Bakhtin is the only one of the three to work from the assumption that epic does in fact belong to princes and that the voices of resistance necessarily take other forms.

We have, then, a disagreement deeper than the generic differences of novel, memoir, and literary theory. Though all three tell parts of the same tale of how honest and subversive voices survive and prevail against the organs of oppression, Pasternak and Nadezhda Mandelstam create heroic memorials to the generation, the nation, and the race. Bakhtin might see these didactic monuments as built on the dead and rotten wood of "epic."

To sort out these disagreements we shall look now separately at Pasternak's fictional (auto)biography, Bakhtin's socio-poetic theory and its resistance to such "epic" projects, and finally Mrs. Mandelstam's synthesis of both modes within the matrix of her own memories.

Pasternak's debts specifically to literary epic go very deep, as we have argued.[22] *Doctor Zhivago* presents a proliferation of allegorical systems laid one upon another. As is evident from the concluding cycle of poems on Christ's Passion, Zhivago projects himself into the roles of Adam, Jesus, and Judas, even as he sees Lara in terms of Eve, Magdalene, and the Virgin Mary. The narrator recounts the poet's three days of descent into hell in a bout of fever; the final poem, "Garden of Gethsemane," ties itself back to the narrative by ending the cycle not with crucifixion or resurrection, but arrest, as is appropriate to the generation being described and to Zhivago himself when he writes at Varykino in anticipation of his own arrest. The use of a poet as an Everyman evokes Dante, as do the "dark forest" and wolves of Varykino. Zhivago's final inspiration, like Dante's, lies in the loss of his *donna*. Dante allusively brings Virgil with him, so that at another level Yurii and Lara play out the tragedy of Aeneas and Dido. Lara, like Dido, offers an interlude between an abandoned first wife, symbol of the old order, and a somewhat faceless second wife, symbol of the new.

---

[21] Pasternak, 369-70.

[22] See the introduction to this volume.

Both Zhivago and Aeneas, denied the dignity of self-immolation, outlive the individuals and the social order dear to them and end their tales as distant, lifeless characters. These curiously passive protagonists make ideal witnesses to the larger mechanisms of a history that may be at war with personal meanings. Pasternak may end up siding more with Virgilian nostalgia than with Dante's sense of deliverance.

Pasternak's allusions evoke not only the *Aeneid* and the *Divine Comedy*, but also their authors' careers, which exemplify the tensions between poetry and authority in Rome and Florence. Both Dante and Virgil started as poets of shorter forms whom events (exile from Florence or the pressure of Augustus) forced to monumental statements. Like Pasternak, these poets saw their worlds turned upside down by civil strife and confronted an order that in some ways they found criminal or inhuman. All three managed to survive where others did not, as seems particularly apparent in the portrayals of Aeneas and Zhivago as regretful survivor-protagonists. Though Aeneas founds a new imperial order, while Zhivago is extruded, both experience an erosion of feeling and a descent into silence.

Concerning the relationship of epic and despotism, Pasternak's own career suggests that some versions of totalitarianism leave no stance for the artist but that of epic writer. Already in 1927 he announced the intention to turn to prose because "epic is what our time inspires."[23] The *bella scuola* of precursors, especially Virgil and Dante, can be proudly invoked as a tradition of doubt and resistance. Princes may then have a role in the creation of monumental art — by virtue of just barely failing to crush its poets. The artists who survive the tyrant may be transformed by the experience from lyric poets into chroniclers of the national experience.

While exploiting the scope and didacticism of prose to make his case, Pasternak will not renounce the claims of the lyric poet, as becomes apparent by the end of the volume. The tale is, after all, that of a poet being silenced; the tragedy of Zhivago is that of the poet who dies before the man, who lives on to be a prolific writer of tracts. The numerous references to Tolstoy, especially in Zhivago's final apocalypse at Varykino, may recall the pitfalls of constructing large, didactic systems in honor of the small, the daily, and the plain. Proceeding without any introduction or annotation from the prose narrative to the cycle of poems printed at the end of *Doctor*

---

[23] Boris Pasternak, *Sochineniya*, vol. III (Ann Arbor: Ardis, 1961), 215-216.

Zhivago, we may wonder what encompasses what: Are the poems a footnote to the main story, an addendum? Or is the prose narrative a prologue to and commentary on the poems, as Mrs. Mandelstam means her memoirs to be? The poems articulate a vision of the Christ-inspired history toward which Zhivago and Lara have struggled. Even the narrative of events at Varykino, the zenith of Zhivago's poetic productivity, begins to erode the boundaries between text and life: "Like the confusion of a first rough draft, the wearisome inactivity of the day was a necessary preparation for the night."[24] Lara has a dissociative sense of their life in this interval: "...and now we bustle around like mad so as not to see that this isn't life, that it's a stage set, that it isn't real, that it's all 'pretend,' as children say, a child's game — just ridiculous."[25] Her protest apparently inspires a reply in "Hamlet" with its conceit of life as a play, and with its ending, "To live life to the end is not a childish task."[26] In giving insight into Zhivago's thoughts at Varykino, the poem's expansive allusions imply worlds of experience within which the preceding biography is a mere footnote: Zhivago casts himself as an actor, perhaps playing a Hamlet who himself plays Jesus. That the creator of Zhivago famously gave Russian voice to Shakespeare's prince may recall the decades of translation that marked the suppression of Pasternak's own lyric voice, for similar ventriloquism now proliferates in the "Hamlet" ode. Pasternak's biography can be taken as a matrix for, or perhaps just a footnote to, Zhivago's poem. The hierarchy of textual authority cannot be established. The narrative of Zhivago's life contains a copious survey of decades and events, but the lyric poems, especially as they modulate into the voice of Jesus, encompass eternities.

This irresolvable tension between poetry and prose, also to be found in the works of Osip and Nadezhda Mandelstam, in the case of *Doctor Zhivago* conforms to Bakhtin's view of the novel as the form that can contain other forms and set them into dialogue with one another. Just as the "novelistic" tendency made a crucial advance through the mixture of prose and poetry in Menippean satire, so Pasternak's prose narrative can be seen as providing a meta-form set around the poems to draw out the ideology so perfectly unvoiced in Zhivago's passionate sincerity. Yet in attaching *Doctor Zhivago*

[24] Pasternak, *Doctor Zhivago*, 366.

[25] Ibid, 360-61.

[26] Ibid, 433.

to the tradition of Virgil and Dante, Pasternak presumably becomes subject
to Bakhtin's assault on "epic," inasmuch as such hybridization of prose and
poetry should not serve the cause of classicism and concerted vision in
the way that *Doctor Zhivago* manifestly does. Guy de Mallac speculates
that Bakhtin would not find Pasternak's novel very "novelistic" since its
speakers, many and various as they are, monophonically express a single
set of opinions.[27] Yet the contradictions in Pasternak's own reaction to
Stalinism — reduced to monumentality notwithstanding himself — raise
suspicions about the neutrality and consistency of Bakhtin's radical anti-
classicism. Though he, unlike Pasternak and the Mandelstams, entirely
concedes epic to the use of princes, his renunciation of the tradition may
be more apparent than real.

Bakhtin, like the others, is a survivor of Stalinism. He spent three
decades exiled from the capitals, mostly barred from publication and
academic appointments. In those decades he produced nine long books,
of which one, on Dostoevsky, was published in 1929, while the next, on
Rabelais, appeared in 1965. Other manuscripts got lost or suppressed or
ripped up for cigarette papers. Like the others he found his influential
"voice" only after Stalin's death. What he wrote under Stalin in various ways
compensates for the freedom and audience denied him.

For the understanding of the novel, these theories are a contribution of
the first rank. We must also note that for students of epic Bakhtin represents
a significant nuisance, since his genre theory, which is also a philosophy of
history, radically simplifies and scapegoats the "epic" as the mouthpiece of
the bad old days, the days of a monolithic, authoritarian, elitist culture.[28] To
some degree, the daunting complexity of Bakhtin's analytical task compels
him to use a straw man of one sort or another: With the "novelistic," as with
other forms of irony, the interpreter who undertakes to chart the quicksilver
movements of its deflation (mockery, subversion, parody, or "dialogizing")
of its targets cannot afford to admit how much these targets themselves

---

[27] Guy de Mallac, *Boris Pasternak: His Life and Art* (Norman: University of Oklahoma
Press, 1981), 297.

[28] For a more extensive critique of Bakhtin's theories of epic and novel, see
Chapter 1 of this volume. For a reading of the *Odyssey* in terms of "novelistic," see now
John Peradotto, "The Social Control of Sexuality: Odyssean Dialogics," *Arethusa* 26 (1993):
173-82.

already use the same ironies (i.e., have their own targets). Plato goes after Aristophanes, who was himself going after Euripides, who was going after Aeschylus, who was going after Homer, who was going after…? Rather than credit infinite chains of ironizing (or "novelizing") in all directions, Bakhtin invents an end to the regress by positing a literature without targets, without irony, without complexity: the monophonic "epic." As the end of the regress, that literature has to be Homer, who is earlier than any other European text. Homer is the only "epic" writer cited.

By making "epic" the straw man, Bakhtin has popularized and reinforced long-discredited simplifications. Uses of *epic* rarely, if ever, conform to Bakhtin's description of a monolithic expression of nationalist orthodoxies and, indeed, are usually quite opposite in tendency. Bakhtin excludes the qualities of melancholy and resistance that Pasternak and the Mandelstams evoke from the tradition, as well as the polyphonies of the uniquely rich intertextuality of the epic tradition. The bard's complicated textual "dialogizing" of predecessors (Dante of Virgil, Virgil of Homer) does not so much make him a cultural imperialist as prevent him from serving the ideologies of his own day in any simple way. As the Mandelstams remind us, Dante is the literature of the prisoners more than of the jailers. Ullrich Langer's category of "boring epic" fits Bakhtin's description and is a reality of literary production, but is not what usually constitutes the canon. The mainstays of that canon — the *Iliad* and *Odyssey*, the *Aeneid*, the *Divine Comedy* — are in their various ages striking experiments in "novelistic" tendency. Canonization, translation, and veneration may have dulled their rough edges and gilded them with oppressive "epic" associations, but these texts all continue to move readers by something other than the "official" tones retrospectively imposed on them.

Bakhtin does parallel Pasternak's and the Mandelstams' view of the relationship of the center and the margins in cultural history. The center (read: "Moscow" or, more specifically, "the Kremlin") is where culture dies, to be redeemed only by resistance at the margins by the irreverent culture of the "people." All these writers would agree on the evils of enforced centralization and cultural homogenization; all give priority to the play of individual voices. Bakhtin further, and largely in opposition to the others, makes the "epic" the literature of the court and has the "novelistic" express the folk laughter of the marketplace. However, his attempt to flesh out this paradigm with names and places succeeds poorly. The only "epic" poet cited, Homer, derived from and became the basis of a widespread popular (indeed, oral) culture. The Homeric poems came from the margins of the Greek-speaking world, Ionia — perhaps at the remove necessary to see Panhellenic culture for the first time as a unity. And "Homer" was the spokesman of a "nation" that existed only in the imagination and for which he does not have a name. Epics do regularly, as Bakhtin observes, express the longing for a cultural center, but it is regularly the lack of same that inspires colonials, exiles, expatriates, and political outsiders to give monumental utterance to those hopes, as we discussed at the outset. If one takes epics as a subspecies of the "novelistic" (as Bakhtin himself does in other essays), his theories of cultural generativity capably account for their origins. If epics are often closer to the dissident voices of the marketplace than Bakhtin quite admits, the populist credentials of the "novelistic" are often questionable. The "novelistic" promotion of popular forms (like the dialogue) into literature regularly served for the amusement of the intelligentsia in the capitals: Plato (Bakhtin mentions only Socrates, who wrote nothing), the Greek novel, Petronius (a courtier of Nero), Rabelais. Writers such as Plato and perhaps Rabelais[29] may, ironically, evoke the life of the streets in support of a new set of elitist values. The popular form of the dialogue became the charter of the institutionalized exclusivity of the Academy. Bakhtin adroitly counters Marxism by finding in the historical circumstances of cultural production a principle to overthrow Marxist orthodoxy, but overlooks the even larger irony that it has often been the established elites (including, as Mrs. Mandelstam notes, Stalin's Union of Writers) that have the leisure to savor and memorialize popular culture. It may be the outsiders and have-nots who need the rallying cry of heroic literature.

Since Bakhtin's own histories, as befits his time, are encoded and polyphonic, it may be a disservice to take him too literally. He may be better served by being read, like Pasternak and Mrs. Mandelstam, in terms of the larger visionary project of constructing a history of voice. Where the other two use the 1920s and 1930s as a lens on preceding centuries, Bakhtin restricts himself to those earlier centuries as a way of talking about an undiscussable present. Though his description of the stultifying

---

[29] See Richard M. Berrong, *Rabelais and Bakhtin: Popular Culture in Gargantua and Pantagruel* (Lincoln and London: University of Nebraska Press, 1986).

uniformity and authoritarianism of "epic" describes the tradition oddly, it applies closely to the socialist realist novel.[30] The deadening authority of an absolutely valorized heroic "then" may be his way of describing the tyranny of Stalinism's heroic "now." Always alerting us to the telling loopholes in any ideological system, Bakhtin himself provides an intriguing loophole concerning this very issue: "It is possible, of course, to conceive even 'my time' as heroic, epic time, when it is seen as historically significant; one can distance it, look at it from afar (not from one's own vantage point but from some point in the future)...."[31] He goes on to describe latter-day "epic," again without examples, in ways that capture the output of the Union of Writers: The later versions of "epic" "...transfer to these [contemporary] events the time-and-value contour of the past, thus attaching them to the world of fathers, of beginnings and peak times — canonizing these events, as it were, while they are still current."[32] Soviet society, with its cults of Lenin and Stalin, had constituted itself as the epoch of the fathers, and its state-generated literature depicted a world (again, Bakhtin is here describing "epic") "...that is inaccessible to personal experience and does not permit an individual, personal point of view or evaluation."[33] What he describes comes not from a traditional society like Archaic Greece but a police state founded on rigid orthodoxy: "The epic world is an utterly finished thing... it is impossible to change, to re-think, to re-evaluate anything in it. It is completed, conclusive and immutable, as a fact, an idea, a value."[34] Even Bakhtin's image of the monolith as a symbol of the "epic" continues to have currency among critics of the regime. Mrs. Mandelstam, writing in the 1960s, and Andrei Sinyavsky both use the Egyptian pyramid as a symbol of the vast, inhuman structure of the Soviet state.[35]

---

[30] Katerina Clark and Michael Holquist, *Mikhail Bakhtin* (Cambridge, Mass. and London: Harvard University Press, 1984), 273.

[31] Mikhail Bakhtin, *The Dialogic Imagination*, ed. Michael Holquist, trans. Caryl Emerson and Michael Holquist (Austin, University of Texas Press, 1981), 14.

[32] Ibid, 14-15.

[33] Ibid, 16.

[34] Ibid, 17.

[35] Nadezhda Mandelstam, 256; Andrei Sinyavsky, *Soviet Civilization*, trans. Joanne Turnbull and Nikolai Formozov (New York: Arcade Publishing, 1990), 267.

It is a long way from the *Iliad* to socialist realism, but Bakhtin facilitates the double reference by leaving the category of the "epic" empty, credited as a generative principle in human culture, but without names attached. In the first, and very dense, twenty-one pages of the essay "Epic and Novel," the form is described in detail without a single "epic" writer being named, though Homer is implied. The essay shifts at that point to the ancient precursors of the novel and in the next paragraph mentions Sophron, Ion of Chios, Critias, Lucilius, Horace, Persius, Juvenal, Petronius, Menippus, and Lucian. Bakhtin is scarcely sparing the general reader the burden of his erudition. In the stark asymmetry between all the famous bards who are not mentioned and the numerous obscure prose writers who are, the unexemplified category of "epic" becomes all the more problematic. The shadowy, eccentrically described "Homer" can be nothing more than a place holder in Bakhtin's system, and the modern "Homers" who canonize the present have been left to be deduced, even as Osip Mandelstam could leave it to the reader to find the unnamed Stalin in the shadow of Farinata and Ulysses. Stalin trained readers well for allegorizing classic texts into "missiles for capturing the future." For "epic," then, read "socialist realism." The loopholes in Bakhtin's description suggest that what defines "epic" is not when it was written (for it can be modern) nor the era that it describes (for it can canonize the present) but rather the ideological rigidity of refusing to allow "then" and "now" to comment on (or "dialogize") one another and claiming one age as the absolute standard of all others.

Bakhtin describes in broad, essentially allegorical terms that great war in history between truth and the lie, between mind and mechanical, deadening force. This is a heroic tale in its own right, and Bakhtin's rhetoric belies his sympathy for the writers who have jovially turned aside from "kings and battles." To excerpt from the 1941 essay "Epic and Novel": "The novel has become the leading hero in the drama of literary development in our time precisely because it best of all reflects the tendencies of a new world still in the making...."[36] (Bakhtin 1981, 7). "[The novel] fights for its own hegemony in literature; wherever it triumphs, the other older genres go into decline" (4), a process later described as "a lengthy battle for the novelization of the other genres" (39).[37] The novel is, in a word,

[36] Bakhtin, 7.

[37] Ibid, 4, 39.

revolutionary: "In the process of becoming the dominant genre, the novel sparks the renovation of all other genres, it infects them with its spirit of process and inconclusiveness. It draws them ineluctably into its orbit precisely because this orbit coincides with the basic direction of literature as a whole" (7).[38] Genres of the world unite! You have nothing to lose but your monophony! The triumph of the "novelistic" has all of the redemptiveness and historical inevitability being claimed in these years for its demon twin, Marxism. Bakhtin ends up describing the overthrow of "epic" as an epic struggle.

Though the "novelistic" is the enemy of the nationalism that propels the "epic," Bakhtin's larger history leads to Russia with a sure aim. The genres that Bakhtin esteems in antiquity — the ironizing, personalistic, seriocomic prose narratives — are the ancestors of forms that have distinguished Russian letters. Bakhtin the iconoclast and anti-classicist may be, in nationalist terms, a pious antiquarian and patriot who gives Russian letters a connection with antiquity that, for want of a Renaissance and Enlightenment, it would seem to lack. Bakhtin creates a canon stretching from the holy fool Socrates to Petronius to Rabelais and onward to Gogol and Dostoevsky. As universal as the "novelistic" tendency is, this is a prehistory that finds its culmination nowhere so clearly as in Russia itself. The irony is familiar: The enemy of theory builds his own theory; the canon-basher substitutes an alternative canon. Though the virtue of the "novelistic" is its focus on the open-ended present, Bakhtin, like any good classicist, finds its essence in its origins. The canon is dead! Long live the canon! Bakhtin has paid the epic tradition the compliment of replacing it with one that functions in much the same way, and one built of even bigger texts, the "loose baggy monsters" most esteemed in Russia.

To sum up, on the topic of epic itself, the extremes of Stalinism drove Bakhtin and Pasternak to what are on the surface opposite answers. Bakhtin links epic with authoritarianism and dances on its grave. Pasternak recalls and revives another tradition wherein epic springs from the resistance to princes and tyrants. In one particular, they show a common inclination: to

---

[38] Ibid, 7. Berrong notes how popular culture "struggles against," "storms," and even "destroys" official culture in Bakhtin (*Rabelais and His World*), a study of Rabelais written during the 1930s and 1940s. Richard M. Berrong, *Rabeleis and Bakhtin: Popular Culture in Gargantua and Pantagruel* (Lincoln and London: University of Nebraska Press, 1986), 11.

give Russian letters a prehistory that leaves them less hostage to the politics of this century. This shared sense of history follows along Christian lines (as remains unstated in Bakhtin's essays) and stands in opposition to the mechanistic and the authoritarian. Bakhtin assembles an anti-canon of iconoclasts, but one strangely like the tradition that it replaces and heroic in its own terms. Pasternak, working in the shadow of Virgil and Dante, seems more aware of the Tolstoyan trap of replacing one kind of heroics with another. Both demonstrate how the society of the future in abolishing the past had given it a ferocious new glamour. Try to make the New Man and he will inevitably long to be the New Adam.

Nadezhda Mandelstam, like her husband, sides with the classicists and invokes "Europe" as the codeword for the humanistic values outlawed by Stalinism. Like Bakhtin she sees cultural history as a logomachy, a clash of discourses, that can be traced by moments of ironic dissonance. Her personal and immediate goal is to assert her true telling of events against the proliferation of self-serving legends, bureaucratic obfuscations and deceits, and naive misperceptions that inevitably surround the suffering and death of a famous poet. Her text is, properly speaking, a polemic, a part of the continuing conflict, and therein lies its immediacy. Her own struggle as a writer exemplifies and comments on the conflict of discourses in Soviet society as the official, centralizing line of the state assaults, but fails to destroy, the honest and irreverent voices of individuals. The depicted struggles of the polyphonic resistance to a dead and deadening unanimity parallel from life the emergence of "the novelistic" into literature.

As an example of her technique of letting language be history, we may take the chapter entitled "The Accomplice," which concerns an "admirer" of Mandelstam's verse, Alexander Fadeyev, a socialist-realist novelist and functionary of the Union of Writers. Fadeyev had both the discrimination to be moved by the verse and the decayed decency to offer praise, consolation, and insincere promises of help. As is observed time and again in the memoirs, the only art left to the complicit intelligentsia is to re-enact eternally the Judas-kiss:

> Less than a year later, during a party in Lavrushinski Street to celebrate the award of the first Government decorations to be given to writers, Fadeyev learned about the death of M[andelstam] and drank to his memory with the words "We have done away with a great poet." Translated

into Soviet idiom, this meant: "You can't make an omelet without breaking eggs."[39]

As would Bakhtin, Mrs. Mandelstam locates the meaning of Fadeyev's utterance in its context, which encompasses a play of discourses, spoken and unspoken. Fadeyev's official and ceremonious tribute translates the homely and unspoken idiom of the maxim. At yet a further level — and here she parts company with Bakhtin — this irreverent fragment of folk wisdom is itself hideously corrupted by public life, a symptom of what outrages her most: the people's passive acceptance of the terror as if (unless one's own family is affected) it mattered no more than omelets and eggs. The great hypocrite Fadeyev implicates the small, unresisting hypocrites (and she excludes no one, not even her husband or herself) who allow the charade to proceed to its lethal outcome. She sees no redemption in the well-policed marketplace. Dismissing both Fadeyev and his collaborators to their native oblivion ("But it scarcely matters who actually signed the sentence..."), she turns the mirror on the audience: "And is it conceivable that people will not learn from our example?"[40]

Mrs. Mandelstam does, like Bakhtin, credit the languages of the people and of daily life (where her husband chose to see himself, "herded with the herd") as the source of truth and moral value. But her reading of polyphony in the society is nearly opposite to Bakhtin's. Polyphony does, as he claims, result from the resistance to authoritarianism, enforced uniformity, and soulless elitism. Yet her memoirs depict this play of voices as pathological, not redemptive: "My name is legion." The attempts to impose the lie or to accept it with enforced Soviet smiles unleash legions of competing discourses: from the ungrounded, comforting, constantly mutating speculations about why acquaintances got arrested ("What for?") to the final monster in the narrative, Tiufiakov, who visits the widow every day with new inventions about her husband's fate — shot, beaten to death, still alive, run off with another woman. Interrogation rooms are identifiable because they have too many doors. Where Bakhtin locates creativity in the circumventing and subverting of authority, Mrs. Mandelstam finds inventiveness mostly in the slips and small emotional self-indulgences (the

[39] Nadezhda Mandelstam, 355.

[40] Ibid, 356.

Judas role) that characterize the universal complicity. The poet's role, and Mrs. Mandelstam's in speaking for her husband, is to assert the unitary truth beneath the proliferation of voices. So much is apparent at the first arrest in 1934: "'*What for*?' Akhmatova would cry indignantly whenever, infected by the prevailing climate, anyone of our circle asked this question. 'What do you mean, *what for*? It's time you understood that people are arrested *for nothing*!'"[41] Though an acute observer of how polyphony is generated by the play of discourses in the culture, Mrs. Mandelstam's aim is to assert the unity of truth. Her moral absolutism is unconcealed.

Though she permits herself scores of *obiter dicta* on literary, historical, moral, and philosophical topics, the force of her argument lies in the gallery of characters that crossed her path between 1934 and 1938, usually set against the false hopes of the 1920s and, *sub specie aeternitatis*, the perspective of the 1960s when, as individuals and groups, they are mostly exterminated, executioners no less than victims. This extraordinary prosopography of individuals set against the absolute claims of death recalls in its scope and format the strings of cameos in the *Iliad* and the *Divine Comedy*. In all three, individuals are given a brief moment on the stage to move under their own energy to the characterizing posture (of dying in Homer, of death in Dante) where they are captured for eternity. Lives distill themselves into a gesture, a word, a deluded hope: Years later, his duplicity revealed, the drunken Fadeyev whispers to the widow in a Moscow elevator the name of her husband's executioner — as if she cared, or would believe him, or respect him even if she did. Cheka interrogators give their victims hard candy — as if those victims could savor being compelled to pretend that there was some human basis to the interchange. The larger argument against historical determinism is not made on the level of theory (its own terms, after all), but in vignettes that open from Marx and end with Dante. Individuals are introduced categorically by the epithets of the new society: "a proletarian," "a non-Party Bolshevik" (which earlier would have been "a fellow traveler"), "a Red professor," an "officer of the Union of Writers." But it is always by free choice that they make the gratuitous and eccentric gestures that fix them for posterity. Even the despised Stalinist sister-in-law Tania finds her memorial not in party ideology (which keeps changing on her) but in telling moments of practice: stealing and selling her comatose

---

[41] Ibid, 11.

stepdaughter's clothing on the day before she dies; uncontrollably turning aside when the unworthy successor Khrushchev drives past on a Leningrad street. Polemical as are her intentions, Mrs. Mandelstam, like Dante, does not overtly sit in judgment so much as catalogue individuals who have gravitated to their own natural positions. She establishes her own credibility, as well as enlivening the ghastly tale with surprise, by spotting vestiges of decency in the persecutors. But these humanizing touches are, as in the *Inferno*, the pinions that affix the damned to their torment. Even the most despicable are characterized not by naked cruelty so much as by the small hypocrisies — the hard candy, the amiable handshake, the praise for the poetry, the consoling word — that acknowledge the victim's humanity and betray the sinner's own conscious choice in proceeding.[42] As in the *Inferno*, it is the humanity and recognizability of the faces that render the vision horrible rather than merely grotesque.

In the struggle over the continuing existence of Mind, the two Josephs, Stalin and Mandelstam, are cast as opponents and antitheses. Yet Mrs. Mandelstam takes care not to counter the Stalinist cult of personality with a comparably false hagiography of her husband. Indeed, she directly debunks the proliferations of legends about martyred poets that come to overshadow their poetry. Her husband remains a shadowy presence, and she does not aggrandize her own participation as anything beyond the future witness.[43] As in the narrative of *Doctor Zhivago*, her prose contains numerous gestures of submission to the poetry. Though her textual authority rests in firsthand experience, she sometimes effaces herself from participant to eavesdropper: "M[andelstam] once asked me (or himself, rather) what it was that made someone a member of the intelligentsia."[44] Her own memory in places is shaped by later reading of his texts, which contain insights that he would not share with her lest she mock him. But then he himself rigorously subjected his own life to the principles articulated in his work. The effect of having Osip Emilevich and Nadezhda Yakovlevna almost disappear from the scenes of their own lives is to keep them from

[42] As Mrs. Mandelstam summarizes the matter: "Probably no other regime ever went in for such niceties in the art of bureaucratic control — apart from all its other qualities, it was distinguished by unparalleled hypocrisy." Ibid, 353.

[43] Ibid, 333.

[44] Ibid, 222.

overshadowing the hero of the tale, the inextinguishable witnessing voice. Mrs. Mandelstam does let victory be proclaimed in the struggle, but only a poet is worthy to make the proclamation:

> But poetry is a law to itself: it is impossible to bury it alive and even a powerful propaganda machinery such as ours cannot prevent it from living on. "I am easy in my mind now," Akhmatova said to me in the sixties. "We have seen how durable poetry is."[45]

In being very nearly one of the missing persons in her own life — a curious absence at the core of what could be autobiography — Mrs. Mandelstam achieves some of the qualities of the omniscient observer and anonymous bard.

Her account is integrated at every level by an ethic of sacrifice that purges the reminiscences of narcissism. As was noted above, Russia itself has in her view been martyred for the cause of truth by living to the fullest the lies of rationalism. Poetry is validated as prophecy by the sufferings of the poet, the one figure most completely exempt from material advantage in a materialist culture. For the poet's wife, marriage becomes the sacrifice of all domestic rituals and comforts. In turn the widow becomes, in her husband's place, Stalin's adversary and bearer of the final victory. The order to "isolate and preserve" gave the poet three more years of life after 1934; the widow is given the injunction, we might say, to "preserve and proclaim."

Mrs. Mandelstam's polemical stance and self-confessed optimism set her apart from the traditional sentimentality of the widow's role. At Zhivago's bier, Lara at last finds independent voice in a lament that echoes images and values of Zhivago's poetry. Her emotionality was "like the choruses and monologues of ancient tragedies, like the language of poetry or music."[46] Her lament recalls that of Igor's wife Euphrosinia from the walls of Putivl in the *Lay of Igor's Campaign*, as well as that of the Virgin Mary over her son. The funereal end of Pasternak's narrative also recalls the end of the *Iliad*, where Andromache, Hecuba, and Helen greet Hector's body as it is returned to Troy. Rather oppositely Mrs. Mandelstam uses tradition as a check on sentimental indulgences like suicide or survivor's guilt or even gestures of humility. She ends the account of the couple's dialogue on suicide

[45] Pasternak, *Doctor Zhivago*, 417.

[46] Nadezhda Mandelstam, 57.

by juxtaposing statements from the great Russian writers Mandelstam and Avvakum:

> When M[andelstam] had gone and I was left alone, I was sustained by the memory of his words "Why do you think you ought to be happy?" and by the passage in the "Life" of the Archpriest Avvakum when his exhausted wife asks him: "How much further must we go?" and he replies: "Until the very grave, woman." Whereupon she gets to her feet and walks on.[47]

Part of the pathos of her position, which she need do nothing to amplify, is that she was never given the widow's due, the lament at the funeral. Her husband vanished, and she was given no body to tend but that of the poetry, which requires of her perseverance rather than deep emotion. In place of a conclusion the second volume of memoirs ends with an unsent letter to her husband from the end of 1938, approximately the time of his death.[48] But, of course, she does not want a conclusion. She is not finished yet.

It is the unsentimental Homer who best anticipates the heroism of her partisanship. That best of wives, Andromache, also finds independent voice at her husband's death. She too confronts the ritual anomaly of being deprived of the corpse as Achilles abuses it. The atrocities of inhuman force leave both women with no ritual and public role, though Andromache is to have it later at Hector's funeral. She is reduced to the simple gesture of burning the clothing that she has prepared for her husband's return. The terms in which she does so are linguistically charged, as she proclaims that this sacrifice will be a *kleos* for him (*Iliad* 22.514). *Kleos*, "fame" or "honor," is the motivating word in the epic and not used often or casually. It is what warriors die for and what bards provide. Had Hector won, he would have had that *kleos*. Achilles has claimed it along with the fallen body that properly belongs to the widow. Yet to a curious degree, the victory in this opposition belongs to Andromache more than Achilles. As gods and men agree, his crazed mutilation of the corpse taints the moment of triumph and vitiates his own *kleos*. At a moment when he could claim the supreme meaning that warrior culture has to offer and shape his own immortal

---

[47] Nadezhda Mandelstam, *Hope Abandoned*, trans. Max Hayward (New York: Athenaeum, 1974), 619-21.

[48] Joseph Brodsky, "Nadezhda Mandelstam (1899-1980): An Obituary," in *Less Than One: Selected Essays*, 145-56 (New York: Farrar, Straus, Giroux, 1986), 154.

memory, he hurtles from the scene like a maniac, dragging the corpse. In his place, it is the widow who is given the privilege of concluding the climax of the work, fixing its meaning, and, in her own terms, prevailing over the self-destructive adversary, who in time, in the great scene with Priam, will accede to her values. In Homer's epic, the victims get the last word.

In similarly deprived and ritually anomalous circumstances, Mrs. Mandelstam claims no role for herself but to purvey *kleos*. Yet this *kleos* is more potent than mere "memory" or setting the documentary record straight. It is a role in the war. Stalin, like Achilles, is the self-cancelling monster of force who has compelled the hero's wife to take up the bard's own role. He has made her not just a widow, but something more. As Joseph Brodsky observed at her death, "She was a widow to culture…." Her impact may lie in the fact that "the status of the modern world vis-à-vis civilization also can be defined as widowhood."[49]

Stalin drove her, like Pasternak and Bakhtin, to a scale of prophecy that none of them might have anticipated in the 1920s. As Brodsky noted, "… she became what she became not because of what took place in Russia in this century but rather in spite of it."[50] That "in spite of" provides one answer to our initial question about the relation of heroic literature to princes. As Anna Akhmatova demonstrated, the step to monumental form was not inevitable, for lyric poets could, if they survived, still recall the terror in lyric poems. But when it happened, this step to a broader canvas and a millennial vision clearly reflected its times. Pasternak said as much in 1927 in declaring that "epic is what our age inspires." The ideological tyranny that instilled Bakhtin's remarkable insight into the voices that can subvert orthodoxy not only called forth description on the broadest historical scale but also kept him from calling the oppressive "epic" forces by name. Mrs. Mandelstam's memoirs make the linkage of epoch and epic fully transparent, for the atrocities of the age provoked her to realize the effects of heroic literature without the need of fiction in a way that may recapture the earliest workings of imperishable *kleos*.

[49] Ibid, 154-55.

[50] On Mrs. Mandelstam's rhetorical position in the text and representation of her role as wife, see the important analysis of Charles Isenberg, "The Rhetoric of Nadezhda Mandelstam's *Hope Against Hope*," in *Autobiographical Statements in Twentieth Century Russian Literature*, ed. Jane Gary Harris (Princeton, N.J.: Princeton University Press, 1990), 192-203.

Works Cited

Afanasev, Viktor, ed. N. *Gnedich, Stikhotvoreniya i poèmy*, Moscow, 1984.

Akhmatova, Anna. Poems of Anna Akhmatova. Translated by Stanley Kunitz and Max Hayward. Boston: Little Brown and Company, 1973.

Alter, Robert. *The Art of Biblical Narrative*. New York: Basic Books, 1981.

Annenkov, P. V. "N. V. Gogol' v Rime letom 1841 goda." In *Gogol' v vospominaniyakh sovremennikov*, edited by S. Mashinskii, 230-316. Moscow, 1952.

Asoyan, A. A. "Zametki o dantovskikh motivakh u Belinskogo i Gogolya." In *Dantovskie Chteniya* 1985, 104-19. Moscow: Nauka, 1985.

Aucouturier, Michel. "The Theory of the Novel in Russia in the 1930s: Lukàcs and Bakhtin." In *The Russian Novel from Pushkin to Pasternak*, edited by John Garrard, 227-40. New Haven and London: Yale University Press, 1983.

Auerbach, Erich. *Mimesis: The Representation of Reality in Western Literature*. Translated by Willard R. Trask. Princeton, N.J.: Princeton University Press, 1953. Reprint, 1974. Originally published as *Mimesis: dargestellte Wirklichkeit in der abendländischen Literatur*. Berne: A. Francke, 1946.

Bakhtin, Mikhail M. *The Dialogic Imagination*. Edited by Michael Holquist. Translated by Caryl Emerson and Michael Holquist. Austin: University of Texas Press, 1981.

————. Rabelais and His World. Translated by Helene Iswolsky. Cambridge, MA: MIT Press, 1968. Reprint. Bloomington: Indiana University Press, 1984.

Barolini, Teodolinda. *Dante's Poets: Textuality and Truth in the Comedy*. Princeton, N.J.: Princeton University Press, 1984.

Baroti, T. "Traditsiya Dante i povest' Gogolya 'Rim.'" *Studia Slavica Hungarica* 29 (1983): 171-83.

Belinsky, V. G. *Sobranie sochinenii v trekh tomakh*. Vol. 2. Moscow, 1948.

Belknap, Robert. *The Structure of* The Brothers Karamazov. The Hague: Mouton. 1967. Reprint. Evanston, Ill.: Northwestern University Press, 1989.

Benjamin, Walter. "The Storyteller." In *Illuminations*. Edited by Hannah Arendt, 83-109. Translated by Harry Zohn. New York: Schocken Books 1969.

Berlin, Isaiah. *The Hedgehog and the Fox*. New York: Simon and Schuster, 1966.

Berrong, Richard M. Rabelais and Bakhtin: Popular Culture in Gargantua and Pantagruel. Lincoln and London: University of Nebraska Press, 1986.

Bersani, Leo. "Against *Ulysses*." *Raritan* 8, no. 2 (Fall 1988): 1-32.

Beye, Charles Rowan. *Epic and Romance in the* Argonautica *of Apollonius.* Literary Structures. Carbondale and Edwardsville: University of Southern Illinois Press, 1982.

Bitsilli, Pavel M. "Pochemu Dostoevskii ne napisal *Zhitie velikogo greshnika*." In *O Dostoevskom. Sbornik statei*, edited by A. L. Bem, 149-54. Paris: AMGA Editions, 1986.

Blessington, Francis C. Paradise Lost *and the Classical Epic.* Boston: Routledge and K. Paul, 1979.

Bloom, Harold. *A Map of Misreading.* New York: Oxford University Press, 1975.

Bolgar, R. R. *The Classical Heritage and Its Beneficiaries.* Cambridge: Cambridge University Press, 1954.

Borges, Jorge Luis. *Borges on Writing.* Edited by Norman T. di Giovanni, Daniel Halpern, and Frank MacShane. New York: Dutton, 1973.

Borghese, Daria. *Gogol a Roma.* Florence: Sansoni, n.d.

Bowie, E. L. "The Greek Novel." In *The Cambridge History of Classical Literature.* Vol. 1, *Greek Literature*, edited by P. E. Easterling and B. M. W. Knox, 683-99. Cambridge: Cambridge University Press, 1985. Reprinted, 1987.

Bowra, Cecil M. *From Virgil to Milton.* London: Macmillan and Co., 1945.

Branch, Watson G., ed. *Melville: The Critical Heritage.* London and Boston: Routledge and Kegan Paul, 1974.

Braun, Maximilian. "*The Brothers Karamazov* as an Expository Novel." *Canadian-American Slavic Studies* 6 (1972): 199-208.

Brecht, Bertolt. "Anmerkungen" to "Aufstieg und Fall der Stadt Mahagonny." In *Stücke*, vol. 3. Berlin: Suhrkamp Verlag, 1955.

_____. *Brecht on Theater: The Development of an Aesthetic.* Translated by John Willet. London and New York: Harcourt, Brace, and World, 1964. Reprint, 1984. Translation with additional materials of *Schriften zum Theater*. Frankfurt: Suhrkamp Verlag, 1957.

Brodsky, Joseph. "Nadezhda Mandelstam (1899-1980): An Obituary." In Less Than One: Selected Essays, 145-56. New York: Farrar, Straus, Giroux, 1986.

Brooks, R. A. "Discolor Aura: Reflections on the Golden Bough." *American Journal of Philology* 74 (1953): 260-80.

Bruss, Neil. "The Sons Karamazov: Dostoevsky's Characters as Freudian Transformations." *The Massachusetts Review* 26, no. 1 (Spring 1986): 40-67.

Burgi, Richard. *A History of the Russian Hexameter*. Hamden, Conn.: The Shoe String Press, 1954.

Butler, Eliza Marian. *The Tyranny of Greece over Germany*. Cambridge: Cambridge University Press, 1935. Reprint, Boston: Beacon Press, 1958.

Christian, R. F. *Tolstoy's War and Peace*. Oxford: Clarendon Press, 1962.

Clark, Katerina, and Michael Holquist. Mikhail Bakhtin. Cambridge, Mass. and London: Harvard University Press, 1984.

Cohen, Ralph. "On the Interrelations of Eighteenth-Century Literary Forms." In *New Approaches to Eighteenth-Century Literature*, edited by Phillip Harth, 33-78. New York and London: Columbia University Press, 1974.

Coleman, Robert. "Ovid and the Anti-Epic." Review of Brooks Otis, *Ovid as an Epic Poet*. In *Classical Review*, n.s. 17 (1967): 46-51.

Comparetti, Domenico. *Vergil in the Middle Ages*. Translated by E. F. M. Benecke. London: Swan Sonnenschein and Company; New York: Macmillan and Company, 1895. Originally published as *Virgilio nel medioevo*. Leghorn: Vigo, 1872.

Curtius, Ernst Robert. *European Literature and the Latin Middle Ages*. Translated by Willard R. Trask. Bollingen Series 36. Princeton, N.J.: Princeton University Press, 1953. Reprint, 1979. Originally published as *Europäische Literatur und lateinisches Mittelalter*. Bern: A. Francke AG Verlag, 1948.

Curtis, James M. "The Function of Imagery in *War and Peace*." *Slavic Review* 29 (1970): 460-80.

de Jonge, Alex. *Dostoevsky and the Age of Intensity*. New York: St. Martin's Press, 1975.

de Mallac, Guy. Boris Pasternak: His Life and Art. Norman: University of Oklahoma Press, 1981.

Dostoevsky, Anna. *Dostoevsky-Reminiscences*. Translated by Beatrice Stillman. New York: Liveright, 1975. Originally published as *Vospominaniya*. Moscow, 1925.

Dostoevsky, Fyodor M. *The Brothers Karamazov*. Translated by Constance Garnett and Ralph Matlaw. Edited by Ralph Matlaw. A Norton Critical Edition. New York: W. W. Norton and Company, 1976.

_____. *F. M. Dostoevskii-Pisma*. Edited by A. S. Dolinin. 4 vols. Moscow-Leningrad, 1928-59.

_____. *Polnoe sobranie sochinenii v 30 tomakh.* Vol. 28, pt. 1. Leningrad: Nauka, 1985.

Driessen, Frederick Christoffel. *Gogol as Short Story Writer.* The Hague: Mouton, 1965.

DuRocher, Richard J. *Milton and Ovid.* Ithaca and London: Cornell University Press, 1985.

Egunov, A. N. "Lomonosov-perevodchik Gomera." In *Literaturnoe tvorchestvo M.V. Lomonosova,* edited by P. N. Berkov and I. Z. Serman, 197-218. Moscow-Leningrad, 1962.

Eikhenbaum, Boris. *Tolstoi in the Sixties.* Translated by Duffield White. Ann Arbor, Mich.: Ardis, 1982.

_____. *Lev Tolstoi, Kniga Vtoraya.* Leningrad, 1931.

Eisenstein, Sergei M. *The Film Sense.* Translated and edited by Jay Leyda. New York: Harcourt, Brace and Company, 1942.

Elley, Derek. *The Epic Film: Myth and History.* London: Routledge and Kegan Paul, 1984.

Erbse, Hartmut. *Beiträge zum Verständnis der Odyssee.* Berlin and New York: De Gruyter, 1972.

Erlich, Victor. *Gogol.* New Haven and London: Yale University Press. 1969.

Ershov, L. F. "Traditsii M. Sholokhova i roman-èpopeya v slavyanskikh stranakh." *Acta Litteraria Academiae Scientiarum Hungaricae* 28, nos. 3-4 (1986): 315-29.

Fáj, Attila. *I Karamazov tra Poe e Vico: Genere poliziesco e concezione ciclica della storia nell'ultimo Dostoevskij.* Studi vichiani, vol. 16. Naples: Guida editori, 1984.

Fanger, Donald. *The Creation of Nikolai Gogol.* Cambridge. Mass.: Harvard University Press, 1979.

_____. *Dostoevsky and Romantic Realism.* Cambridge, Mass.: Harvard University Press, 1965.

_____. "Influence and Tradition in the Russian Novel." In *The Russian Novel from Pushkin to Pasternak,* edited by John Garrard, 29-50. New Haven and London: Yale University Press, 1983.

Fiedler, Leslie A. *The Inadvertent Epic.* New York: Simon and Schuster, 1979.

Finch, Chauncey E. "Tolstoy as a Student of the Classics." *Classical Journal* 47 (1952): 205-10.

_____. "Classical Influence on N. V. Gogol." *Classical Journal* 48 (1953): 291-96.

Finley, John H., Jr. *Homer's* Odyssey. Cambridge, Mass., and London: Harvard University Press, 1978.

Foerster, Donal M. *The Fortunes of Epic Poetry: A Study in English and American Criticism 1750-1950*. Washington, D.C.: Catholic University Press, 1962.

Fowler, Alastair. "The Life and Death of Literary Forms." *In New Directions in Literary History*, edited by Ralph Cohen, 77-94. Baltimore: The Johns Hopkins University Press, 1974.

Frankel. Hermann. *Early Greek Poetry and Philosophy*. Translated by Moses Hadas and James Willis. New York and London: Harcourt Brace Jovanovich, 1975. Originally published as *Dichtung und Philosophie des frühen Griechentums*. Munich: C. H. Beck'sche Verlagsbuchhandlung, 1962.

Frazer, Sir James. *Balder the Beautiful*. In *The Golden Bough*. Vol. 11. London: Macmillan and Co., 1914.

Freccero, John. "Dante's Ulysses: From Epic to Novel." In *Concepts of the Hero in the Middle Ages and the Renaissance*, edited by Norman T. Burns and Christopher J. Reagan, 101-19. Albany: SUNY Press, 1975. Reprinted in John Freccero, *Dante: The Poetics of Conversion*. Edited and with an introduction by Rachel Jacoff, 136-51. Cambridge, Mass.: Harvard University Press, 1986.

Gerschenkron, Alexander. "Notes on Doctor Zhivago." *Modern Philology* 58 (1961): 194-200.

Giamatti, A. Bartlett. *The Earthly Paradise and the Renaissance Epic*. Princeton N.J.: Princeton University Press, 1966.

Gide, André. *Dostoevsky*. New York: New Directions, 1961. Originally published as *Dostoievsky: articles et causeries*. Paris: Pion, 1923. Gippius. V. V. Gogol. Edited and translated by Robert A. Maguire. Ann Arbor, Mich.: Ardis, 1981.

Gifford, Henry. *Pasternak: A Critical Study*. Cambridge: Cambridge University Press, 1977.

Girard, René. *Violence and the Sacred*. Translated by Patrick Gregory. Baltimore: The Johns Hopkins University Press, 1977. Originally published as *Violence et le sacré*. Paris: B. Grasset, 1972.

Godard, Jean-Luc. *Godard on Godard*. Translated by Tom Milne. Edited by Jean Narboni and Tom Milne. New York and London: Viking, 1972. Reprint. New York: Da Capo Press, 1986. Originally published as *Jean-Luc Godard par Jean-Luc Godard*. Paris: B. Belfond, 1968.

Goethe, J. W. [von], and J. C. F. [von] Schiller. "Über epische und dramatische Dichtung." In *Goethes Werke*, edited by Erich Trunz. Hamburger Ausgabe in Bänden. Vol. 12, pp. 249-51. 12th ed., 1981.

Gogol, Nikolai V. *Dead Souls*. Translated by Bernard Guilbert Guerney (as *Chichikov's Journeys*: or, *Home Life in Old Russia*). New York: The Readers Club, 1942.

_____. *Dead Souls*. Translated by George Reavy. New York: W. W. Norton, 1971.

_____. *Mirgorod*. Translated by David Magarshack. New York: Noonday. 1962.

_____. *Nikolai Gogol: A Selection*. Translated by Christopher English. Moscow: Progress Publishers, 1981.

_____. *"The Overcoat" and Other Tales of Good and Evil*. Translated by David Magarshack. New York: W. W. Norton and Company, 1965.

_____. *Polnoe sobranie sochinenii*. 14 vols. Moscow, 1937-52.

_____. *Selected Passages from Correspondence with Friends*. Translated by Jesse Zeldin. Nashville, Tenn.: Vanderbilt University Press, 1969.

_____. *Sobranie sochinenii v semi tomakh*. 7 vols. Moscow, 1966- 67.

Gorky, Maxim. *Reminiscences of Tolstoy, Chekhov and Andreyev*. Translated by Katherine Mansfield, S.S. Koteliansky, and Leonard Woolf. London: Hogarth Press, 1948.

Greene, Thomas. *The Descent from Heaven*. New Haven and London: Yale University Press, 1963.

Griffin, Jasper. *Homer on Life and Death*. Oxford: Clarendon Press, 1980. Reprint, 1983.

Griffiths, F. T., and S. J. Rabinowitz. "*Doctor Zhivago* and the Tradition of National Epic." *Comparative Literature* 32 (1980): 63-79.

_____. "Tolstoy and Homer." *Comparative Literature* 35 (1983): 97-125.

Grossman, Joan Delaney. "Tolstoy's Portrait of Anna: Keystone in the Arch." *Criticism* 18 (1976): 1-14.

Gusev, N. N. *Letopis' zhizni i tvorchestva L'va Nikalaevicha Tolstogo*. Moscow: Gosudarstvennoe izdatelstvo khudozhestvennoi literatury, 1958.

Hagan, John. "A Pattern of Character Development in *War and Peace*: Prince Andrej." *Slavic and East European Journal* 13 (1969): 164-90.

Halliwell, Stephen. *Aristotle's Poetics*. Chapel Hill: The University of North Carolina Press, 1986.

Hamburger, Käte. *Leo Tolstoi, Gestalt und Problem*. Bern: A. Francke, 1950.

Havelock, Eric A. "The Homeric Encyclopedia." *In Preface to Plato*. New York: Grosset & Dunlap, 1967.

_____. *Preface to Plato*. Cambridge, Mass.: Harvard University Press, and Oxford: Basil Blackwell, 1963. Reprint. New York: Bantam, 1982.

Hegel, G. W. F. *The Philosophy of Fine Arts*. Translated by F. P. B. Osmaston. Vol. 4. London: G. Bell and Sons, 1920.

Holquist, James Michael. "The Burden of Prophecy: Gogol's Conception of Russia." *Review of National Literatures* 3, no. 1 (Spring 1972): 39-55.

_____. "Did Tolstoj Write Novels?" In *American Contributions to the Eighth International Congress of Slavists*. Vol. 2. Edited by Victor Terras. 272-79. Columbus, Ohio: Slavica Publishers, 1978.

_____. *Dostoevsky and the Novel*. Princeton, N.J.: Princeton University Press, 1977; rpt., Evanston, Ill.: Northwestern University Press, 1986.

Homer, *The Iliad*. Translated by Richmond Lattimore. Chicago and London: The University of Chicago Press, 1951. Reprint, 1976.

Isenberg, Charles. "The Rhetoric of Nadezdha Mandelstam's Hope Against Hope." In *Autobiographical Statements in Twentieth Century Russian Literature*, edited by Jane Gary Harris, 192-203. Princeton: Princeton University Press, 1990.

Ivinskaya, Olga. *A Captive of Time*. Translated by Max Hayward. New York: Doubleday, 1978.

Jackson, Robert Louis. "The Second Birth of Pierre Bezukhov." *Canadian-American Slavic Studies* 12 (1978), 535-42.

Jepsen, Laura. *From Achilles to Christ: The Myth of the Hero in Tolstoy's War and Peace*. (N.P., 1978).

Jong, Alex de. *Dostoevsky and the Age of Intensity*. New York: St. Martin's Press, 1975.

Karlinsky, Simon. *The Sexual Labyrinth of Nikolai Gogol*. Cambridge, Mass.: Harvard University Press, 1976.

Kermode, Frank. *The Classic: Literary Images of Permanence and Change*. New York: Viking, 1975.

Kirk, Geoffrey S. *The Songs of Homer*. Cambridge: Cambridge University Press, 1962.

Knauer, Georg. *Die Aeneas und Homer.* Gottingen: Vandenhoeck and Ruprecht, 1964.

Koster, Severin. *Antike Epostheorien.* Palingenesia, vol. 5. Wiesbaden: Franz Steiner Verlag, 1970.

Kristeva, Julia. *Sēmeiōtikē: recherches pour une sémanalyse.* Collection "Tel Quel." Paris: Editions du Seuil, 1969.

Lamont, Rosette C. "Joseph Brodsky: A Poet's Classroom." *The Massachusetts Review* 15, no. 4 (Autumn 1974): 553-77.

Lattimore, Richard. *The Iliad of Homer.* Chicago and London: University of Chicago Press, 1951.

Leavis, F. R. *The Great Tradition: George Eliot, Henry James, Joseph Conrad.* London: Chatto and Windus, 1950.

Lord, George deForest. *Heroic Mockery: Variations on Epic Themes from Homer to Joyce.* Newark: University of Delaware Press, 1977.

Lubbock, Percy. Preface to *The Tragic Muse*, by Henry James. New York: Charles Scribner's Sons, 1908.

_____. *The Craft of Fiction.* New York: Viking, 1957.

Lukács, Georg. *Werke.* Vol. VI: *Probleme des Realismus.* Vol. III: Der historische Roman. Edited by Peter Christian Ludz, Frank Benseler, György Márkus. Berlin: Luchterhand, 1965.

_____. *The Theory of the Novel.* Translated by Anna Bostock. Cambridge, Mass.: MIT Press, 1971. Originally published as *Die Theorie des Romans.* Berlin: P. Cassirer. 1920.

Macaulay, Thomas Babington. *Critical and Historical Essays Contributed to the Edinburgh Review.* Trevelyan Edition. Vol. 1. London: Longmans, Green, and Company, 1909.

McLean, Hugh. "Gogol and the Whirling Telescope." In *Russia: Essays in History and Literature*, edited by G. Lyman and M. Legters, 79-99. Leiden: Brill, 1972.

Madelénat, Daniel. *L' Epopée.* Paris: Presses universitaires de France, 1986.

Mailer, Norman. *Advertisements for Myself.* New York: Putnam, 1959.

Mandelstam, Nadezhda. Hope Against Hope. Translated by Max Hayward. New York: Atheneum, 1970.

_____. Hope Abandoned. Translated by Max Hayward. New York: Athenaeum, 1974.

Mandelstam, Osip. *Osip Mandelstam: Selected Essays*. Translated by Sidney Monas. Austin and London: University of Texas Press, 1977.

Mann, Yurii. *Poètika Gogolya*. Moscow: Khudozhestvennaya Literatura, 1978.

Manzoni, Alessandro. *On the Historical Novel*. Translated by Sandra Bermann. Lincoln and London: The University of Nebraska Press, 1984. Originally published as *Del romanzo storico*. Milan, 1845.

Markov, Vladimir. "Notes on Pasternak's Doctor Zhivago," *Russian Review* 18 (1959): 14-22.

Martz, Louis L. *Poet of Exile: A Study of Milton's Poetry*. New Haven and London: Yale University Press, 1980.

Masing-Delic, I. 1989. "Capitalist Bread and Socialist Spectacle: The Janus Face of 'Rome' in Pasternak's Doctor Zhivago." In Boris Pasternak and his Times: Selected Papers from the Second International Symposium on Pasternak, edited by Lazar Fleishman, 372-85. Modern Literature and Culture: Studies and Texts, 25. Oakland: Berkeley Slavic Specialties, 1989.

Matlaw, Ralph E. "Recurrent Imagery in Dostoevskij." *Harvard Slavic Studies* 3 (1956): 201-25.

_____. "Mechanical Structure and Inner Form: A Note on *War and Peace* and *Doctor Zhivago*." Symposium 17 (1962): 291. Reprint in Tolstoy, ed. Gibian.

Merchant, Paul. *The Epic*. The Critical Idiom, vol. 17. London: Methuen and Company, 1971. Reprint, 1979.

Meyer, Priscilla, and Stephen Rudy, eds. *Dostoevsky and Gogol*. Ann Arbor, Mich.: Ardis, 1979.

Mooney. Harry J., Jr. *Tolstoy's Epic Vision: A Study of War and Peace and Anna Karenina*. Tulsa, Okla.: University of Tulsa Press, 1968.

Morson, Gary Saul. *Hidden in Plain View: Narrative and Creative Potentials in* War and Peace. Stanford: Stanford University Press, 1987.

Mynors. R. A. B. P. *Vergilii Maronis Opera*. Oxford: Claredonianus, 1969.

Nagy, Gregory. *The Best of the Achaeans*. Baltimore and London: The Johns Hopkins University Press, 1979. Reprint, 1981.

Nimis, Stephen A. *Narrative Semiotics in the Epic Tradition: The Simile*. Bloomington and Indianapolis: Indiana University Press, 1987.

Norden, Eduard. P. *Vergilius Moro Aeneis Buch VI*. Leipzig: B.G. Teubner, 1903.

Olson, Paul A. "The Epic and Great Plains Literature: Rølvaag, Cather, and Neihardt." *Prairie Schooner* 55 (1981): 263-85.

Otis, Brooks. *Ovid as an Epic Poet.* Cambridge: Cambridge University Press, 1966. 2d ed., 1970.

Page, Denys. *The Homeric Odyssey.* Oxford: Clarendon Press, 1955.

Parry, Adam. "The Two Voices of Virgil's Aeneid." *Arion* 2 (Winter, 1963): 66-80.

————. "The Language of Achilles." *Transactions and Proceedings of the American Philological Association* 87 (1956): 1-7. Reprinted in *The Language and Background of Homer: Some Recent Studies and Controversies,* selected and introduced by Geoffrey S. Kirk, 48-54. Cambridge: Heifer; New York: Barnes and Noble, 1964. Also reprinted in *Homer,* edited by Harold Bloom, 109-13. Modern Critical Views. New York: Chelsea House Publishers, 1986.

Pasternak, Boris. *Doctor Zhivago.* Prose translated by Max Hayward and Manya Harari. Poems translated by Bernard Guerney. New York: Pantheon, 1958. Reprint. New York: Bantam, 1985.

————. *Sochineniya.* Vol. III. Ann Arbor, Mich.: University of Michigan Press, 1961.

Peace, Richard. *The Enigma of Gogol.* Cambridge: Cambridge University Press, 1981.

Pedrotti, Louis. "The Architecture of Love in Gogol's *Rome.*" *California Slavic Studies* 6 (1971): 17-27.

Peradotto, John. "The Social Control of Sexuality: Odyssean Dialogics." *Arethusa* 26 (1993): 173-82.

Perlina, Nina. *Varieties of Poetic Utterance: Quotations in* The Brothers Karamazov. Lanham, Md.: University Press of America, 1985. Poggioli, Renato. "Gogol's 'Old-Fashioned Landowners': An Inverted Eclogue." *Indiana Slavic Studies* 3 (19631: 54-72.

Pevear, Richard. "On the Memoirs of Nadezhda Mandelstam." *The Hudson Review* 24, no. 3 (1971): 427-40.

Poggioli, Renato. "Boris Pasternak." *Partisan Review* 25 (1958): 541-54.

————. *The Poets of Russia.* Cambridge, Mass.: Harvard University Press, 1960.

Proffer, Carl. *The Simile and Gogol's* Dead Souls. The Hague: Mouton, 1967.

Proust, Marcel. *Remembrance of Things Past.* Vol. 3, *The Captive.* Translated by C.K. Scott Moncrieff and Terence Kilmartin, and by Andreas Mayor. New York:

Random House, 1981. Originally published as *A la recherche du temps perdu*. Vol. 6, *La Prisonnière*. Paris: Editions Gallimard, 1923.

Pucci, Pietro. Odysseus Polutropos: Intertextual Readings in the Odyssey and the Iliad. Ithaca and London: Cornell University Press, 1987.

Ray, Robert. *A Certain Tendency of the Hollywood Cinema, 1930-1980*. Princeton, N.J.: Princeton University Press, 1985.

Redfield, James M. *Nature and Culture in the* Iliad: *The Tragedy of Hector*. Chicago and London: The University of Chicago Press, 1975.

Richter, Sigrid. "Rom und Gogol': Gogol's Romerlebnis und sein Fragment 'Rim.'" Dissertation, University of Hamburg, 1964.

Ruskin, John. *The Works of John Ruskin*. Vol. 5. Edited by E. T. Cook and Alexander Wedderburn. New York: Longmans, Greene and Co., 1904.

Russo, Joseph, and Bennett Simon. "Homeric Psychology and the Oral Epic Tradition." *Journal of the History of Ideas* 29 (1968): 485-98.

Shapiro, Marianne. "Gogol and Dante." *Modern Language Studies* 17, no. 2 (Spring 1987): 37-54. Reprinted in Michael Shapiro and Marianne Shapiro, *Figuration in Verbal Art*, 191-211. Princeton, N.J.: Princeton University Press, 1988.

Simon, Bennett. *Mind and Madness in Ancient Greece: The Classical Roots of Modern Psychiatry*. Ithaca and London: Cornell University Press, 1978.

Simonsuuri, Kirsti. *Homer's Original Genius: Eighteenth-Century Notions of the Early Greek Epic* (1688-1798). Cambridge: Cambridge University Press, 1979.

Sinyavsky, Andrei. *Soviet Civilization*. Translated by Joanne Turnbull and Nikolai Formozov. New York: Arcade Publishing, 1990.

Solzhenitsyn, Aleksandr I. *The First Circle*. Translated by Thomas P. Whitney. New York: Harper and Row, 1968.

Stam, Robert. *Reflexivity in Film and Literature from Don Quixote to Jean-Luc Godard*. Studies in Cinema, vol. 31. Ann Arbor. Mich.: UMI Research Press, 1985.

Stanford, W. B. *The Ulysses Theme*. 2nd ed. New York: Blackwell, 1963.

Steiner, George. *Tolstoy or Dostoevsky*. New York: Knopf, 1959.

Stenbock-Fermor, Elisabeth. *The Architecture of* Anna Karenina. Lisse: Peter de Ridder Press, 1975.

Steussy, R. E. "The Myth Behind Doctor Zhivago." *Russian Review* 19 (1959): 184-98.

Strakhov, Nikolai. "The Russian Idea in *War and Peace*." In *War and Peace*. Edited by George Gibian. Translated by Louise Maude, Aylmer Maude, and GeorgeGibian. New York: W.W. Norton & Co., 1966.

Terras, Victor. *A Karamazov Companion*. Madison: University of Wisconsin Press, 1981.

Terz, Abram [Andrei Sinvayskii]. *V teni Gogolya*. London: Collins, 1975.

Tillyard, E. M. W. *The English Epic and Its Background*. New York: Oxford University Press, 1954.

_____. *The Epic Strain in the English Novel*. London: Chatto and Windus, 1958.

Todorov, Tzvetan. *Mikhail Bakhtin: The Dialogical Principle*. Translated by Wlad Godzich. *Theory and History of Literature*, vol. 13. Minneapolis: University of Minnesota Press. 1980. Originally published as *Mikhail Bakhtine: le principe dialogique*. Paris: Editions du Seuil, 1981.

Tolstoy, Leo. *Polnoe sobranie sochinenii*. Vol. 62. Edited by. V.G. Chertkova. Moscow: Gosudarstvennoe izdatel'stvo khudozhestvennoi literatury, 1928-1964.

_____. *War and Peace*. Edited by George Gibian. Translated by Louise Maude, Aylmer Maude, and George Gibian. A Norton Critical Edition. New York: W.W. Norton & Co., 1966.

_____. *"What Is Art" and "Essays on Art."* Translated by Aylmer Maude. London: Oxford University Press, 1929.

Ulis, Rose-Marie R. "Has the Historical Novel Replaced the Epic?" *Classical Bulletin* 40 (1964): 50-52.

Vermeule, Emily T. *Greece in the Bronze Age*. Chicago and London: The University of Chicago Press, 1964.

Veselovsky, A. "'Mertvye Dushi': Glava iz ètiuda o Gogole." *Vestnik Evropy* 3 (1891): 68-102.

Vogüé, E. M. de. *The Russian Novel*. Translated by H. A. Sawyer. London: Chapman and Hall, 1913. Originally published as *Le Roman russe*. Paris, 1880.

Webber, Joan. *Milton and His Epic Tradition*. Seattle: University of Washington Press, 1979.

Wender, Dorothea. *The Last Scenes of the Odyssey*. Leyden: E.J. Brill, 1978.

Whitman, Cedric H. *Homer and the Homeric Tradition*. Cambridge, Mass.: Harvard University Press, 1958.

Yeats, W.B. *The Variorum Edition of the Poems of W. B. Yeats.* Edited by Peter Allt and Russell K. Alspach. New York: Macmillan, 1957.

Yelistratova, Anna. *Nikolai Gogol and the West European Novel.* Translated by Christopher English. Moscow: Raduga Publishers, 1984. Originally published as *Nikolai Gogol i problemy zapadnoevropeiskogo romana.* Moscow, 1972.

INDEX

234

Index

Lomonosov, M. V. 17, 33
Lubbock, P. 144
Lucan 27, 36, 38, 209
Lucilius 209
Lukács, G. 22, 28, 31, 42, 47, 154n20
Lukas, G.
  — *Star Wars* 23, 24n30
  — *Indiana Jones* 24n30

Mailer, N. 144
Mandelstam, N. Ya. 9, 195, 197–200, 202, 207, 208, 211–215, 217
Mandelstam, O. E. 197–199, 201, 202, 209, 211, 214, 216
  — "Conversations about Dante" 196
  — "Ode" 197
Mandelstams 204–206
Manzoni, A. 20
Markov, V. 179
Masing-Delic, I. 196n3
Matlaw, R. 169n3
Maykov, A. N. 117
Melville, H. 21
  — *Moby Dick* 20, 21
Menippus 209
Milton, J. 19, 22, 26, 31, 34, 38–42, 47, 55n12, 57, 60, 127, 147, 150, 163, 165, 173–175, 180, 195
  — "Lycidas" 41
  — *Paradise Lost* 41, 127, 149
  — *Paradise Regained* 174
Mitchell, M.
  — *Gone with the Wind* 144
Morson, G. S. 34
Mussolini, B. 195

Napoleon 12, 87, 90, 128, 152, 154, 155, 163, 164, 169, 173, 195
Nero 36, 207
Nietzsche, F. 35, 40

Odoevsky, V. F. 9
  — *Russian Nights* 9
Ossian 21, 163, 195
Outland, T. 26
  — *The Professor's House* 26
Ovid 17, 19, 27, 32, 34, 38, 39, 52, 59, 71, 72, 97, 106, 202
  — *Metamorphoses* 72

Palance, J. 23
Pasternak, B. L. 13, 26, 53, 128, 175–182, 184, 185, 189–207, 210, 211, 215, 217
  — *Doctor Zhivago* 9, 13, 162n24, 176–178, 180, 181, 183n15, 186, 189, 191–194, 197, 198, 202–205, 214
  — "Garden of Gethsemane" 202
  — "Hamlet" 182, 204
  — *Nineteen Five* 176
Pedrotti, L. 64n25
Pericles 26n33
Perlina, N. 121
Persius 209
Petronius 36, 207, 209, 210
Pevear, R. 200
Philotheus, monk 11, 17, 197
Plato 22, 34, 35, 36, 44n62, 160, 206, 207
  — *Symposium* 35
Pletnev, P. A. 50
Poggioli, R. 58, 177
Polevoi, N. A. 17
Pound, E. 195
Prokopovich, N. Y. 51n7
Proust, M. 129n19, 146
  — *Remembrance of Things Past* 129n19, 146
Pseudo-Longinus 41
Pushkin, A. S. 9, 17, 33, 51, 57n15, 73, 77, 81, 100, 111–113, 120, 121n13, 176, 184, 202
  — *Eugene Onegin* 73, 81, 176

www.ingramcontent.com/pod-product-compliance
Lightning Source LLC
Chambersburg PA
CBHW051105030726
47504CB00006B/1803